THIS
BOOK
PLACES
AN
INDICTMENT
ON
THE
FEDERAL
GOVERNMENT
AND
16TH
AMENDMENT!!!

—

DANIEL H. MARCHI

AuthorHouse™
1663 Liberty Drive
Bloomington, IN 47403
www.authorhouse.com
Phone: 1-800-839-8640

Published by AuthorHouse 6/7/2012

ISBN: 978-1-4685-8406-6 (sc)
ISBN: 978-1-4685-8405-9 (e)

Library of congress Control Number: 2012907136

Any people depicted in stock imagery provided by Thinkstock are models,
and such images are being used for illustrative purposes only.
Certain stock imagery © Thinkstock.

This book is printed on acid-free paper.

Because of the dynamic nature of the Internet, any web addresses or links contained in this book may have changed
since publication and may no longer be valid. The views expressed in this work are solely those of the author and do
not necessarily reflect the views of the publisher, and the publisher hereby disclaims any responsibility for them.

A
POWERFUL
MATHEMATICAL
ALGORYTHM
HAS
BEEN
DERIVED
THAT
DESCRIBES
THE
PATH
OF
TAXATION!!!

CORPORATIONS AND COMPANIES DON'T

PAY TAXES

CORPORATIONS AND COMPANIES

TAXES

CONVERT

TO

SALES

TAXES

LEADING

AMERICAN PEOPLE

TO

BONDANGE!!!

THE 16TH AMENDMENT PRODUCED
AN INCOME TAX
SOCIAL SECURITY WAGE TAX
MEDICARE WAGE TAX
AN UNEMPLOYMENT TAX

INCOME TAX CONVERTS TO
A SALES TAX
SOCIAL SECURITY TAX
CONVERTS TO
A SALES TAX
MEDICARE TAX
CONVERTS TO
A SALES TAX
UNEMPLOYMENT TAX
CONVERTS TO
A SALES TAX
"MULTI TAXATION"
ENSLAVES
PEOPLE

TODAY!!!

EVERY PERSON IN THE UNITED STATES PAYS THESE HIDDEN SALES TAXES:

COMPANY TAX
INCOME TAX
SOCIAL SECURITY WAGE TAX
MEDICARE WAGE TAX
UNEMPLOYMENT WAGE TAX
SNOWBALL COMPANY TAX
SNOWBALL INCOME TAX
SNOWBALL SOCIAL SECURITY WAGE TAX
SNOWBALL MEDICARE WAGE TAX
SNOWBALL UNEMPLOYMENT TAX

A PRODUCT OF THE 16TH AMENDMENT!!!

CORPORATIONS

AND

FEDERAL GOVERNMENT

BENEFIT!!!

WHERE DO THESE SALES' TAXES GO?

THE FOLLOWING PRESENTATION OF THE MATHEMATICAL ALGORYTHIM DERIVATION IS WRITTEN IN A COMPUTER PROGRAMMING LANGUAGE STYLE!!!

INTRODUCTION

As a "gross wage earners," your company stripped the "16th amendment wage tax" from your "gross wage" and passed the "16th amendment wage tax" to the Government. You are relegated to the status of being a "net wage earner."

Commencing with a bit of reality, you go to a grocery store.

The "grocery company" has transferred the following taxes to the government on an hourly basis:

"company tax"

"16th amendment wage tax"

To insure a profit on groceries being bought, the following taxes are presented at the grocery's checkout counter:

"grocery company tax"

"16th amendment wage tax"

"snowball company tax" ("mathematical algorithm")

"snowball 16th amendment wage tax" ("mathematical algorithm")

You place yourself at the grocery checkout counter watching the cashier as she passes each item over the octal reader in the process of totaling your grocery bill.

At that very moment, while the cashier rings up your grocery's bill, the following taxes are added to groceries' purchases:

"grocery company tax"

"16th amendment wage tax"

"snowball company tax" ("mathematical algorithm")

"snowball 16th amendment wage tax" ("mathematical algorithm")

You place your visa card in the card reader and the card reader finally displays the total price of your grocery bill containing the following taxes on items in your grocery cart:

"grocery company tax"

"16th amendment wage tax"

"snowball company tax" ("mathematical algorithm")

"snowball 16th amendment wage tax" ("mathematical algorithm")

As a "net wage earner," you are going to pay "triple taxation" on the following taxes according to the mathematical algorithm in this book:

"grocery company tax"

"16th amendment wage tax"

"snowball company tax" ("mathematical algorithm")

"snowball 16th amendment wage tax" ("mathematical algorithm")

If you are a non-wage earner, then you are going to pay "double taxation" on the following taxes according to the mathematical algorithm in this book:

"grocery company tax"

"16th amendment wage tax"

"snowball company tax" ("mathematical algorithm")

"snowball 16th amendment wage tax" ("mathematical algorithm")

Moreover, persons who use the following to purchase items will pay "double taxation" on the same Items according to the mathematical algorithm:

"unemployed employed worker"

"food stamps"

"stimulus money"

"medicare recipient"

"social security recipient"

Who benefits from "double taxation" and "triple taxation" otherwise known "multi taxation?"

The government and company do not pay taxes; therefore both government and company profit from "multi taxation."

10TH AMENDMENT
powers of the states and people
("reserve power clause")
ratified 12/15/1791

The powers not delegated to the United States of America by the Constitution, nor prohibited by it to the States, are reserved ("Reserve Power Clause") to the States respectively, or to the people.

The "delegated to the United States of America" sentence in the 10th Amendment" must not be altered. Any substitution within violates the 10th Amendment!

10TH AMENDMENT RESERVES POWER CLAUSE

The 10th Amendment states "the powers not delegated to the United States of America by the constitution, nor prohibited by it to the states, are reserved to the states respectively, or to the people."

In other words, "the powers not delegated to the United States of America by the constitution, or not prohibited (not allowed) by it to the states, are reserved to the states respectively, or to the people."

In other words, "the powers not delegated to the United States of America by the constitution, or not not allowed by it to the states, are reserved to the states respectively, or to the people."

In other words, "the powers not delegated to the United States of America by the constitution, or allowed by it to the states, are reserved to the states respectively, or to the people."

The part "the powers not delegated to the United States of America by the constitution" is a "logical constant expression" designating amendments that may not be substituted or changed. Amendments may be only substituted or added in a Constitutional Convention setting. The most important part of the 10th Amendment is the logical variable expression "are reserved to the states respectively or to the people" that allows amendments to be rescinded, repealed, or added.

The 10th Amendment "Reserves Power Clause" "are reserved to the states respectively or to the people" is the most important implementable part of the 10th Amendment. The 10th Amendment Reserves Power Clause may be executed in the following two ways:

10th Amendment "Reserves Power Clause" as pertains to the State Government (Legislature)

10th Amendment "Reserves Power Clause" as pertains to the people

AMENDMENT 16 RATIFIED 2/3/1913

The Congress shall have power to lay and collect taxes on incomes, from whatever source derived, without apportionment among the several States, and without regard to any census or enumeration.

The 16th Amendment replaces "Article I Section 2, Clause 3." "Representatives and direct Taxes shall be apportioned among the several States which may be included within this Union, according to their respective Numbers, which shall be determined by adding to the whole Number of free Persons, including those bound to Service for a Term of Years, and excluding Indians not taxed, three fifths of all other Persons."

The 16th amendment violates the "delegated to the United States of America" sentence in the 10th Amendment" and the bill of rights.

DIRECT TAX

The "direct tax" was legal and Constitutional. The "direct tax" is directly on a person or person's property satisfying the person's inalienable property rights. The planners of the constitution had rejected income taxes (or any other direct taxes) unless they were apportioned to each state according to population.

16 AMENDMENT NOTES

- The 16th Amendment tax allows direct taxation without apportionment according the population of to each state.
- The 16th Amendment taxes corporate profit.
- The 16th Amendment allows Income received from the inalienable rights of property (rents from real estate) or (income from labor or personal investments) to be taxed without apportionment.
- The 16th Amendment forced the people of the United States to lose their inalienable rights of property for excise taxable privileges.
- The 16th Amendment forced the people of the United States to lose their person's inalienable property rights for entitlement (social security, medicare, unemployment) taxable privileges.
- The 16th Amendment substituted an "indirect tax" on income for a "direct tax."
- The 16th Amendment asserts taxes are collected on incomes without apportionment similar to an indirect tax collection.
- The 16th Amendment allows the Federal Government to equally impose social insurance taxes on employers and employees.
- The 16th Amendment allows the Federal Government to collect the social security wage tax from an employee's "gross income wage" making him a "net wage earner."
- The 16th Amendment allows the Federal Government to collect the medicare wage tax from an employee's "gross income wage" making him a "net wage earner."
- The 16th Amendment allows the Federal Government to collect the unemployment tax from an employee's "gross income wage" making him a "net wage earner."
- The 16th Amendment allows the Federal Government to collect corporate and company income taxes temporary changing the status of the corporation and company income from "gross income" to "net income" (the corporation and company recoups by transferring the taxes to the market place introducing "multi taxation" (corporations and companies don't pay taxes!).

AMENDMENT 17 RATIFIED 4/8/1913

The Senate of the United States shall be composed of two Senators from each State, elected by the people thereof, for six years; and each Senator shall have one vote.

The 17th Amendment supersedes Article 1 Section 3 "The Senate of the United States shall be composed of two Senators from each State, chosen by the Legislature thereof, for six Years; and each Senator shall have one Vote."

Immediately after they shall be assembled in Consequence of the first Election, they shall be divided as equally as may be into three Classes. The Seats of the Senators of the first Class shall be vacated at the expiration of the second year, of the second class at the expiration of the fourth year, and of the third class at the expiration of the sixth year, so that one third may be chosen every second year.

The 17th amendment violates the "delegated to the United States of America" sentence of the 10th Amendment.

FEDERAL RESERVE BANK

Powers of Congress: To coin Money, regulate the Value thereof, and of foreign Coin, and fix the Standard of Weights and Measures.

- Federal Reserve Bank is allowed to print money.
- Federal Reserve Bank violates the "delegated to the United States of America" sentence of the 10th amendment.

PREAMBLE

(The right to "alter or abolish" a government)

We hold these truths to be self-evident, that all men are created equal, that they are endowed by their Creator with certain unalienable Rights that among these are Life, Liberty and the pursuit of Happiness. That to secure these rights, Governments are instituted among Men, deriving their just powers from the consent of the governed, That whenever any Form of Government becomes destructive of these ends, it is the Right of the People to alter or to abolish it, and to institute new Government, laying its foundation on such principles and organizing its powers in such form, as to them shall seem most likely to affect their Safety and Happiness. Prudence, indeed, will dictate that Governments long established should not be changed for light and transient causes; and accordingly all experience hath shown, that mankind are more disposed to suffer, while evils are sufferable, than to right themselves by abolishing the forms to which they are accustomed. But when a long train of abuses and usurpations, pursuing invariably the same Object evinces a design to reduce them under absolute Despotism, it is their right, it is their duty, to throw off such Government, and to provide new guards for their future security.

RID 16TH AND 17TH AMENDMENT

The 13 colonies fought for representation and the power of taxation. Both go hand in hand as was the situation prior to the American Revolutionary War.

Today, the people's assembly districts or the States Governments Legislatures have lost both representation and the power of taxation.

The "17th Amendment" created the present day "Federalism" system of government which took away representation; and the "16th amendment wage tax" took away the power of taxation. The Federal Reserve siphons dollars to slowly inflate the purchasing power of the dollar.

The following tri-punch of the 1913 conspiracy of the progressive period has brought "Federalism to its knees;

- "16th amendment wage tax"
- "17th amendment"
- "Federal reserve"

States Governments' Legislatures must apply the "reserves power clause to repeal:

- "17th amendment"
- "16th amendment" (taxation returns to states governments' Legislatures)
- "Federal Reserve Bank" (Future "Central Bank" profits must remain within the confines of the United States Government and operated by the government.)

The situation is in the hands of the States Governments' Legislatures! Are the States Governments' legislatures capable???

Remember, at one time, the States Governments' legislatures had the power of being able to impeach the President of the United States as well as States Governors!

PRIVATIZE

Another course of action to take is to privatize all entitlement taxes including the following:

- "medicare wage taxes"
- "social security wage taxes"
- "unemployment wage taxes"

This action will convert a socialistic system to a complete capitalistic one!

PONZI SCHEME

A "Ponzi Scheme" is an economic arrangement where the money paid into the system by later entrants is paid right back out as benefits to earlier entrants.

Social Security did not fit that precise "Ponzi Scheme" definition during the Great Depression. Social Security was created during the Great Depression by President Franklin Roosevelt.

Receiving benefits from "social security wages' taxes" immediately, defies the "Ponzi Scheme." President Roosevelt realized that the money makers during the depression were companies selling items for profit. At that time, the current "company tax" and "social security wage tax" were put on items to be sold.

The following tax was sent to the government on a weekly basis:

- "company tax"
- "social security wage tax"

To add to a company's profit, a company transmits the following tax to the market place:

- "company tax"
- "snowball company tax" ("mathematical algorithm")
- "social security wage tax"
- "snowball social security wage tax" ("mathematical algorithm")

Since the country was experiencing a severe depression, the "social security tax'" money including the following taxes on items in the market place went to paying "Social Security retired recipients:

- "company tax"
- "snowball company tax" ("mathematical algorithm")
- "social security wage tax"
- "snowball social security wage tax" ("mathematical algorithm")

Retirees began receiving benefits immediately, without having paid into the program themselves through taxing current companies and their workers from the following taxes in the country's market place:

- "company tax"
- "snowball company tax" ("mathematical algorithm")
- "social security wage tax"
- "snowball social security wage tax" ("mathematical algorithm")

Moreover, the retired poor people who received the "social security" benefits actually paid a "double tax" on items purchased. The following taxes convert to hidden sales taxes that produced a "multi taxation" situation:

- "company tax"
- "snowball company tax" ("mathematical algorithm")
- "social security wages' tax"
- "snowball social security wage tax" ("mathematical algorithm")

The benefits of "multi taxation" went to the government; and, President Roosevelt, knowing it or not, gave needed income to the "retired recipients" from the profits of "multi taxation."

The "Ponzi Scheme" definition did not apply to the Social Security wage tax on an item during the great depression!

Want happens today?

The following taxes are deducted from the company's and worker's income and sent to the government on a weekly basis:

- "company tax"
- "16th Amendment wage tax"
- "social security wage tax"
- "medicare wage tax"
- "unemployment wage tax"

The status of a "gross wage earner" becomes "net wage earner;"

To add to a company's profit, the following taxes are transmitted to the market place becoming hidden, sales taxes.

- "company tax"
- "16th Amendment wage tax"
- "social security wage taxes"
- "medicare wage taxes"
- "unemployment wage taxes"
- "snowball company tax" ("mathematical algorithm")
- "snowball 16th Amendment wage tax" ("mathematical algorithm")
- "snowball social security wage taxes" ("mathematical algorithm")
- "snowball medicare wage taxes" ("mathematical algorithm")
- "snowball unemployment wage taxes" ("mathematical algorithm")

These taxes are placed on an item being sold throughout the country's market place indicating that the company does not pay taxes leaving the paying of taxes to the people in the market place producing "multi taxation."

A "net wage earner" who purchases in the market place would be subject to a "triple taxation" and any other person would be subjected to a "double taxation." Since the government and company do not pay taxes, the benefit of "multi taxation" goes to the government and companies.

Every person, citizen or not, rich or poor, pays these taxes every time a purchase is made.

The government's "multi taxation" profit reverts to other purposes like stimulus packages, growth of government…etc.

Under a non-Republic Federal Government, in other words, "Federalism" the "Ponzi Scheme" dominates for social security.

AN ALGORITHMIC MATHEMATICAL MODEL
PROVES
"COMPANY TAXES"
AND
"WAGE TAXES"
CONVERT
TO
"SALES TAXES"

TWO DIMENSIONAL VENN DIAGRAM

INCLUDE

TRANSMIT COMPANY TAX
TRANSMIT 16TH AMENDMENT WAGE TAX
TRANSMIT SOCIAL SECURITY WAGE TAX
TRANSMIT MEDICARE WAGE TAX
TRANSMIT UNEMPLOYMENT WAGE TAX
SNOWBALL COMPANY TAX
SNOWBALL COMPANY AND 16TH AMENDMENT WAGE TAX
SNOWBALL COMPANY AND SOCIALSECURITY WAGE TAX
SNOWBALL COMPANY AND MDEICARE WAGE TAX
SNOWBALL COMPANY AND UNEMPLOYMENT TAX
MAIN COMPANY SUBSETS

"n" NUMBER OF COMPANIES' SUBSETS THAT
MANUFACTURED

OR

HANDLED A "MAIN COMPANY" ITEM

SNOW BALLING BEGINS!

SNOWBALL COMPANY TAX
SUIT (CLOTHING)

COMPANY TAX (1)

SUIT* COMPANY* TAX	PANTS* COMPANY* TAX	JACKET* COMPANY* TAX	VEST* COMPANY* TAX

"COMPANY TAX (2)"

PANTS* BUTTONS* COMPANY* TAX	PANTS* WOOL* WEAVE COMPANY* TAX	PANTS* ZIPPER* COMPANY* TAX	VEST* BUTTONS* COMPANY* TAX	VEST* SILK* CLOTH COMPANY* TAX	VEST* WOOL* CLOTH COMPANY* TAX

JACKET* BUTTONS* COMPANY* TAX	JACKET* SILK* CLOTH COMPANY* TAX	JACKET* WOOL* CLOTH COMPANY* TAX

"COMPANY TAX (3)"

BUTTONS* COMPANY* TAX	SILK* WEAVER COMPANY* TAX	WOOL* WEAVER COMPANY* TAX	ZIPPER* METAL COMPANY* TAX	ZIPPER* METAL* COMPANY* TAX

ONE SUIT
SIMPLE HYPTHETICAL CASE
"snowball company tax"="company tax (1)" +"company tax (2)" +"company tax (3)"

ONE ITEM
ALGORITHM
"SNOWBALL COMPANY TAX"

n equals number of companies whom manufactured or handled the item to be bought.

"snowball company tax"=
    "company tax"
    +"company tax (1)"
    +"company tax (2)"
    +"company tax (3)"
       +
       +
       +
    +"company tax (n)"

"gross income"=
    "company tax"
    +"snowball company tax"
    +"company expenses"
    +"profit"

> **Taxes of companies 1 thru n are added resulting in the production of an item through the delivering of a product or providing a service. All taxes are sent to the market place through the company's "gross income" as a "snowball company tax" that produced the item increasing the price of the item.**

> **Since company's "gross income" includes the "company tax" and "snowball company tax" the "gross income" increases!**

- The "company tax" and the "snowball company tax" will be passed to all consumers within the United States territories.
- For States Government, the "company tax" and the "snowball company tax" will be passed to all consumers within the States Government's territory.
- For County Government, the "company tax" and the "snowball company tax" will be passed to all consumers within the County Government's territory.
- For City Government, the "company tax" and the "snowball company tax" will be passed to all consumers within the City Government's territory.
- For Town Government, the "company tax" and the "snowball company tax" will be passed to all consumers within the Town Government's territory.
  - Any increase to the "company tax" will increase the "gross income."
  - Any decrease to the "company tax" will decrease the "gross income."

TRANSMIT COMPANY TAX

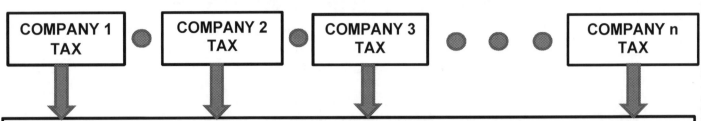

| COMPANY 1 TAX | COMPANY 2 TAX | COMPANY 3 TAX | COMPANY n TAX |

COMPANIES WEEKLY SEND "COMPANY TAXES" TO THE GOVERNMENT. "COMPANY TAXES" AND "SNOWBALL COMPANY TAXES" ARE ADDED TO COMPANY'S GROSS PROFITS. TO SECURE A PROFIT TO THEIR PRODUCTS, COMPANIES TRANSMIT "COMPANY TAXES" AND "SNOWBALL COMPANY TAXES" TO THE MARKET PLACE. "COMPANY TAXES" TURN OUT TO BE SALES' TAXES.

1

SNOWBALL COMPANY TAX

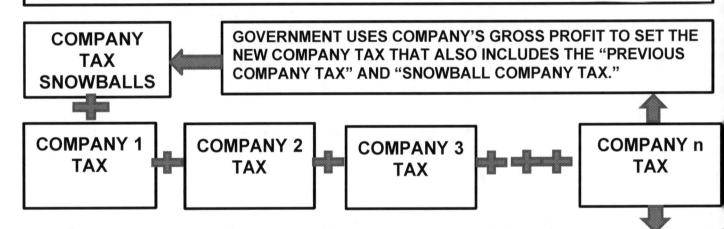

COMPANY TAX SNOWBALLS

GOVERNMENT USES COMPANY'S GROSS PROFIT TO SET THE NEW COMPANY TAX THAT ALSO INCLUDES THE "PREVIOUS COMPANY TAX" AND "SNOWBALL COMPANY TAX."

| COMPANY 1 TAX | COMPANY 2 TAX | COMPANY 3 TAX | COMPANY n TAX |

THE COMPANY WEEKLY SENDS THE "COMPANY TAX" TO THE GOVERNMENT; AND, THE COMPANY'S "COMPANY TAX" IS CONSIGNED TO THE MARKET PLACE.
THE "COMPANY TAX" PRODUCES A "SNOWBALL COMPANY TAX." BOTH THE "COMPANY TAX" AND THE "SNOWBALL COMPANY TAX" ARE INCLUDED IN THE PRICE OF THE ITEM PERMITTING THE ITEM'S COST TO INCREASE.
BOTH "COMPANY TAX" AND THE "SNOWBALL COMPANY TAX" ARE ADDED TO THE COMPANY'S GROSS PROFIT.
SINCE THE "NEW "COMPANY TAX" INCLUDES THE "OLD COMPANY TAX" AND THE "SNOWBALL COMPANY TAX," THE "NEW COMPANY TAX" SNOWS BALLS.
THE PAYMENT OF THE "COMPANY TAX" AND "SNOWBALL COMPANY TAX" IS LEFT TO THE CONSUMER INDICATING THAT THE "COMPANY TAX" IS ACTUALLY A SALES TAX.

SNOWBALL COMPANY
AND
16TH AMENDMENT
WAGE TAX
SUIT (CLOTHING)
"COMPANY TAX (1)"

SUIT* COMPANY* TAX	JACKET* COMPANY* TAX	VEST* COMPANY* TAX	PANTS* COMPANY* TAX

"16TH AMENDMENT WAGE TAX (1)"

PANTS* 16TH AMENDMENT WAGE* TAX	PANTS* BUTTONS* 16TH AMENDMENT WAGE* TAX	PANTS* WOOL* CLOTH 16TH AMENDMENT WAGE* TAX	PANTS* ZIPPER* 16TH AMENDMENT WAGE* TAX
JACKET* 16TH AMENDMENT WAGE* TAX	JACKET* BUTTONS* 16TH AMENDMENT WAGE* TAX	JACKET* SILK* CLOTH 16TH AMENDMENT WAGE* TAX	JACKET* WOOL* CLOTH 16TH AMENDMENT WAGE* TAX
VEST* 16TH AMENDMENT WAGE* TAX	VEST* BUTTONS* 16TH AMENDMENT WAGE* TAX	VEST* SILK* CLOTH 16TH AMENDMENT WAGE* TAX	VEST* WOOL* CLOTH 16TH AMENDMENT WAGE* TAX

"COMPANY TAX (2)"

BUTTONS* COMPANY* TAX	SILK* WEAVER COMPANY* TAX	WOOL* WEAVER COMPANY* TAX	ZIPPER* MEDALS COMPANY* TAX	ZIPPER MEDALS* COMPANY* TAX

"16TH AMENDMENT WAGE TAX (2)"

BUTTONS* 16TH AMENDMENT WAGE* TAX	SILK* WEAVER 16TH AMENDMENT WAGE* TAX	WOOL* WEAVER 16TH AMENDMENT WAGE* TAX	METAL* 16TH AMENDMENT WAGE* TAX

ONE SUIT
SIMPLE HYPTHETICAL CASE

"snowball tax (1)"="company tax (1)" +"16th amendment wage tax (1)"
"snowball tax (2)"="company tax (2)" +"16th amendment wage tax (2)"
"snowball tax"="snowball tax (1)" +"snowball tax (2)"+"company tax"

ONE ITEM
ALGORITHM
COMPANY AND 16TH AMENDMENT WAGE SNOWBALL TAX!

n equals number of companies whom manufactured or handled the item to be bought.

"snowball company tax"=
    "company tax"
    +"company tax (1)"
    +"company tax (2)"
    +"company tax (3)"
       +
       +
       +
    +"company tax (n)"

> Taxes of companies 1 thru n are added resulting in the production of an item through the delivering of a product or providing a service. All taxes are sent to the market place through the company's "gross income" as a "snowball company gross tax" that produced the item increasing the price of the item.

k1, k2, k3,,,kn equals the number of workers whom manufactured or handled the item to be bought in 1,2,3,,,, n companies.

"snowball 16th amendment wage tax (1)"=
    "16th amendment wage tax (1, 1)"
    +"16th amendment wage tax (1, 2)"
    +"16th amendment wage tax (1, 3)"
       +
       +
       +
    +"16th amendment wage tax (1, k1)"

> k1 is the number of worker's 16th amendment wage taxes in company (1) that are included in the "gross income" of the item. The k1 worker 16th amendment wage taxes are delivered to the market place.

"snowball 16th amendment wage tax (2)"=
    "16th amendment wage tax (2, 1)"
    +"16th amendment wage tax (2, 2)"
    +"16th amendment wage tax (2, 3)"
       +
       +
       +
    +"16th amendment wage tax (2, k2)"

> k_2 is the number of worker's 16th amendment wage taxes in company (2) that are included in the "gross income" of the item. The k_2 worker 16th amendment wage taxes are delivered to the market place.

"snowball 16th amendment wage tax (3)"=
    "16th amendment wage tax (3, 1)"
    +"16th amendment wage tax (3, 2)"
    +"16th amendment wage tax (3, 3)"
       +
       +
       +
    +"16th amendment wage tax (3, k3)"
       +
       +
       +
       +

> k_3 is the number of worker's 16th amendment wage taxes in company (3) that are included in the "gross income" of the item. The k_3 worker 16th amendment wage taxes are delivered to the market place.

"snowball 16th amendment wage tax (n)"=
    "16th amendment wage tax (n, 1)"
    +"16th amendment wage tax (n, 2)"
    +"16th amendment wage tax (n, 3)"
       +
       +
       +
    +"16th amendment wage tax (n, kn)"

> k_n is the number of worker's 16th amendment wage taxes in company (n) that are included in the "gross income" of the item. The k_n worker 16th amendment wage taxes are delivered to the market place.

"snowball 16th amendment wage tax"=
    "snowball 16th amendment wage tax (1)"
    +"snowball 16th amendment wage tax (2)"
    +"snowball 16th amendment wage tax (3)"
       +
       +
       +
    +"snowball 16th amendment wage tax (kn)"

> The total snowball worker's 16th amendment wage taxes are included in the item's "gross income" and are delivered to the market place.

"gross income"=
    "company tax"
    +"16th amendment tax"
    +"snowball company tax"
    +"snowball 16th amendment tax"
    +"company expenses"
    +"profit"

> Since company's ""gross income"" includes the "company tax," "snowball company tax," "16th amendment tax" and "snowball 16th amendment tax," the cost of the item increases!

- The "company tax," "snowball company tax," "16th amendment tax" and "snowball 16th amendment tax" will be passed to all consumers within the United States territories.
- For States Government, the "company tax," "snowball company tax," "16th amendment tax" and "snowball 16th amendment tax" will be passed to all consumers within the States Government's territory.
- For County Government, the "company tax," "snowball company tax," "16th amendment tax" and "snowball 16th amendment tax" will be passed to all consumers within the County Government's territory.
- For City Government, the "company tax," "snowball company tax," "16th amendment tax" and "snowball 16th amendment tax" will be passed to all consumers within the City Government's territory.
- For Town Government, the "company tax," "snowball company tax," "16th amendment tax" and "snowball 16th amendment tax" will be passed to all consumers within the Town Government's territory.
  - Any increase to the "company tax" will increase "gross income."
  - Any increase to the "16th amendment wage tax" will increase the "gross income."
  - Any decrease to the "company tax" will decrease "gross income."
  - Any decrease to the "16th amendment wage tax" will decrease the "gross income."

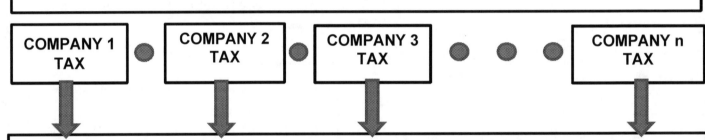

TRANSMIT 16TH AMENDMENT WAGE TAX

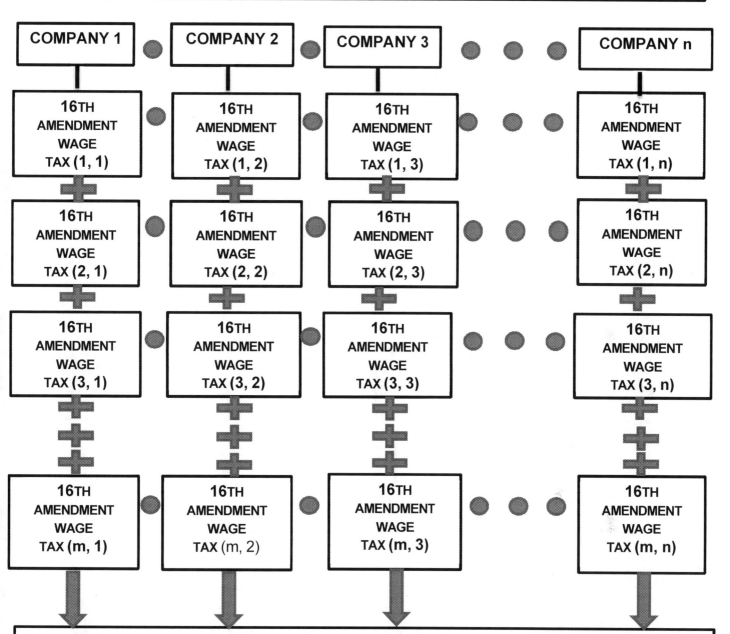

COMPANIES WEEKLY SEND "16TH AMENDMENT TAXES" TO THE GOVERNMENT. "16TH AMENDMENT TAXES" AND "SNOWBALL 16TH AMENDMENT TAXES" ARE ADDED TO COMPANY'S GROSS PROFITS. TO SECURE A PROFIT TO THEIR PRODUCTS, COMPANIES TRANSMIT "16TH AMENDMENT TAXES" AND "SNOWBALL 16TH AMENDMENT TAXES" TO THE MARKET PLACE. "16TH AMENDMENT TAX" TURNS OUT TO BE A SALES' TAX.

SNOWBALL COMPANY AND 16TH AMENDMENT WAGE TAX

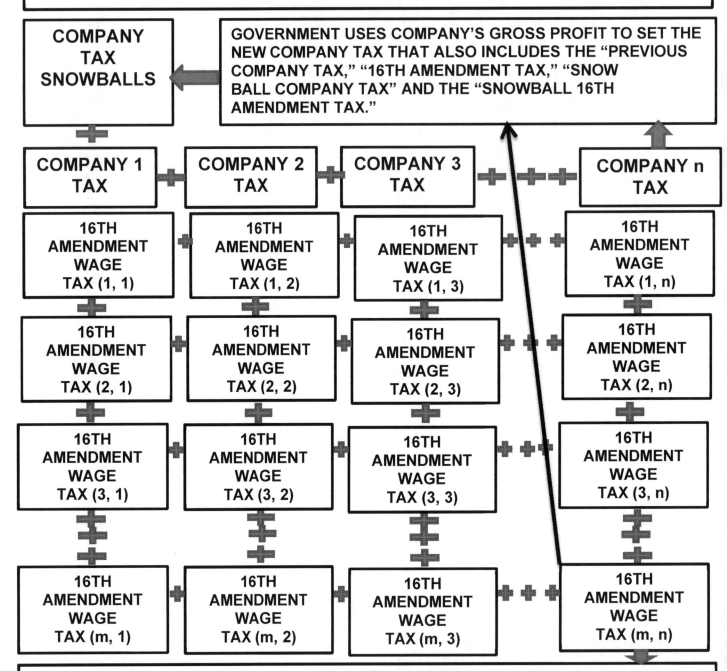

COMPANY TAX SNOWBALLS

GOVERNMENT USES COMPANY'S GROSS PROFIT TO SET THE NEW COMPANY TAX THAT ALSO INCLUDES THE "PREVIOUS COMPANY TAX," "16TH AMENDMENT TAX," "SNOW BALL COMPANY TAX" AND THE "SNOWBALL 16TH AMENDMENT TAX."

COMPANY 1 TAX **COMPANY 2 TAX** **COMPANY 3 TAX** **COMPANY n TAX**

16TH AMENDMENT WAGE TAX (1, 1) — 16TH AMENDMENT WAGE TAX (1, 2) — 16TH AMENDMENT WAGE TAX (1, 3) — 16TH AMENDMENT WAGE TAX (1, n)

16TH AMENDMENT WAGE TAX (2, 1) — 16TH AMENDMENT WAGE TAX (2, 2) — 16TH AMENDMENT WAGE TAX (2, 3) — 16TH AMENDMENT WAGE TAX (2, n)

16TH AMENDMENT WAGE TAX (3, 1) — 16TH AMENDMENT WAGE TAX (3, 2) — 16TH AMENDMENT WAGE TAX (3, 3) — 16TH AMENDMENT WAGE TAX (3, n)

16TH AMENDMENT WAGE TAX (m, 1) — 16TH AMENDMENT WAGE TAX (m, 2) — 16TH AMENDMENT WAGE TAX (m, 3) — 16TH AMENDMENT WAGE TAX (m, n)

THE "COMPANY TAX," "SNOWBALL COMPANY TAX;" "16TH AMENDMENT TAX" AND "SNOWBALL 16TH AMENDMENT TAX" ARE INCLUDED IN THE PRICE OF THE ITEM PERMITTING THE ITEM'S COST TO INCREASE. THE COMPANY WEEKLY SENDS THE "COMPANY TAX" AND "16TH AMENDMENT TAX" TO THE GOVERNMENT.

THE "COMPANY TAX" AND "16TH AMENDMENT TAX" ARE ALSO CONSIGNED TO THE MARKET PLACE. THE PAYMENT OF THE "COMPANY TAX," "16TH AMENDMENT TAX," "SNOWBALL COMPANY TAX" AND "SNOWBALL16TH AMENDMENT TAX" ARE LEFT TO THE CONSUMER INDICATING THAT THE "COMPANY TAX" AND "16TH AMENDMENT TAX" ACTUALLY ARE SALES' TAXES.

SNOWBALL COMPANY AND SOCIAL SECURITY WAGE TAX SUIT (CLOTHING)

"COMPANY TAX (1)"

SUIT* COMPANY* TAX	JACKET* COMPANY* TAX	VEST* COMPANY* TAX	PANTS* COMPANY* TAX

"SOCIAL SECURITY WAGE TAX (1)"

PANTS* SOCIAL SECURITY WAGE* TAX	PANTS* BUTTONS* SOCIAL SECURITY WAGE* TAX	PANTS* WOOL* CLOTH SOCIAL SECURITY WAGE* TAX	PANTS* ZIPPER* SOCIAL SECURITY WAGE* TAX
JACKET* SOCIAL SECURITY WAGE* TAX	JACKET* BUTTONS* SOCIAL SECURITY WAGE* TAX	JACKET* SILK* CLOTH SOCIAL SECURITY WAGE* TAX	JACKET* WOOL* CLOTH SOCIAL SECURITY WAGE* TAX
VEST* SOCIAL SECURITY WAGE* TAX	VEST* BUTTONS* SOCIAL SECURITY WAGE* TAX	VEST* SILK* CLOTH SOCIAL SECURITY WAGE* TAX	VEST* WOOL* CLOTH SOCIAL SECURITY WAGE* TAX

"COMPANY TAX (2)"

BUTTONS* COMPANY* TAX	SILK* WEAVE COMPANY* TAX	WOOL* WEAVE COMPANY* TAX	ZIPPER* MEDAL COMPANY* TAX	ZIPPER MEDAL* COMPANY* TAX

"SOCIAL SECURITY WAGE TAX (2)"

BUTTONS* SOCIAL SECURITY WAGE* TAX	SILK* WEAVER* SOCIAL SECURITY WAGE* TAX	WOOL* WEAVER* SOCIAL SECURITY WAGE* TAX	ZIPPER* METAL* SOCIAL SECURITY WAGE* TAX

ONE SUIT
SIMPLE HYPTHETICAL CASE

"snowball tax (1)"="company tax (1)" +"social security wage tax (1)"
"snowball tax (2)"="company tax (2)" +"social security wage tax (2)"
"snowball tax"="snowball tax (1)" +"snowball tax (2)" + "company tax"

ONE ITEM
ALGORITHM
COMPANY AND SOCIAL SECURITY WAGE SNOWBALL TAX!

n equals number of companies whom manufactured or handled the item to be bought.

"snowball company tax"=
   "company tax"
   +"company tax (1)"
   +"company tax (2)"
   +"company tax (3)"
      +
      +
      +
   +"company tax (n)"

> **Taxes of companies 1 thru n are added resulting in the production of an item through the delivering of a product or providing a service. All taxes are sent to the market place through the company's "gross income" as a "snowball company gross tax" that produced the item increasing the price of the item.**

k1, k2, k3,,,kn equals the number of workers whom manufactured or handled the item to be bought in 1,2,3,,,, n companies.

"snowball social security wage tax (1)"=
   "social security wage tax (1, 1)"
   +"social security wage tax (1, 2)"
   +"social security wage tax (1, 3)"
      +
      +
      +
   +"social security wage tax (1, k1)"

"snowball social security wage tax (2)"=
   "social security wage tax (2, 1)"
   +"social security wage tax (2, 2)"
   +"social security wage tax (2, 3)"
      +
      +
      +
   +"social security wage tax (2, k2)"

> **k1 is the number of worker's social security wage taxes in company (1) that are included in the "gross income" of the item. The k1 worker social security wage taxes are delivered to the market place.**

> **k2 is the number of worker's social security wage taxes in company (2) that are included in the "gross income" of the item. The k2 worker social security wage taxes are delivered to the market place.**

"snowball social security wage tax (3)"=
    "social security wage tax (3, 1)"
    +"social security wage tax (3, 2)"
    +"social security wage tax (3, 3)"
       +
       +
       +
    +"social security wage tax (3, k3)"
       +
       +
       +

k3 is the number of worker's social security wage taxes in company (3) that are included in the "gross income" of the item. The k3 worker social security wage taxes are delivered to the market place.

"snowball social security wage tax (n)"=
    "social security wage tax (n, 1)"
    +"social security wage tax (n, 2)"
    +"social security wage tax (n, 3)"
       +
       +
       +
    +"social security wage tax (n, kn)"

kn is the number of worker's social security wage taxes in company (n) that are included in the "gross income" of the item. The kn worker social security wage taxes are delivered to the market place.

"snowball social security wage tax"=
    "snowball social security wage tax (1)"
    +"snowball social security wage tax (2)"
    +"snowball social security wage tax (3)"
       +
       +
       +
    +"snowball social security wage tax (kn)"

The total snowball worker's social security wage taxes are included in the item's "gross income" and are delivered to the market place.

"gross income"=
    "company tax"
    +"social security wage tax"
    +"snowball company tax"
    +"snowball social security wage tax"
    +"company expenses"
    +"profit"

Since company's "gross income" includes the "company tax," "snowball company tax," "social security wage tax" and "snowball social security wage tax" the cost of the item increases!

- The "company tax," "snowball company tax," "social security wage tax" and "snowball social security wage tax" will be passed to all consumers within the United States territories.
- For States Government, the "company tax," "snowball company tax," "social security wage tax" and "snowball social security wage tax" will be passed to all consumers within the States Government's territory.
- For County Government, the "company tax," "snowball company tax," "social security wage tax" and "snowball social security wage tax" will be passed to all consumers within the County Government's territory.
- For City Government, the "company tax," "snowball company tax,"" "social security wage tax" and "snowball social security wage tax" will be passed to all consumers within the City Government's territory.
- For Town Government, the "company tax," "snowball company tax," "social security wage tax" and "snowball social security wage tax" will be passed to all consumers within the Town Government's territory.

- Any increase to the "company tax" will increase "gross income."
- Any increase to the "social security tax" will increase the "gross income."
- Any decrease to the "company tax" will decrease "gross income."
- Any decrease to the "social security tax" will decrease the "gross income."

TRANSMIT COMPANY TAX

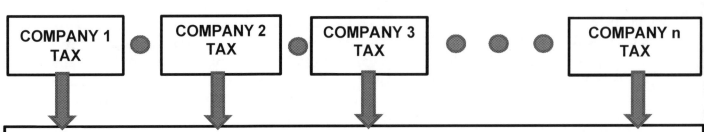

| COMPANY 1 TAX | COMPANY 2 TAX | COMPANY 3 TAX | | COMPANY n TAX |

COMPANYS WEEKLY SEND "COMPANY TAXES" TO THE GOVERNMENT. "COMPANY TAXES" AND "SNOWBALL COMPANY TAXES" ARE ADDED TO COMPANY'S GROSS PROFITS. TO SECURE A PROFIT TO THEIR PRODUCTS, COMPANIES TRANSMIT "COMPANY TAXES" AND "SNOWBALL COMPANY TAXES" TO THE MARKET PLACE. "COMPANY TAXES" TURN OUT TO BE SALES' TAXES.

TRANSMIT SOCIAL SECURITY WAGE TAX

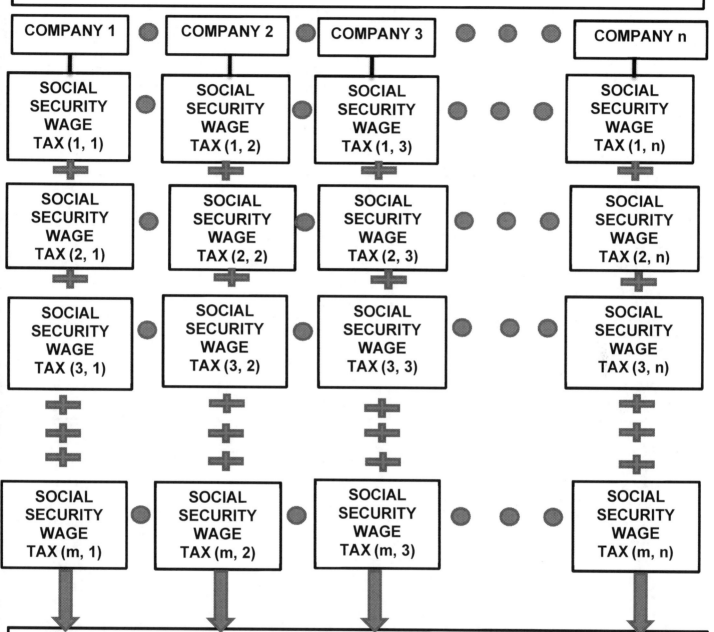

COMPANIES WEEKLY SEND "SOCIAL SECURITY TAXES" TO THE GOVERNMENT. "SOCIAL SECURITY TAXES" AND "SNOWBALL SOCIAL SECURITY TAXES" ARE ADDED TO COMPANY'S GROSS PROFITS. TO SECURE A PROFIT TO THEIR PRODUCTS, COMPANIES TRANSMIT "SOCIAL SECURITY TAXES" AND "SNOWBALL SOCIAL SECURITY TAXES" TO THE MARKET PLACE. "SOCIAL SECURITY TAXES" TURN OUT TO BE SALES' TAXES.

SNOWBALL COMPANY AND SOCIAL SECURITY WAGE TAX

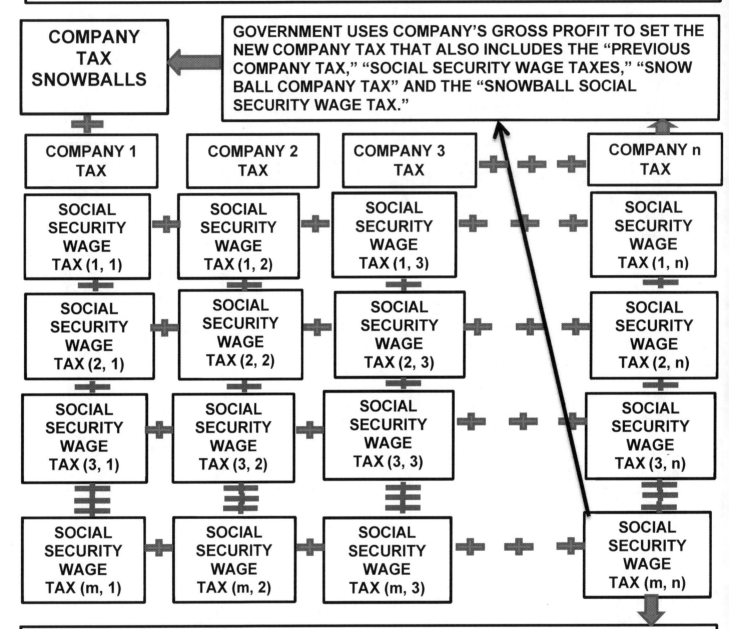

COMPANY TAX SNOWBALLS

GOVERNMENT USES COMPANY'S GROSS PROFIT TO SET THE NEW COMPANY TAX THAT ALSO INCLUDES THE "PREVIOUS COMPANY TAX," "SOCIAL SECURITY WAGE TAXES," "SNOW BALL COMPANY TAX" AND THE "SNOWBALL SOCIAL SECURITY WAGE TAX."

| COMPANY 1 TAX | COMPANY 2 TAX | COMPANY 3 TAX | COMPANY n TAX |

| SOCIAL SECURITY WAGE TAX (1, 1) | SOCIAL SECURITY WAGE TAX (1, 2) | SOCIAL SECURITY WAGE TAX (1, 3) | SOCIAL SECURITY WAGE TAX (1, n) |

| SOCIAL SECURITY WAGE TAX (2, 1) | SOCIAL SECURITY WAGE TAX (2, 2) | SOCIAL SECURITY WAGE TAX (2, 3) | SOCIAL SECURITY WAGE TAX (2, n) |

| SOCIAL SECURITY WAGE TAX (3, 1) | SOCIAL SECURITY WAGE TAX (3, 2) | SOCIAL SECURITY WAGE TAX (3, 3) | SOCIAL SECURITY WAGE TAX (3, n) |

| SOCIAL SECURITY WAGE TAX (m, 1) | SOCIAL SECURITY WAGE TAX (m, 2) | SOCIAL SECURITY WAGE TAX (m, 3) | SOCIAL SECURITY WAGE TAX (m, n) |

THE "COMPANY TAX," "SNOWBALL COMPANY TAX;" "SOCIAL SECURITY WAGE TAX" AND "SNOWBALL SOCIAL SECURITY WAGE TAX" ARE INCLUDED IN THE PRICE OF THE ITEM PERMITTING THE ITEM'S COST TO INCREASE. THE COMPANY WEEKLY SENDS THE "COMPANY TAX" AND "SOCIAL SECURITY WAGE TAX" TO THE GOVERNMENT.

THE "COMPANY TAX" AND "SOCIAL SECURITY WAGE TAX" ARE ALSO CONSIGNED TO THE MARKET PLACE. THE PAYMENT OF THE "COMPANY TAX," "SOCIAL SECURITY WAGE TAX," "SNOWBALL COMPANY TAX" AND "SNOWBALL SOCIAL SECURITY WAGE TAX" ARE LEFT TO THE CONSUMER INDICATING THAT THE "COMPANY TAX" AND "SOCIAL SECURITY WAGE TAX" ACTUALLY ARE SALES' TAXES.

SNOWBALL COMPANY
AND
MEDICARE WAGE TAX
SUIT (CLOTHING)

"COMPANY TAX (1)"

SUIT* COMPANY* TAX	JACKET* COMPANY* TAX	VEST* COMPANY* TAX	PANTS* COMPANY* TAX

"MEDICARE WAGE TAX (1)"

PANTS* MEDICARE WAGE* TAX	PANTS* BUTTONS* MEDICARE WAGE* TAX	PANTS* WOOL* CLOTH MEDICARE WAGE* TAX	PANTS* ZIPPER* MEDICARE WAGE* TAX
JACKET* MEDICARE WAGE* TAX	JACKET* BUTTONS* MEDICARE WAGE* TAX	JACKET* SILK* CLOTH MEDICARE WAGE* TAX	JACKET* WOOL* CLOTH MEDICARE WAGE* TAX
VEST* MEDICARE WAGE* TAX	VEST* BUTTONS* MEDICARE WAGE* TAX	VEST* SILK* CLOTH MEDICARE WAGE* TAX	VEST* WOOL* CLOTH MEDICARE WAGE* TAX

"COMPANY TAX (2)"

BUTTONS COMPANY TAX	SILK WEAVE COMPANY TAX	WOOL WEAVE COMPANY TAX	ZIPPER MEDALS COMPANY TAX	ZIPPER MEDALS COMPANY TAX

"MEDICARE WAGE TAX (2)"

BUTTONS* MEDICARE WAGE* TAX	SILK* WEAVER* MEDICARE WAGE* TAX	WOOL* WEAVER* MEDICARE WAGE* TAX	ZIPPER^ METAL MEDICARE WAGE* TAX	ZIPPER^ METAL* MEDICARE WAGE* TAX

ONE SUIT
SIMPLE HYPTHETICAL CASE

"snowball tax (1)"="company tax (1)" +"medicare wage tax (1)"
"snowball tax (2)"="company tax (2)" +"medicare wage tax (2)"
"snowball tax"="snowball tax (1)" +"snowball tax (2)" + "company tax"

ONE ITEM
ALGORITHM
COMPANY AND MEDICARE WAGE SNOWBALL TAX!

n equals number of companies whom manufactured or handled the item to be bought.

"snowball company tax"=
   "company tax"
   +"company tax (1)"
   +"company tax (2)"
   +"company tax (3)"
      +
      +
      +
   +"company tax (n)"

> Taxes of companies 1 thru n are added resulting in the production of an item through the delivering of a product or providing a service. All taxes are sent to the market place through the company's "gross income" as a "snowball company gross tax" that produced the item increasing the price of the item.

k1, k2, k3,,,kn equals the number of workers whom manufactured or handled the item to be bought in 1,2,3,,,, n companies.

"snowball medicare wage tax (1)"=
   "medicare wage tax (1, 1)"
   +"medicare wage tax (1, 2)"
   +"medicare wage tax (1, 3)"
      +
      +
      +
   +"medicare wage tax (1, k1)"
"snowball medicare wage tax (2)"=
   "medicare wage tax (2, 1)"
   +"medicare wage tax (2, 2)"
   +"medicare wage tax (2, 3)"
      +
      +
      +
   +"medicare wage tax (2, k2)"

> k1 is the number of worker's medicare wage taxes in company (1) that are included in the "gross income" of the item. The k1 worker medicare wage taxes are delivered to the market place.

> k2 is the number of worker's medicare wage taxes in company (2) that are included in the "gross income" of the item. The k2 worker medicare wage taxes are delivered to the market place.

"snowball medicare wage tax (3)"=
"medicare wage tax (3, 1)"
+"medicare wage tax (3, 2)"
+"medicare wage tax (3, 3)"
+
+
+
+"medicare wage tax (3, k3)"
+
+
+

"snowball medicare wage tax (n)"=
"medicare wage tax (n, 1)"
+"medicare wage tax (n, 2)"
+"medicare wage tax (n, 3)"
+
+
+
+"medicare wage tax (n, kn)"
"snowball medicare wage tax"=
"snowball medicare wage tax (1)"
+"snowball medicare wage tax (2)"
+"snowball medicare wage tax (3)"
+
+
+
+"snowball medicare wage tax (n)"
"gross income"=
"company tax"
+"medicare wage tax "
+"snowball company tax"
+"snowball medicare wage tax "
+"company expenses"
+"profit"

k3 is the number of worker's medicare wage taxes in company (3) that are included in the "gross income" of the item. The k3 worker medicare wage taxes are delivered to the market place.

kn is the number of worker's medicare wage taxes in company (n) that are included in the "gross income" of the item. The kn worker medicare wage taxes are delivered to the market place.

The total snowball worker's wage taxes are included in the item's "gross income" and are delivered to the market place.

Since company's "gross income" includes the "company tax," "snowball company tax," "medicare wage tax" and "snowball medicare wage tax" the cost of the item increases!

- The "company tax," "snowball company tax," "medicare wage tax" and "snowball medicare wage tax " will be passed to all consumers within the United States territories.
- For States Government, the "company tax," "snowball company tax," "medicare wage tax" and "snowball medicare wage tax" will be passed to all consumers within the States Government's territory.
- For County Government, the "company tax," "snowball company tax," "medicare wage tax" and "snowball medicare wage tax" will be passed to all consumers within the County Government's territory.
- For City Government, the "company tax," "snowball company tax," "medicare wage tax" and "snowball medicare wage tax" will be passed to all consumers within the City Government's territory.
- For Town Government, the "company tax," "snowball company tax," "medicare wage tax" and "snowball medicare wage tax" will be passed to all consumers within the Town Government's territory.
  - Any increase to the "company tax" will increase "gross income."
  - Any increase to the "medicare wage tax" will increase the "gross income."
  - Any decrease to the "company tax" will decrease "gross income."
  - Any decrease to the "medicare wage tax" will decrease the "gross income."

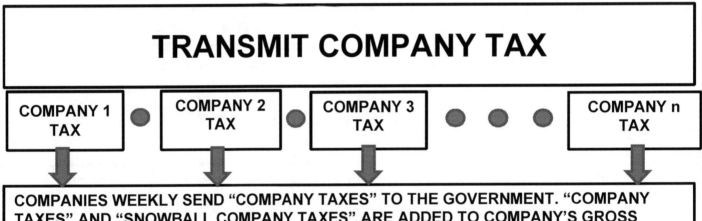

TRANSMIT COMPANY TAX

| COMPANY 1 TAX | COMPANY 2 TAX | COMPANY 3 TAX | COMPANY n TAX |

COMPANIES WEEKLY SEND "COMPANY TAXES" TO THE GOVERNMENT. "COMPANY TAXES" AND "SNOWBALL COMPANY TAXES" ARE ADDED TO COMPANY'S GROSS PROFITS. TO SECURE A PROFIT TO THEIR PRODUCTS, COMPANIES TRANSMIT "COMPANY TAXES" AND "SNOWBALL COMPANY TAXES" TO THE MARKET PLACE. "COMPANY TAXES" TURN OUT TO BE SALES' TAXES.

TRANSMIT MEDICARE WAGE TAX

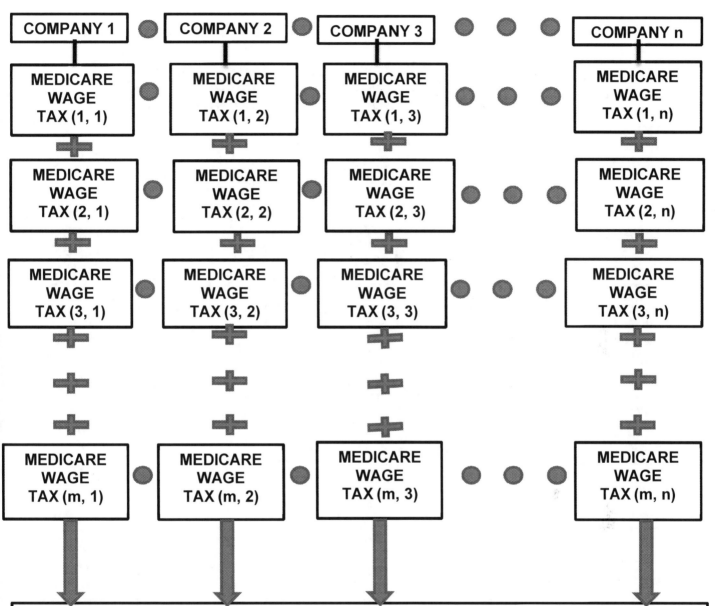

COMPANIES WEEKLY SEND "MEDICARE TAXES" TO THE GOVERNMENT. "MEDICARE TAXES" AND "SNOWBALL MEDICARE TAXES" ARE ADDED TO COMPANY'S "GROSS PROFITS." TO SECURE A PROFIT TO THEIR PRODUCTS, COMPANIES TRANSMIT "MEDICARE TAXES" AND "SNOWBALL MEDICARE TAXES" TO THE MARKET PLACE. "MEDICARE TAXES" TURN OUT TO BE SALES' TAXES.

SNOWBALL COMPANYAND MEDICARE WAGE TAX

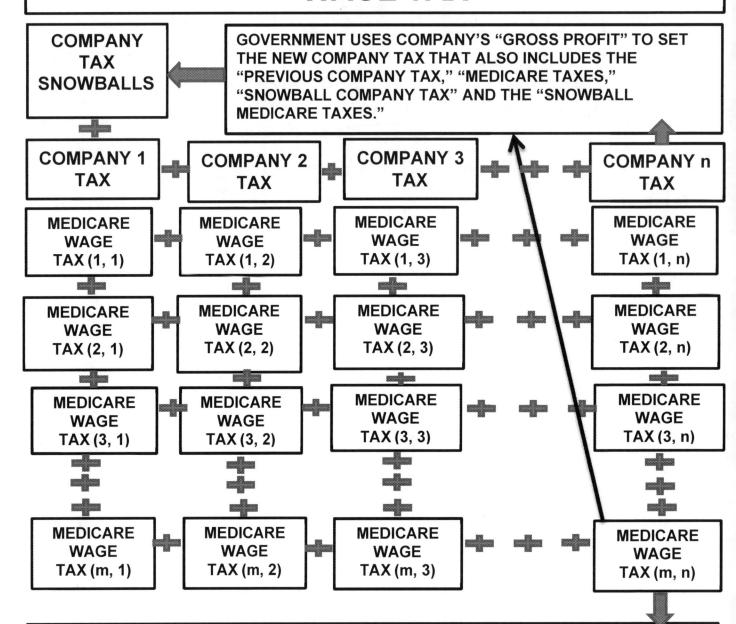

COMPANY TAX SNOWBALLS

GOVERNMENT USES COMPANY'S "GROSS PROFIT" TO SET THE NEW COMPANY TAX THAT ALSO INCLUDES THE "PREVIOUS COMPANY TAX," "MEDICARE TAXES," "SNOWBALL COMPANY TAX" AND THE "SNOWBALL MEDICARE TAXES."

COMPANY 1 TAX

COMPANY 2 TAX

COMPANY 3 TAX

COMPANY n TAX

MEDICARE WAGE TAX (1, 1)

MEDICARE WAGE TAX (1, 2)

MEDICARE WAGE TAX (1, 3)

MEDICARE WAGE TAX (1, n)

MEDICARE WAGE TAX (2, 1)

MEDICARE WAGE TAX (2, 2)

MEDICARE WAGE TAX (2, 3)

MEDICARE WAGE TAX (2, n)

MEDICARE WAGE TAX (3, 1)

MEDICARE WAGE TAX (3, 2)

MEDICARE WAGE TAX (3, 3)

MEDICARE WAGE TAX (3, n)

MEDICARE WAGE TAX (m, 1)

MEDICARE WAGE TAX (m, 2)

MEDICARE WAGE TAX (m, 3)

MEDICARE WAGE TAX (m, n)

THE "COMPANY TAX," "SNOWBALL COMPANY TAX;" "MEDICARE TAX" AND "SNOWBALL MEDICARE TAX" ARE INCLUDED IN THE PRICE OF THE ITEM PERMITTING THE ITEM'S COST TO INCREASE. THE COMPANY WEEKLY SENDS THE "COMPANY TAX" AND "MEDICARE TAX" TO THE GOVERNMENT.

THE "COMPANY TAX" AND "MEDICARE TAX" ARE ALSO CONSIGNED TO THE MARKET PLACE. THE PAYMENT OF THE "COMPANY TAX," "MEDICARE TAX," "SNOWBALL COMPANY TAX" AND "SNOWBALLMEDICARE TAX" ARE LEFT TO THE CONSUMER INDICATING THAT THE "COMPANY TAX" AND "MEDICARE TAX" ACTUALLY ARE SALES' TAXES.

SNOWBALL COMPANY
AND
UNEMPLOYMENT WAGE TAX
SUIT (CLOTHING)
"COMPANY TAX (1)"

SUIT* COMPANY* TAX	JACKET* COMPANY* TAX	VEST* COMPANY* TAX	PANTS* COMPANY* TAX

"UNEMPLOYMENT WAGE TAX (1)"

PANTS* UNEMPLOYMENT WAGE* TAX	PANTS* BUTTONS* UNEMPLOYMENT WAGE* TAX	PANTS* WOOL* CLOTH UNEMPLOYMENT WAGE* TAX	PANTS* ZIPPER* UNEMPLOYMENT WAGE* TAX
JACKET* UNEMPLOYMENT WAGE* TAX	JACKET* BUTTONS* UNEMPLOYMENT WAGE* TAX	JACKET& SILK* CLOTH UNEMPLOYMENT WAGE* TAX	JACKET* WOOL* CLOTH UNEMPLOYMENT WAGE* TAX
VEST* UNEMPLOYMENT WAGE* TAX	VEST* BUTTONS* UNEMPLOYMENT WAGE* TAX	VEST* SILK* CLOTH UNEMPLOYMENT WAGE* TAX	VEST* WOOL* CLOTH UNEMPLOYMENT WAGE* TAX

"COMPANY TAX (2)"

BUTTONS* COMPANY* TAX	SILK* WEAVER COMPANY* TAX	WOOL* WEAVER COMPANY* TAX	ZIPPER* MEDALS COMPANY* TAX	ZIPPER MEDALS* COMPANY* TAX

"UNEMPLOYMENT WAGE TAX (2)"

BUTTONS* UNEMPLOYMENT WAGE* TAX	SILK* WEAVER UNEMPLOYMENT WAGE* TAX	WOOL* WEAVER UNEMPLOYMENT WAGE* TAX	METAL* UNEMPLOYMENT WAGE* TAX

SIMPLE HYPTHETICAL CASE

"snowball tax (1)"="company tax (1)" +"unemployment wage tax (1)"
"snowball tax (2)"="company tax (2)" +"unemployment wage tax (2)"
"snowball tax"="snowball tax (1)" +"snowball tax (2)"+"company tax"

ONE ITEM
ALGORITHM
COMPANY AND UNEMPLOYMENT WAGE SNOWBALL TAX!

n equals number of companies whom manufactured or handled the item to be bought.

"snowball company tax"=
 "company tax"
 +"company tax (1)"
 +"company tax (2)"
 +"company tax (3)"
  +
  +
  +
 +"company tax (n)"

Taxes of companies 1 thru n are added resulting in the production of an item through the delivering of a product or providing a service. All taxes are sent to the market place through the company's "gross income" as a "snowball company gross tax" that produced the item increasing the price of the item.

k1, k2, k3,,,kn equals the number of workers whom manufactured or handled the item to be bought in 1,2,3,,,, n companies.

"snowball unemployment wage tax (1)"=
 "unemployment wage tax (1, 1)"
 +"unemployment wage tax (1, 2)"
 +"unemployment wage tax (1, 3)"
  +
  +
  +
 +"unemployment wage tax (1, k1)"

"snowball unemployment wage tax (2)"=
 "unemployment wage tax (2, 1)"
 +"unemployment wage tax (2, 2)"
 +"unemployment wage tax (2, 3)"
  +
  +
  +
 +"unemployment wage tax (2, k2)"

k1 is the number of worker's unemployment wage taxes in company (1) that are included in the "gross income" of the item. The k1 worker "unemployment wage taxes" are delivered to the market place.

k2 is the number of worker's unemployment wage taxes in company (2) that are included in the "gross income" of the item. The k2 worker "unemployment wage taxes" are delivered to the market place.

"snowball unemployment wage tax (3)"=
    "unemployment wage tax (3, 1)"
    +"unemployment wage tax (3, 2)"
    +"unemployment wage tax (3, 3)"
        +
        +
        +
    +"unemployment wage tax (3, k3)"
        +
        +
        +

k3 is the number of worker's unemployment wage taxes in company (3) that are included in the "gross income" of the item. The k3 worker unemployment wage taxes are delivered to the market place.

"snowball unemployment wage tax (n)"=
    "unemployment wage tax (n, 1)"
    +"unemployment wage tax (n, 2)"
    +"unemployment wage tax (n, 3)"
        +
        +
        +
    +"unemployment wage tax (n, kn)"

kn is the number of worker's unemployment wage taxes in company (n) that are included in the "gross income" of the item. The kn worker unemployment wage taxes are delivered to the market place.

"snowball unemployment wage tax"=
    "snowball unemployment wage tax (1)"
    +"snowball unemployment wage tax (2)"
    +"snowball unemployment wage tax (3)"
        +
        +
        +
    +"snowball unemployment wage tax (kn)"

The total snowball worker's unemployment wage taxes are included in the item's "gross income" and are delivered to the market place.

"gross income"=
    "company tax"
    +"unemployment tax"
    +"snowball company tax"
    +"snowball unemployment tax"
    +"company expenses"
    +"profit"

Since company's "gross income" includes the "company tax," "snowball company tax," "unemployment tax" and "snowball unemployment tax," the cost of the item increases!

- The "company tax," "snowball company tax," "unemployment tax" and "snowball unemployment tax" will be passed to all consumers within the United States territories.
- For States Government, the "company tax," "snowball company tax," "unemployment tax" and "snowball unemployment tax" will be passed to all consumers within the States Government's territory.
- For County Government, the "company tax," "snowball company tax," "unemployment tax" and "snowball unemployment tax" will be passed to all consumers within the County Government's territory.
- For City Government, the "company tax," "snowball company tax," "unemployment tax" and "snowball unemployment tax" will be passed to all consumers within the City Government's territory.
- For Town Government, the "company tax," "snowball company tax," "unemployment tax" and "snowball unemployment tax" will be passed to all consumers within the Town Government's territory.
  - Any increase to the "company tax" will increase "gross income."
  - Any increase to the "unemployment wage tax" will increase the "gross income."
  - Any decrease to the "company tax" will decrease "gross income."
  - Any decrease to the "unemployment wage tax" will decrease the "gross income."

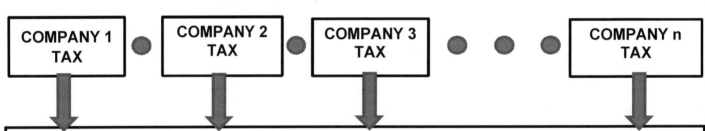

TRANSMIT COMPANY TAX

| COMPANY 1 TAX | | COMPANY 2 TAX | | COMPANY 3 TAX | | | | COMPANY n TAX |

COMPANIES WEEKLY SEND "COMPANY TAXES" TO THE GOVERNMENT. "COMPANY TAXES" AND "SNOWBALL COMPANY TAXES" ARE ADDED TO COMPANY'S GROSS PROFITS. TO SECURE A PROFIT TO THEIR PRODUCTS, COMPANIES TRANSMIT "COMPANY TAXES" AND "SNOWBALL COMPANY TAXES" TO THE MARKET PLACE. "COMPANY TAXES" TURN OUT TO BE SALES' TAXES.

TRANSMIT UNEMPLOYMENT WAGE TAX

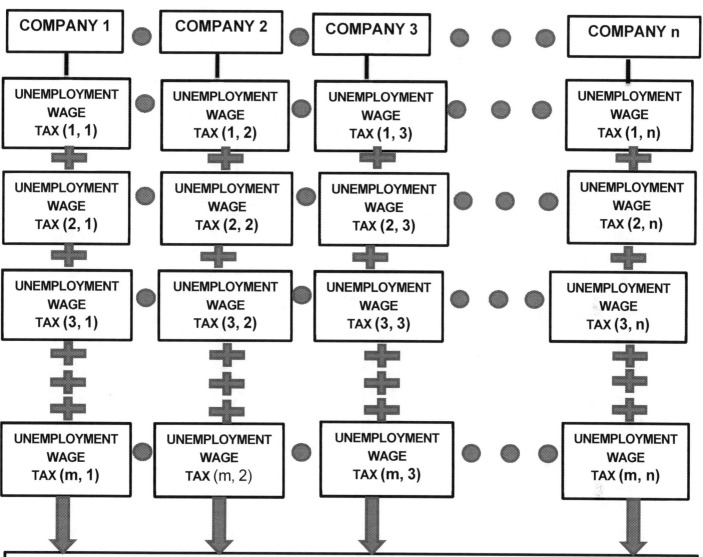

COMPANIES WEEKLY SEND "UNEMPLOYMENT TAXES" TO THE GOVERNMENT. "UNEMPLOYMENT TAXES" AND "SNOWBALL UNEMPLOYMENT TAXES" ARE ADDED TO COMPANY'S GROSS PROFITS. TO SECURE A PROFIT TO THEIR PRODUCTS, COMPANIES TRANSMIT "UNEMPLOYMENT TAXES" AND "SNOWBALL UNEMPLOYMENT TAXES" TO THE MARKET PLACE. "UNEMPLOYMENT TAXES" TURN OUT TO BE SALES' TAXES.

SNOWBALL COMPANY AND UNEMPLOYMENT WAGE TAX

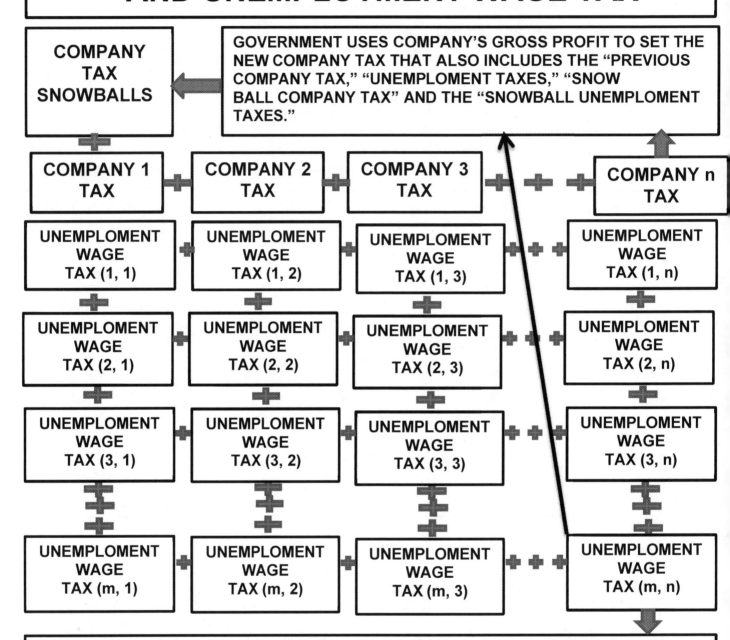

COMPANY TAX SNOWBALLS

GOVERNMENT USES COMPANY'S GROSS PROFIT TO SET THE NEW COMPANY TAX THAT ALSO INCLUDES THE "PREVIOUS COMPANY TAX," "UNEMPLOYMENT TAXES," "SNOW BALL COMPANY TAX" AND THE "SNOWBALL UNEMPLOMENT TAXES."

| COMPANY 1 TAX | COMPANY 2 TAX | COMPANY 3 TAX | COMPANY n TAX |

| UNEMPLOMENT WAGE TAX (1, 1) | UNEMPLOMENT WAGE TAX (1, 2) | UNEMPLOMENT WAGE TAX (1, 3) | UNEMPLOMENT WAGE TAX (1, n) |

| UNEMPLOMENT WAGE TAX (2, 1) | UNEMPLOMENT WAGE TAX (2, 2) | UNEMPLOMENT WAGE TAX (2, 3) | UNEMPLOMENT WAGE TAX (2, n) |

| UNEMPLOMENT WAGE TAX (3, 1) | UNEMPLOMENT WAGE TAX (3, 2) | UNEMPLOMENT WAGE TAX (3, 3) | UNEMPLOMENT WAGE TAX (3, n) |

| UNEMPLOMENT WAGE TAX (m, 1) | UNEMPLOMENT WAGE TAX (m, 2) | UNEMPLOMENT WAGE TAX (m, 3) | UNEMPLOMENT WAGE TAX (m, n) |

The "company tax," "snowball company tax;" "unemployment tax" and "snowball unemployment tax" are included in the price of the item permitting the item's cost to increase. the company weekly sends the "company tax" and "unemployment tax" to the government.

The "company tax" and "unemployment tax" are also consigned to the market place. The payment of the "company tax," "unemployment tax," "snowball company tax" and "snowball unemployment tax" are left to the consumer indicating that the "company tax" and "unemployment tax" actually are sales' taxes.

16TH AMENDMENT" "SOCIAL SECURITY"
"MEDICARE" "UNEMPLOYMENT"
SUIT (CLOTHING)
"16TH SOCIAL MED UNEMPLOY WAGE TAX (1)"

PANTS* 16TH AMENDMENT SOCIAL SECURITY MEDICARE UNEMPLOYMENT WAGE* TAX	PANTS* BUTTONS* 16TH AMENDMENT SOCIAL SECURITY MEDICARE UNEMPLOYMENT WAGE* TAX	PANTS* ZIPPER* 16TH AMENDMENT SOCIAL SECURITY MEDICARE UNEMPLOYMENT WAGE* TAX	PANTS* WOOL* CLOTH 16TH AMENDMENT SOCIAL SECURITY MEDICARE UNEMPLOYMENT WAGE* TAX
JACKET* 16TH AMENDMENT SOCIAL SECURITY MEDICARE UNEMPLOYMENT WAGE* TAX	JACKET* BUTTONS* 16TH AMENDMENT SOCIAL SECURITY MEDICARE UNEMPLOYMENT WAGE* TAX	JACKET* SILK* CLOTH 16TH AMENDMENT SOCIAL SECURITY MEDICARE UNEMPLOYMENT WAGE* TAX	JACKET* WOOL* CLOTH 16TH AMENDMENT SOCIAL SECURITY MEDICARE UNEMPLOYMENT WAGE* TAX
VEST* 16TH AMENDMENT SOCIAL SECURITY MEDICARE UNEMPLOYMENT WAGE TAX	VEST* BUTTONS* 16TH AMENDMENT SOCIAL SECURITY MEDICARE UNEMPLOYMENT WAGE* TAX	VEST* SILK* CLOTH 16TH AMENDMENT SOCIAL SECURITY MEDICARE UNEMPLOYMENT WAGE* TAX	VEST* WOOL* CLOTH 16TH AMENDMENT SOCIAL SECURITY MEDICARE UNEMPLOYMENT WAGE* TAX
SUIT^ 16TH AMENDMENT SOCIAL SECURITY MEDICARE UNEMPLOYMENT WAGE* TAX			

"16TH AMENDMENT" "SOCIAL SECURITY" "MEDICARE" "UNEMPLOYMENT"

"16TH SOCIAL MED UNEMPLOY WAGE TAX (2)"

BUTTONS*	SILK*	WOOL*	ZIPPER*
16TH AMENDMENT	WEAVER*	WEAVER*	METAL*
SOCIAL SECURITY	16TH AMENDMENT	16TH AMENDMENT	16TH AMENDMENT
MEDICARE	SOCIAL SECURITY	SOCIAL SECURITY	SOCIAL SECURITY
UNEMPLOYMENT	MEDICARE	MEDICARE	MEDICARE
WAGE*	UNEMPLOYMENT	UNEMPLOYMENT	UNEMPLOYMENT
TAX	WAGE*	WAGE*	WAGE*
	TAX	TAX	TAX

ONE SUIT
SIMPLE HYPTHETICAL CASE

"snowball tax"= "company tax"

+"company tax (1)"

+"company tax (2)"

+"16th social med unemploy wage tax (1)"

+"16th social med unemploy wage tax (2)"

ONE ITEM
ALGORITHM
SNOWBALL COMPANY, 16TH AMENDMENT, SOCIAL SECURITY, MEDICARE AND WAGE UNEMPLOYMENT WAGE TAX!

n equals number of companies whom manufactured or handled the item to be bought.

"snowball company tax"=

"company tax"

+"company tax (1)"

+"company tax (2)"

+"company tax (3)"

+

+

+

+"company tax (n)"

Taxes of companies 1 thru n are added resulting the production of an item through the delivering of a product or providing a service. All taxes are sent to the market place through the company's "gross income" as a "snowball company gross tax" that produced the item increasing the price of the item.

k1, k2, k3,,,kn equals the number of workers whom manufactured or handled the item to be bought in 1,2,3,,,, n companies.

"snowball 16th amendment wage tax (1)"=
    "16th amendment wage tax (1, 1)"
    +"16th amendment wage tax (1, 2)"
    +"16th amendment wage tax (1, 3)"
        +
        +
        +
    +"16th amendment wage tax (1, k1)"
"snowball 16th amendment wage tax (2)"=
    "16th amendment wage tax (2, 1)"
    +"16th amendment wage tax (2, 2)"
    +"16th amendment wage tax (2, 3)"
        +
        +
        +
    +"16th amendment wage tax (2, k2)"
"snowball 16th amendment wage tax (3)"=
    "16th amendment wage tax (3, 1)"
    +"16th amendment wage tax (3, 2)"
    +"16th amendment wage tax (3, 3)"
        +
        +
        +
    +"16th amendment wage tax (3, k3)"
        +
        +
        +
"snowball 16th amendment wage tax (n)"=
    "16th amendment wage tax (n, 1)"
    +"16th amendment wage tax (n, 2)"
    +"16th amendment wage tax (n, 3)"
        +
        +
        +
    +"16th amendment wage tax (n, kn)"

k1 is the number of worker's 16th amendment wage taxes in company (1) that are included in the "gross income" of the item. The k1 worker 16th amendment wage taxes are delivered to the market place.

k2 is the number of worker's 16th amendment wage taxes in company (2) that are included in the "gross income" of the item. The k2 worker 16th amendment wage taxes are delivered to the market place.

k3 is the number of worker's 16th amendment wage taxes in company (3) that are included in the "gross income" of the item. The k3 worker 16th amendment wage taxes are delivered to the market place.

kn is the number of worker's 16th amendment wage taxes in company (n) that are included in the "gross income" of the item. The kn worker 16th amendment wage taxes are delivered to the market place.

"snowball 16th amendment wage tax"=
     "snowball 16th amendment wage tax (1)"
     +"snowball 16th amendment wage tax (2)"
     +"snowball 16th amendment wage tax (3)"
         +
         +
         +
     +"snowball 16th amendment wage tax (kn)"
"snowball social security tax (1)"=
     "social security wage tax (1, 1)"
     +"social security wage tax (1, 2)"
     +"social security wage tax (1, 3)"
         +
         +
         +
     +"social security wage tax (1, k1)"
"snowball social security tax (2)"=
     "social security wage tax (2, 1)"
     +"social security wage tax (2, 2)"
     +"social security wage tax (2, 3)"
         +
         +
         +
     +"social security wage tax (2, k2)"
"snowball social security tax (3)"=
     "social security wage tax (3, 1)"
     +"social security wage tax (3, 2)"
     +"social security wage tax (3, 3)"
         +
         +
         +
     +"social security wage tax (3, k3)"
         +
         +
         +
"snowball social security tax (n)"=
     "social security wage tax (n, 1)"
     +"social security wage tax (n, 2)"
     +"social security wage tax (n, 3)"
         +
         +
         +
     +"social security wage tax (n, kn)"

The total snowball worker's 16th amendment wage taxes are included in the item's "gross income" and are delivered to the market place.

k1 is the number of worker's social security wage taxes in company (1) that are included in the "gross income" of the item. The k1 worker social security wage taxes are delivered to the market place.

k2 is the number of worker's social security wage taxes in company (2) that are included in the "gross income" of the item. The k2 worker social security wage taxes are delivered to the market place.

k3 is the number of worker's social security wage taxes in company (3) that are included in the "gross income" of the item. The k3 worker social security wage taxes are delivered to the market place.

kn is the number of worker's social security wage taxes in company (n) that are included in the "gross income" of the item. The kn worker social security wage taxes are delivered to the market place.

"snowball social security wage tax"=
    "snowball social security wage tax (1)"
    +"snowball social security wage tax (2)"
    +"snowball social security wage tax (3)"
        +
        +
        +
+"snowball social security wage tax (kn)"
    "snowball medicare tax (1)"=
    "medicare wage tax (1, 1)"
    +"medicare wage tax (1, 2)"
    +"medicare wage tax (1, 3)"
        +
        +
        +
    +"medicare wage tax (1, k1)"
"snowball medicare tax (2)"=
    "medicare wage tax (2, 1)"
    +"medicare wage tax (2, 2)"
    +"medicare wage tax (2, 3)"
        +
        +
        +
    +"medicare wage tax (2, k2)"
"snowball medicare tax (3)"=
    "medicare wage tax (3, 1)"
    +"medicare wage tax (3, 2)"
    +"medicare wage tax (3, 3)"
        +
        +
        +
    +"medicare wage tax (3, k3)"
        +
        +
        +
"snowball medicare tax (n)"=
    "medicare wage tax (n,1)"
    +"medicare wage tax (n, 2)"
    +"medicare wage tax (n, 3)"
        +
        +
        +
    +"medicare wage tax (n, kn)"

The total snowball worker's social security wage taxes are included in the item's "gross income" and are delivered to the market place.

k1 is the number of worker's medicare wage taxes in company (1) that are included in the "gross income" of the item. The k1 worker medicare wage taxes are delivered to the market place.

k2 is the number of worker's medicare wage taxes in company (2) that are included in the "gross income" of the item. The k2 worker medicare wage taxes are delivered to the market place.

k3 is the number of worker's medicare wage taxes in company (3) that are included in the "gross income" of the item. The k3 worker medicare wage taxes are delivered to the market place.

kn is the number of worker's medicare wage taxes in company (n) that are included in the "gross income" of the item. The kn worker medicare wage taxes are delivered to the market place.

"snowball medicare wage tax"=
    "snowball medicare wage tax (1)"
    +"snowball medicare wage tax (2)"
    +"snowball medicare wage tax (3)"
       +
       +
       +
    +"snowball medicare wage tax (kn)"
"snowball unemployment tax (1)"=
    "unemployment wage tax (1, 1)"
    +"unemployment wage tax (2, 1)"
    +"unemployment wage tax (3, 1)"
       +
       +
       +
    +"unemployment wage tax (n, k1)"
"snowball unemployment tax (2)"=
    "unemployment wage tax (1, 2)"
    +"unemployment wage tax (2, 2)"
    +"unemployment wage tax (3, 2)"
       +
       +
       +
    +"unemployment wage tax (n, k 2)"
"snowball unemployment tax (3)"=
    "unemployment wage tax (1, 3)"
    +"unemployment wage tax (2, 3)"
    +"unemployment wage tax (3, 3)"
       +
       +
       +
    +"unemployment wage tax (n, k3)"
       +
       +
       +
"snowball unemployment tax (n)"=
    "unemployment wage tax (n, 1)"
    +"unemployment wage tax (n, 2)"
    +"unemployment wage tax (n, 3)"
       +
       +
       +
    +"unemployment wage tax (n, kn)"

The total snowball worker's medicare wage taxes are included in the item's "gross income" and are delivered to the market place.

k1 is the number of worker's unemployment wage taxes in company (1) that are included in the "gross income" of the item. The k1 worker unemployment wage taxes are delivered to the market place.

k2 is the number of worker's unemployment wage taxes in company (2) that are included in the "gross income" of the item. The k2 worker unemployment wage taxes are delivered to the market place.

k3 is the number of worker's unemployment wage taxes in company (3) that are included in the "gross income" of the item. The k3 worker unemployment wage taxes are delivered to the market place.

kn is the number of worker's unemployment wage taxes in company (n) that are included in the "gross income" of the item. The kn worker unemployment wage taxes are delivered to the market place.

"snowball unemployment wage tax"=
>"snowball unemployment wage tax (1)"
>+"snowball unemployment wage tax (2)"
>+"snowball unemployment wage tax (3)"
>+
>+
>+
>+"snowball unemployment wage tax (kn)"

"gross income"=
>"company tax"
>+"16th amendment wage tax"
>+"social security wage tax"
>+"medicare wage tax"
>+"unemployment wage tax"
>+"snowball company tax"
>+"snowball 16th amendment wage tax"
>+"snowball social security wage tax"
>+"snowball medicare wage tax"
>+"snowball unemployment wage tax"
>+"company expenses"
>+"profit"

The total snowball worker's unemployment wage taxes are included in the item's "gross income" and are delivered to the market place.

Since company's "gross income" includes the "company tax," "16th amendment wage tax," "social security wage tax," "medicare wage tax," "unemployment wage tax," "snowball company tax," "snowball 16th amendment wage tax," "snowball social security wage tax," "snowball medicare wage tax" and "snowball unemployment wage tax," "gross income" increases!

- The "company tax," "16th amendment wage tax," "social security wage tax," "medicare wage tax" and "unemployment wage tax" will be passed to all consumers within the United States territories.
- For States Government, the "company tax," "16th amendment wage tax," "social security wage tax," "medicare wage tax" and "unemployment wage tax" will be passed to all consumers within the States Government's territory.
- For County Government, the "company tax," "16th amendment wage tax," "social security wage tax," "medicare wage tax" and "unemployment wage tax" will be passed to all consumers within the County Government's territory.
- For City Government, the "company tax," "16th amendment wage tax," "social security wage tax," "medicare wage tax" and "unemployment wage tax" will be passed to all consumers within the City Government's territory.
- For Town Government, the "company tax," "16th amendment wage tax," "social security wage tax," "medicare wage tax" and "unemployment wage tax" will be passed to all consumers within the Town Government's territory.
- Any increase to the "company tax" will increase "gross income."
- Any increase to the "16th amendment wage tax" will increase the "gross income."
- Any increase to the "social security tax" will increase the "gross income."
- Any increase to the "medicare wage tax" will increase the "gross income."
- Any increase to the "unemployment wage tax" will increase the "gross income."
- Any decrease to the "company tax" will decrease "gross income."
- Any decrease to the "16th amendment wage tax" will decrease the "gross income."
- Any decrease to the "social security tax" will decrease the "gross income."
- Any decrease to the "medicare wage tax" will decrease the "gross income."
- Any decrease to the "unemployment wage tax" will decrease the "gross income."

TRANSMIT COMPANY TAX

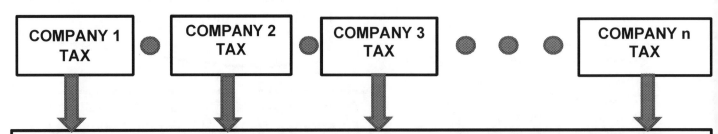

| COMPANY 1 TAX | COMPANY 2 TAX | COMPANY 3 TAX | COMPANY n TAX |

COMPANIES WEEKLY SEND "COMPANY TAXES" TO THE GOVERNMENT. "COMPANY TAXES" AND "SNOWBALL COMPANY TAXES" ARE ADDED TO COMPANY'S PROFITS. TO SECURE A PROFIT TO THEIR PRODUCTS, COMPANIES TRANSMIT "COMPANY TAXES" AND "SNOWBALL COMPANY TAXES" TO THE MARKET PLACE. "COMPANY TAXES" TURN OUT TO BE SALES' TAXES.

TRANSMIT 16TH AMENDMENT WAGE TAX

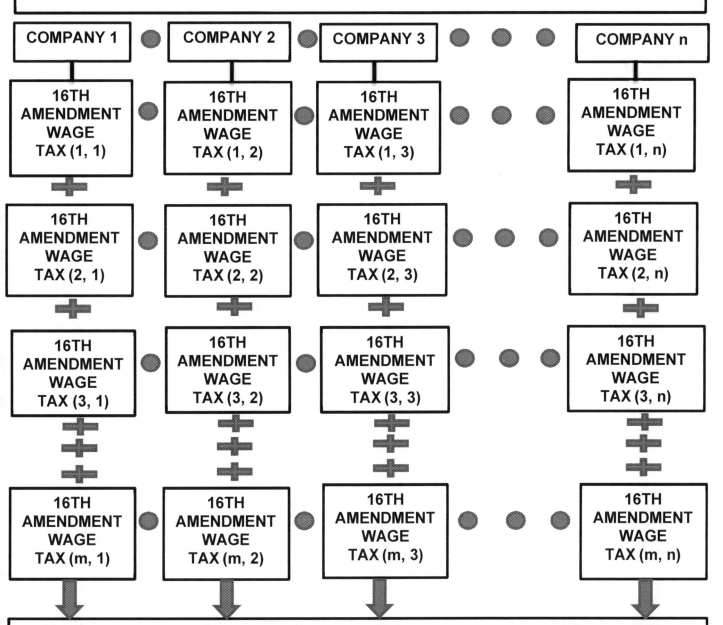

COMPANIES WEEKLY SEND "16TH AMENDMENT TAXES" TO THE GOVERNMENT. "16TH AMENDMENT TAXES" AND "SNOWBALL 16TH AMENDMENT TAXES" ARE ADDED TO COMPANY'S GROSS PROFITS. TO SECURE A PROFIT TO THEIR PRODUCTS, COMPANIES TRANSMIT "16TH AMENDMENT TAXES" AND "SNOWBALL 16TH AMENDMENT TAXES" TO THE MARKET PLACE. "16TH AMENDMENT TAXES" TURN OUT TO BE SALES' TAXES

TRANSMIT SOCIAL SECURITY WAGE TAX

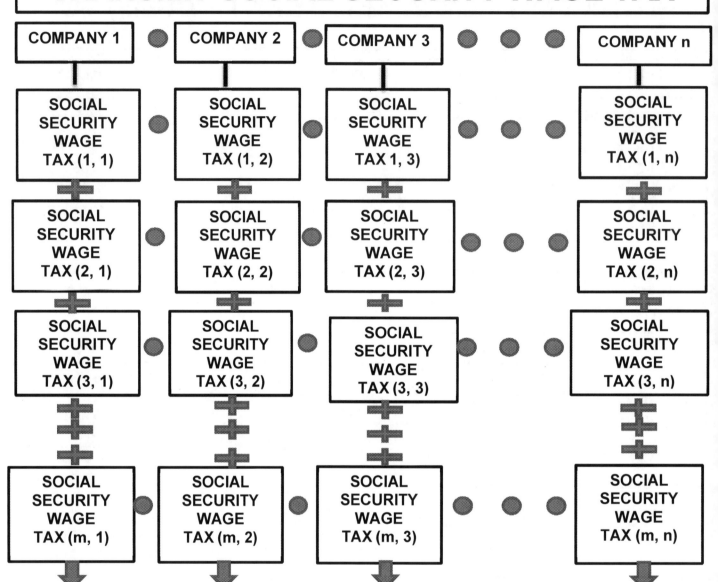

COMPANIES WEEKLY SEND "SOCIAL SECURITY TAXES" TO THE GOVERNMENT. "SOCIAL SECURITY TAXES" AND "SNOWBALL SOCIAL SECURITY TAXES" ARE ADDED TO COMPANY'S GROSS PROFITS. TO SECURE A PROFIT TO THEIR PRODUCTS, COMPANIES TRANSMIT "SOCIAL SECURITY TAXES" AND "SNOWBALL SOCIAL SECURITY TAXES" TO THE MARKET PLACE. "SOCIAL SECURITY TAXES" TURN OUT TO BE SALES' TAXES.

TRANSMIT MEDICARE WAGE TAX

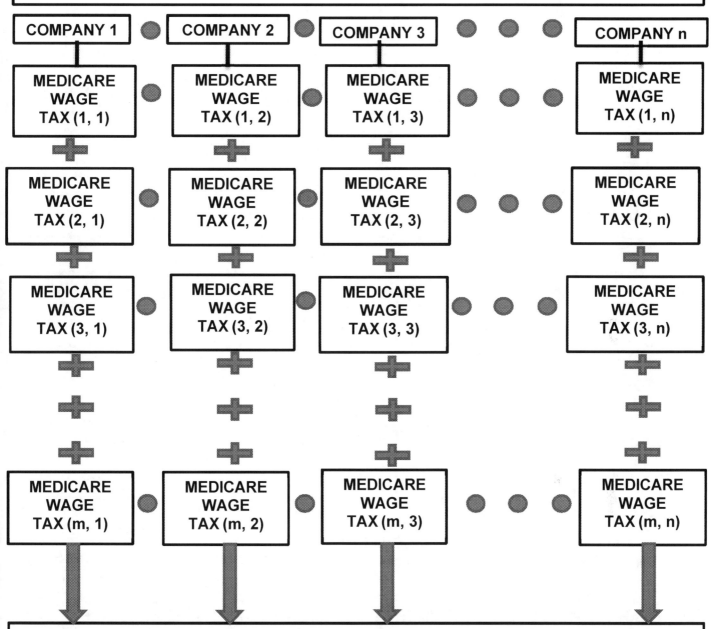

COMPANIES WEEKLY SEND "MEDICARE TAXES" TO THE GOVERNMENT. "MEDICARE TAXES" AND "SNOWBALL MEDICARE TAXES" ARE ADDED TO COMPANY'S GROSS PROFITS. TO SECURE A PROFIT TO THEIR PRODUCTS, COMPANIES TRANSMIT "MEDICARE TAXES" AND "SNOWBALL MEDICARE TAXES" TO THE MARKET PLACE. "MEDICARE TAXES" TURN OUT TO BE SALES' TAXES.

TRANSMIT UNEMPLOYMENT WAGE TAX

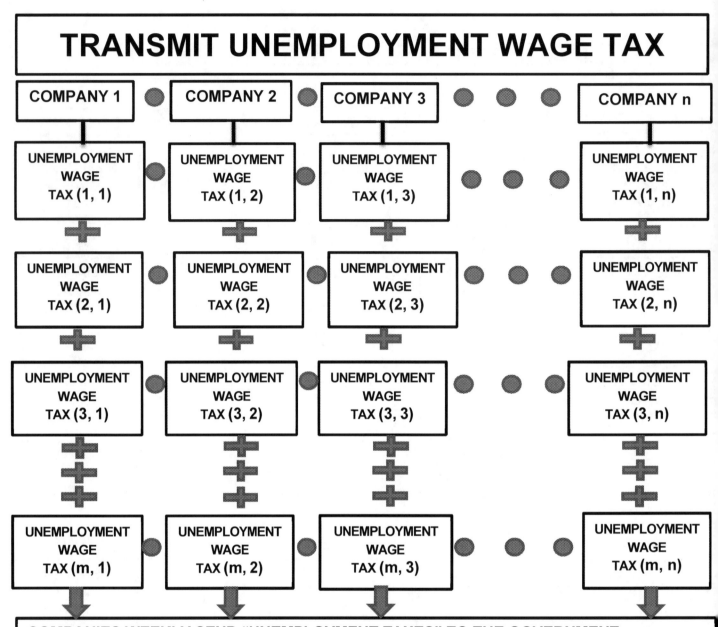

COMPANIES WEEKLY SEND "UNEMPLOYMENT TAXES" TO THE GOVERNMENT. "UNEMPLOYMENT TAXES" AND "SNOWBALL UNEMPLOYMENT TAXES" ARE ADDED TO COMPANY'S GROSS PROFITS. TO SECURE A PROFIT TO THEIR PRODUCTS, COMPANIES TRANSMIT "UNEMPLOYMENT TAXES" AND "SNOWBALL UNEMPLOYMENT TAXES" TO THE MARKET PLACE. "UNEMPLOYMENT TAXES" TURN OUT TO BE SALES' TAXES.

SNOWBALL COMPANY AND 16TH AMENDMENT WAGE

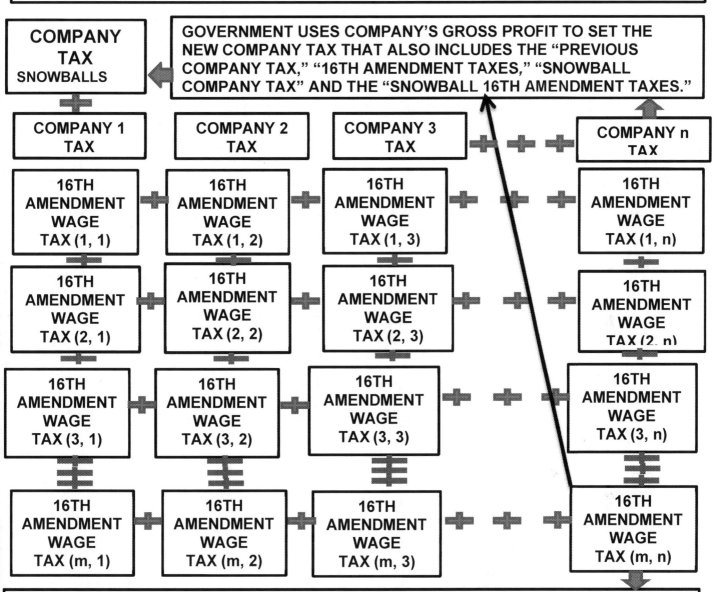

COMPANY TAX SNOWBALLS

GOVERNMENT USES COMPANY'S GROSS PROFIT TO SET THE NEW COMPANY TAX THAT ALSO INCLUDES THE "PREVIOUS COMPANY TAX," "16TH AMENDMENT TAXES," "SNOWBALL COMPANY TAX" AND THE "SNOWBALL 16TH AMENDMENT TAXES."

COMPANY 1 TAX	COMPANY 2 TAX	COMPANY 3 TAX	COMPANY n TAX
16TH AMENDMENT WAGE TAX (1, 1)	16TH AMENDMENT WAGE TAX (1, 2)	16TH AMENDMENT WAGE TAX (1, 3)	16TH AMENDMENT WAGE TAX (1, n)
16TH AMENDMENT WAGE TAX (2, 1)	16TH AMENDMENT WAGE TAX (2, 2)	16TH AMENDMENT WAGE TAX (2, 3)	16TH AMENDMENT WAGE TAX (2, n)
16TH AMENDMENT WAGE TAX (3, 1)	16TH AMENDMENT WAGE TAX (3, 2)	16TH AMENDMENT WAGE TAX (3, 3)	16TH AMENDMENT WAGE TAX (3, n)
16TH AMENDMENT WAGE TAX (m, 1)	16TH AMENDMENT WAGE TAX (m, 2)	16TH AMENDMENT WAGE TAX (m, 3)	16TH AMENDMENT WAGE TAX (m, n)

THE COMPANY WEEKLY SENDS THE "16TH AMENDMENT TAX" AND THE "COMPANY TAX" TO THE GOVERNMENT. THE COMPANY'S "16TH AMENDMENT TAX" AND THE "COMPANY TAX" ARE CONSIGNED TO THE MARKET PLACE. THE "COMPANY TAX" PRODUCES A "SNOWBALL COMPANY TAX." THE "16TH AMENDMENT TAX" PRODUCES A "SNOWBALL 16TH AMENDMENT TAX." THE "COMPANY TAX, "COMPANY SNOWBALL TAX," "16TH AMENDMENT TAX" AND THE "SNOWBALL 16TH AMENDMENT TAX" ARE INCLUDED IN THE PRICE OF THE ITEM PERMITTING THE ITEM'S COST TO INCREASE. THE "COMPANY TAX," "COMPANY SNOWBALL GROSS TAX," "16TH AMENDMENT TAX" AND "SNOWBALL 16TH AMENDMENT TAX" ARE ADDED TO THE COMPANY'S GROSS PROFIT. THE PAYMENT OF THE 16TH AMENDMENT TAX AND COMPANY TAX IS LEFT TO THE CONSUMER INDICATING THAT THE "COMPANY TAX" AND "16TH AMENDMENT TAX" ARE ACTUALLY SALES' TAXES.

SNOWBALL COMPANY
AND SOCIAL SECURITY WAGE

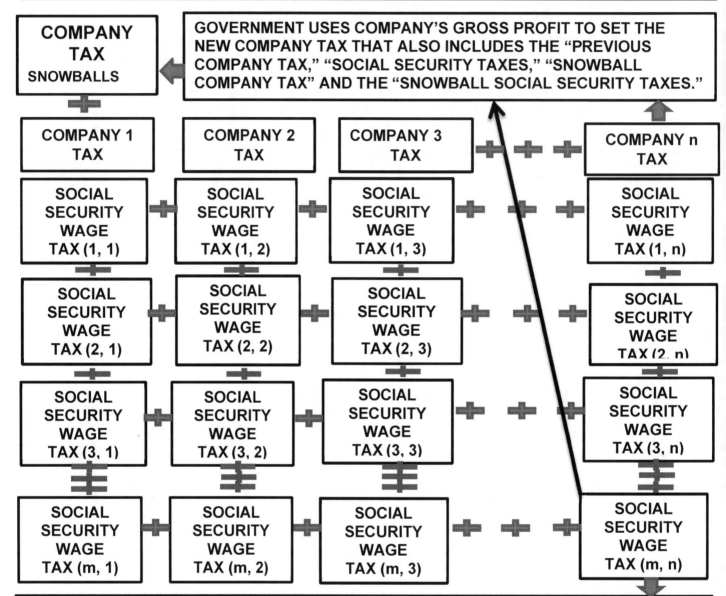

COMPANY TAX SNOWBALLS	GOVERNMENT USES COMPANY'S GROSS PROFIT TO SET THE NEW COMPANY TAX THAT ALSO INCLUDES THE "PREVIOUS COMPANY TAX," "SOCIAL SECURITY TAXES," "SNOWBALL COMPANY TAX" AND THE "SNOWBALL SOCIAL SECURITY TAXES."

THE COMPANY WEEKLY SENDS THE "SOCIAL SECURITY TAX" AND THE "COMPANY TAX" TO THE GOVERNMENT. THE COMPANY'S "SOCIAL SECURITY TAX" AND THE "COMPANY TAX" ARE CONSIGNED TO THE MARKET PLACE. THE "COMPANY TAX" PRODUCES A "SNOWBALL COMPANY TAX." THE "SOCIAL SECURITY TAX" PRODUCES A "SNOWBALL SOCIAL SECURITY TAX." THE "COMPANY TAX, "COMPANY SNOWBALL TAX," "SOCIAL SECURITY TAX" AND THE "SNOWBALL SOCIAL SECURITY TAX" ARE INCLUDED IN THE PRICE OF THE ITEM PERMITTING THE ITEM'S COST TO INCREASE. THE "COMPANY TAX," "COMPANY SNOWBALL GROSS TAX," "SOCIAL SECURITY TAX" AND "SNOWBALL SOCIAL SECURITY TAX" ARE ADDED TO THE COMPANY'S GROSS PROFIT. THE PAYMENT OF THE SOCIAL SECURITY TAX AND COMPANY TAX IS LEFT TO THE CONSUMER INDICATING THAT THE "COMPANY TAX" AND "SOCIAL SECURITY TAX" ARE ACTUALLY SALES' TAXES.

SNOWBALL COMPANY AND MEDICARE WAGE

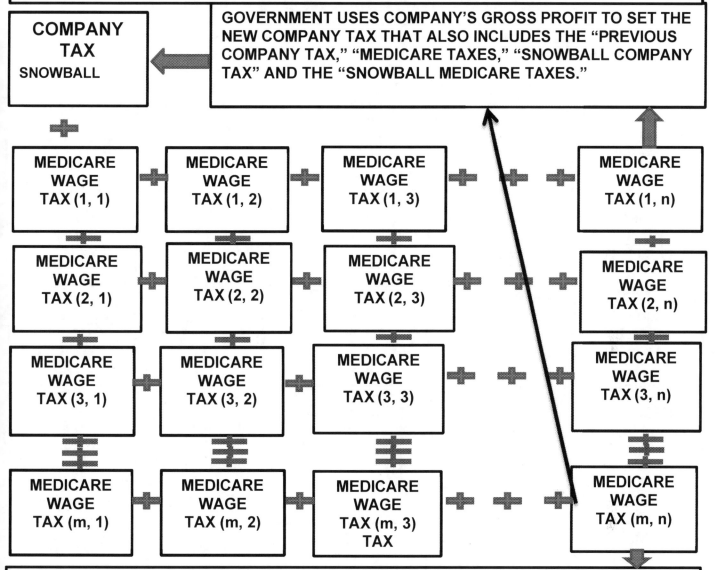

COMPANY TAX
SNOWBALL

GOVERNMENT USES COMPANY'S GROSS PROFIT TO SET THE NEW COMPANY TAX THAT ALSO INCLUDES THE "PREVIOUS COMPANY TAX," "MEDICARE TAXES," "SNOWBALL COMPANY TAX" AND THE "SNOWBALL MEDICARE TAXES."

MEDICARE WAGE TAX (1, 1) — MEDICARE WAGE TAX (1, 2) — MEDICARE WAGE TAX (1, 3) — MEDICARE WAGE TAX (1, n)

MEDICARE WAGE TAX (2, 1) — MEDICARE WAGE TAX (2, 2) — MEDICARE WAGE TAX (2, 3) — MEDICARE WAGE TAX (2, n)

MEDICARE WAGE TAX (3, 1) — MEDICARE WAGE TAX (3, 2) — MEDICARE WAGE TAX (3, 3) — MEDICARE WAGE TAX (3, n)

MEDICARE WAGE TAX (m, 1) — MEDICARE WAGE TAX (m, 2) — MEDICARE WAGE TAX (m, 3) TAX — MEDICARE WAGE TAX (m, n)

THE COMPANY WEEKLY SENDS THE "MEDICARE TAX" AND THE "COMPANY TAX" TO THE GOVERNMENT. THE COMPANY'S "MEDICARE TAX" AND THE "COMPANY TAX" ARE CONSIGNED TO THE MARKET PLACE. THE "COMPANY TAX" PRODUCES A "SNOWBALL COMPANY TAX." THE "MEDICARE TAX" PRODUCES A "SNOWBALL MEDICARE TAX." THE "COMPANY TAX, "COMPANY SNOWBALL TAX," "MEDICARE TAX" AND THE "SNOWBALL MEDICARE TAX" ARE INCLUDED IN THE PRICE OF THE ITEM PERMITTING THE ITEM'S COST TO INCREASE. THE "COMPANY TAX," "COMPANY SNOWBALL GROSS TAX," "MEDICARE TAX" AND "SNOWBALL MEDICARE TAX" ARE ADDED TO THE COMPANY'S GROSS PROFIT. THE PAYMENT OF THE MEDICARE TAX AND COMPANY TAX IS LEFT TO THE CONSUMER INDICATING THAT THE "COMPANY TAX" AND "MEDICARE TAX" ARE ACTUALLY SALES' TAXES.

SNOWBALL COMPANY
AND UNEMPLOYMENT WAGE

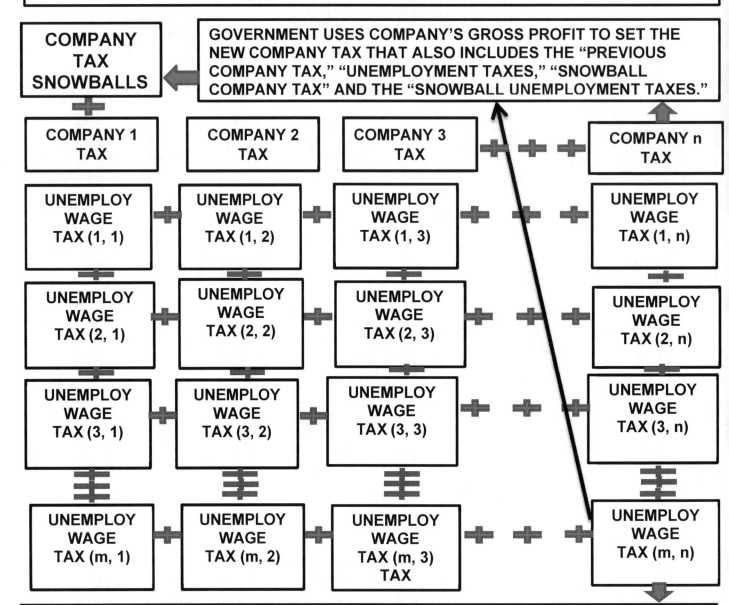

COMPANY TAX SNOWBALLS	GOVERNMENT USES COMPANY'S GROSS PROFIT TO SET THE NEW COMPANY TAX THAT ALSO INCLUDES THE "PREVIOUS COMPANY TAX," "UNEMPLOYMENT TAXES," "SNOWBALL COMPANY TAX" AND THE "SNOWBALL UNEMPLOYMENT TAXES."

COMPANY 1 TAX	COMPANY 2 TAX	COMPANY 3 TAX	COMPANY n TAX
UNEMPLOY WAGE TAX (1, 1)	UNEMPLOY WAGE TAX (1, 2)	UNEMPLOY WAGE TAX (1, 3)	UNEMPLOY WAGE TAX (1, n)
UNEMPLOY WAGE TAX (2, 1)	UNEMPLOY WAGE TAX (2, 2)	UNEMPLOY WAGE TAX (2, 3)	UNEMPLOY WAGE TAX (2, n)
UNEMPLOY WAGE TAX (3, 1)	UNEMPLOY WAGE TAX (3, 2)	UNEMPLOY WAGE TAX (3, 3)	UNEMPLOY WAGE TAX (3, n)
UNEMPLOY WAGE TAX (m, 1)	UNEMPLOY WAGE TAX (m, 2)	UNEMPLOY WAGE TAX (m, 3) TAX	UNEMPLOY WAGE TAX (m, n)

THE COMPANY WEEKLY SENDS THE "UNEMPLOYMENT TAX" AND THE "COMPANY TAX" TO THE GOVERNMENT. THE COMPANY'S "UNEMPLOYMENT TAX" AND THE "COMPANY TAX" ARE CONSIGNED TO THE MARKET PLACE. THE "COMPANY TAX" PRODUCES A "SNOWBALL COMPANY TAX." THE "UNEMPLOYMENT TAX" PRODUCES A "SNOWBALL UNEMPLOYMENT TAX." THE "COMPANY TAX, "COMPANY SNOWBALL TAX," "UNEMPLOYMENT TAX" AND THE "SNOWBALL UNEMPLOYMENT TAX" ARE INCLUDED IN THE PRICE OF THE ITEM PERMITTING THE ITEM'S COST TO INCREASE. THE "COMPANY TAX," "COMPANY SNOWBALL GROSS TAX," "UNEMPLOYMENT TAX" AND "SNOWBALL UNEMPLOYMENT TAX" ARE ADDED TO THE COMPANY'S GROSS PROFIT. THE PAYMENT OF THE UNEMPLOYMENT TAX AND COMPANY TAX IS LEFT TO THE CONSUMER INDICATING THAT THE "COMPANY TAX" AND "UNEMPLOYMENT TAX" ARE ACTUALLY SALES' TAXES.

SNOWBALL 16TH AMENDMENT WAGE TAX
(NO COMPANY TAX)
SUIT (CLOTHING)

"16TH AMENDMENT WAGE TAX (1)"

PANTS* 16TH AMENDMENT WAGE* TAX	PANTS* BUTTONS* 16TH AMENDMENT WAGE* TAX	PANTS* WOOL* CLOTH 16TH AMENDMENT WAGE* TAX	PANTS* ZIPPER* 16TH AMENDMENT WAGE* TAX
JACKET* 16TH AMENDMENT WAGE* TAX	JACKET* BUTTONS* 16TH AMENDMENT WAGE* TAX	JACKET* SILK* CLOTH 16TH AMENDMENT WAGE* TAX	JACKET* WOOL* CLOTH 16TH AMENDMENT WAGE* TAX
VEST* 16TH AMENDMENT WAGE* TAX	VEST* BUTTONS* 16TH AMENDMENT WAGE* TAX	VEST* SILK* CLOTH 16TH AMENDMENT WAGE* TAX	VEST* WOOL* CLOTH 16TH AMENDMENT WAGE* TAX

"16TH AMENDMENT WAGE TAX (2)"

BUTTONS* 16TH AMENDMENT WAGE* TAX	SILK* WEAVER 16TH AMENDMENT WAGE* TAX	WOOL* WEAVER 16TH AMENDMENT WAGE* TAX	METAL* 16TH AMENDMENT WAGE* TAX

ONE SUIT
SIMPLE HYPTHETICAL CASE
"snowball 16th amendment wage tax"="16th amendment wage tax (1)"
+"16th amendment wage tax (2)"

ONE ITEM
ALGORITHM
16TH AMENDMENT WAGE SNOWBALL TAX!

k1, k2, k3,,,kn equals the number of workers whom manufactured or handled the item to be bought in 1,2,3,,,, n companies.

"snowball 16th amendment wage tax (1)"=
    "16th amendment wage tax (1, 1)"
    +"16th amendment wage tax (1, 2)"
    +"16th amendment wage tax (1, 3)"
    +
    +
    +
    +"16th amendment wage tax (1, k1)"

k1 is the number of worker's 16th amendment wage taxes in company (1) that are included in the "gross income" of the item. The k1 worker 16th amendment wage taxes are delivered to the market place.

"snowball 16th amendment wage tax (2)"=
    "16th amendment wage tax (2, 1)"
    +"16th amendment wage tax (2, 2)"
    +"16th amendment wage tax (2, 3)"
    +
    +
    +
    +"16th amendment wage tax (2, k2)"

k2 is the number of worker's 16th amendment wage taxes in company (2) that are included in the "gross income" of the item. The k2 worker 16th amendment wage taxes are delivered to the market place.

"snowball 16th amendment wage tax (3)"=
    "16th amendment wage tax (3, 1)"
    +"16th amendment wage tax (3, 2)"
    +"16th amendment wage tax (3, 3)"
    +
    +
    +
    +"16th amendment wage tax (3, k3)"
    +
    +
    +

k3 is the number of worker's 16th amendment wage taxes in company (3) that are included in the "gross income" of the item. The k3 worker 16th amendment wage taxes are delivered to the market place.

"snowball 16th amendment wage tax (n)"=
    "16th amendment wage tax (n, 1)"
    +"16th amendment wage tax (n, 2)"
    +"16th amendment wage tax (n, 3)"
    +
    +
    +
    +"16th amendment wage tax (n, kn)"

kn is the number of worker's 16th amendment wage taxes in company (n) that are included in the "gross income" of the item. The kn worker 16th amendment wage taxes are delivered to the market place.

"snowball 16th amendment wage tax"=
  "snowball 16th amendment wage tax (1)"
  +"snowball 16th amendment wage tax (2)"
  +"snowball 16th amendment wage tax (3)"
      +
      +
      +
  +"snowball 16th amendment wage tax (kn)"
"gross income"=
  "16th amendment tax"
  +"snowball 16th amendment tax"
  +"company expenses"
  +"profit"

> **The total snowball worker's 16th amendment wage taxes are included in the item's "gross income" and are delivered to the market place.**

> **Since company's "gross income" includes the "16th amendment tax" and "snowball 16th amendment tax," the "gross income" increases!**

- The "16th amendment tax" and "snowball 16th amendment tax" will be passed to all consumers within the United States territories.
- For States Government, the "16th amendment tax" and "snowball 16th amendment tax" will be passed to all consumers within the States Government's territory.
- For County Government, the "16th amendment tax" and "snowball 16th amendment tax" will be passed to all consumers within the County Government's territory.
- For City Government, the "16th amendment tax" and "snowball 16th amendment tax" consumers within the City Government's territory.
- For Town Government, the "16th amendment tax" and "snowball 16th amendment tax" will be passed to all consumers within the Town Government's territory.
- Any increase to the "16th amendment wage tax" will increase the "gross income."
- Any decrease to the "16th amendment wage tax" will decrease the "gross income."

TRANSMIT 16TH AMENDMENT WAGE TAX

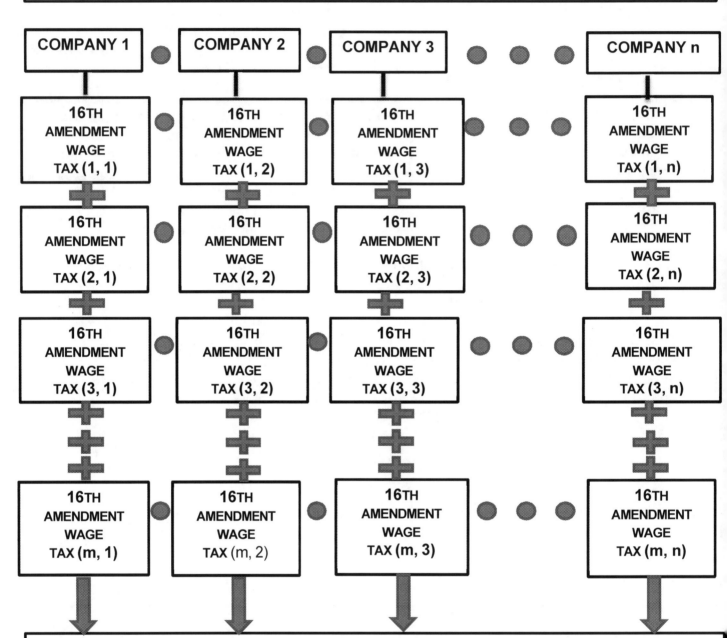

COMPANIES WEEKLY SEND "16TH AMENDMENT TAXES" TO THE GOVERNMENT. "16TH AMENDMENT TAXES" AND "SNOWBALL 16TH AMENDMENT TAXES" ARE ADDED TO COMPANY'S GROSS PROFITS. TO SECURE A PROFIT TO THEIR PRODUCTS, COMPANIES TRANSMIT "16TH AMENDMENT TAXES" AND "SNOWBALL 16TH AMENDMENT TAXES" TO THE MARKET PLACE. "16TH AMENDMENT TAXES" TURN OUT TO BE SALES' TAXES.

SNOWBALL 16TH AMENDMENT WAGE TAX

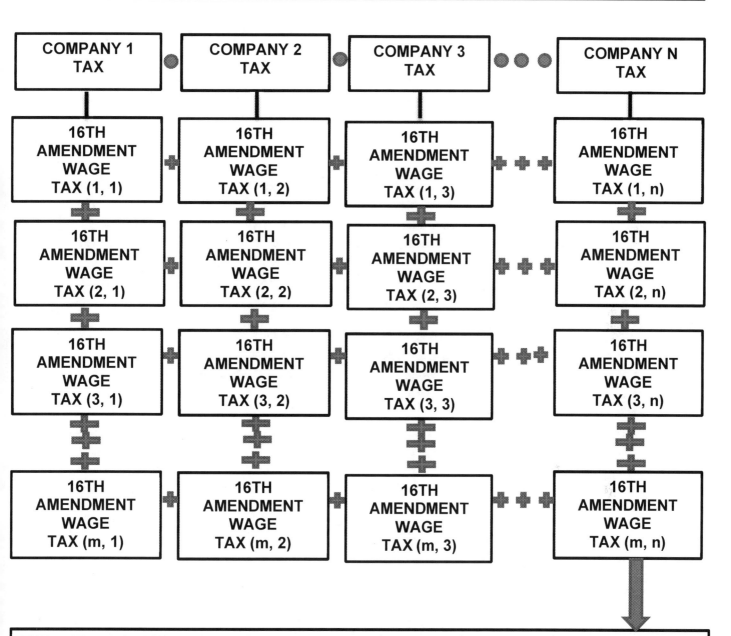

THE "16TH AMENDMENT TAX" AND "SNOWBALL 16TH AMENDMENT TAX" ARE INCLUDED IN THE PRICE OF THE ITEM PERMITTING THE ITEM'S COST TO INCREASE. THE COMPANY WEEKLY SENDS THE 16TH AMENDMENT TAX" TO THE GOVERNMENT.

THE "16TH AMENDMENT TAX" IS CONSIGNED TO THE MARKET PLACE. THE PAYMENT OF THE "16TH AMENDMENT TAX" AND "SNOWBALL 16TH AMENDMENT TAX" ARE LEFT TO THE CONSUMER INDICATING THAT THE 16TH AMENDMENT TAX" IS ACTUALLY A SALE'S TAX.

SNOWBALL SOCIAL SECURITY WAGE TAX
(NO COMPANY TAX)
SUIT (CLOTHING)
"SOCIAL SECURITY WAGE TAX (1)"

PANTS* SOCIAL SECURITY WAGE* TAX	PANTS* BUTTONS* SOCIAL SECURITY WAGE* TAX	PANTS* WOOL* CLOTH SOCIAL SECURITY WAGE* TAX	PANTS* ZIPPER* SOCIAL SECURITY WAGE* TAX
JACKET* SOCIAL SECURITY WAGE* TAX	JACKET* BUTTONS* SOCIAL SECURITY WAGE* TAX	JACKET* SILK* CLOTH SOCIAL SECURITY WAGE* TAX	JACKET* WOOL* CLOTH SOCIAL SECURITY WAGE* TAX
VEST* SOCIAL SECURITY WAGE* TAX	VEST* BUTTONS* SOCIAL SECURITY WAGE* TAX	VEST* SILK* CLOTH SOCIAL SECURITY WAGE* TAX	VEST* WOOL* CLOTH SOCIAL SECURITY WAGE* TAX

"SOCIAL SECURITY WAGE TAX (2)"

BUTTONS* SOCIAL SECURITY WAGE* TAX	SILK* WEAVER* SOCIAL SECURITY WAGE* TAX	WOOL* WEAVER* SOCIAL SECURITY WAGE* TAX	ZIPPER* METAL* SOCIAL SECURITY WAGE* TAX

ONE SUIT
SIMPLE HYPTHETICAL CASE

"snowball social security wage tax"="social security wage tax (1)" +"social security wage tax (2)"

ONE ITEM
ALGORITHM
SOCIAL SECURITY WAGE SNOWBALL TAX

k1, k2, k3,,,kn equals the number of workers whom manufactured or handled the item to be bought in 1,2,3,,,, n companies.

"snowball social security wage tax (1)"=
    "social security wage tax (1, 1)"
    +"social security wage tax (1, 2)"
    +"social security wage tax (1, 3)"
       +
       +
       +
    +"social security wage tax (1, k1)"
"snowball social security wage tax (2)"=
    "social security wage tax (2, 1)"
    +"social security wage tax (2, 2)"
    +"social security wage tax (2, 3)"
       +
       +
       +
    +"social security wage tax (2, k2)"
"snowball social security wage tax (3)"=
    "social security wage tax (3, 1)"
    +"social security wage tax (3, 2)"
    +"social security wage tax (3, 3)"
       +
       +
       +
    +"social security wage tax (3, k3)"
       +
       +
       +
    "snowball social security wage tax (kn)"=
"social security wage tax (n, 1)"
    +"social security wage tax (n, 2)"
    +"social security wage tax (n, 3)"
       +
       +
       +
    +"social security wage tax (n, kn)"

k1 is the number of worker's social security wage taxes in company (1) that are included in the "gross income" of the item. The k1 social security wage taxes are delivered to the market place.

k2 is the number of worker's social security wage taxes in company (2) that are included in the "gross income" of the item. The k2 worker social security wage taxes are delivered to the market place.

k3 is the number of worker's social security wage taxes in company (3) that are included in the "gross income" of the item. The k3 worker social security wage taxes are delivered to the market place.

kn is the number of worker's social security wage taxes in company (n) that are included in the "gross income" of the item. The kn worker social security wage taxes are delivered to the market place.

"snowball social security wage tax"=
    "snowball social security wage tax (1)"
    +"snowball social security wage tax (2)"
    +"snowball social security wage tax (3)"
         +
         +
         +
    +"snowball social security wage tax (kn)"
"gross income"=
    "social security wage tax"
    +"snowball social security wage tax"
    +" expenses"
    +"profit"

The total snowball worker's social security wage taxes are included in the item's "gross income" and are delivered to the market place.

Since company's "gross income" includes the "social security wage tax" and "snowball social security social security wage tax" the cost of the item increases!

- The "social security wage tax" and "snowball social security wage tax" will be passed to all consumers within the United States territories.
- For States Government, the "social security wage tax" and "snowball social security wage tax" will be passed to all consumers within the States Government's territory.
- For County Government, the "social security wage tax" and "snowball social security wage tax" will be passed to all consumers within the County Government's territory.
- For City Government, the "social security wage tax" and "snowball social security wage tax" will be passed to all consumers within the City Government's territory.
- For Town Government, the "social security wage tax" and "snowball social security wage tax" will be passed to all consumers within the Town Government's territory.
- Any increase to the "social security tax" will increase the "gross income."
- Any decrease to the "social security tax" will decrease the "gross income."

TRANSMIT SOCIAL SECURITY WAGE TAX

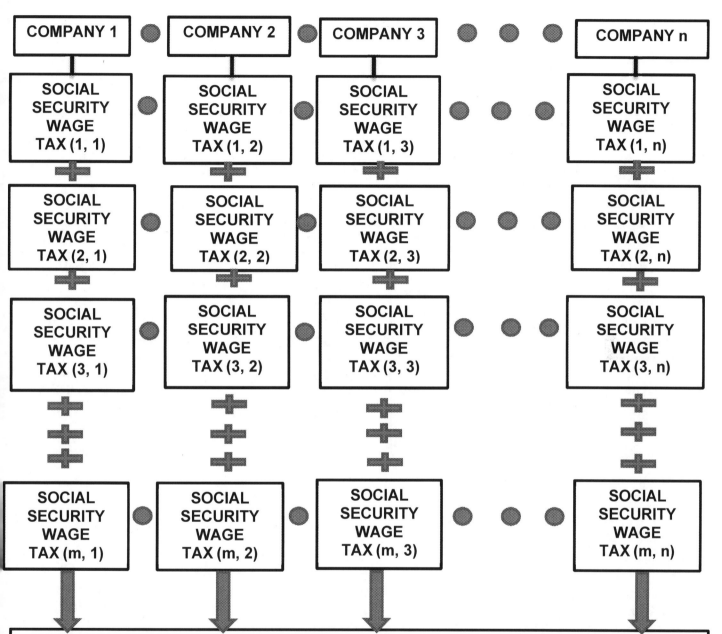

COMPANY 1	●	COMPANY 2	●	COMPANY 3	● ● ●	COMPANY n
SOCIAL SECURITY WAGE TAX (1, 1)	●	SOCIAL SECURITY WAGE TAX (1, 2)	●	SOCIAL SECURITY WAGE TAX (1, 3)	● ●	SOCIAL SECURITY WAGE TAX (1, n)
SOCIAL SECURITY WAGE TAX (2, 1)	●	SOCIAL SECURITY WAGE TAX (2, 2)	●	SOCIAL SECURITY WAGE TAX (2, 3)	● ●	SOCIAL SECURITY WAGE TAX (2, n)
SOCIAL SECURITY WAGE TAX (3, 1)	●	SOCIAL SECURITY WAGE TAX (3, 2)	●	SOCIAL SECURITY WAGE TAX (3, 3)	● ●	SOCIAL SECURITY WAGE TAX (3, n)
SOCIAL SECURITY WAGE TAX (m, 1)	●	SOCIAL SECURITY WAGE TAX (m, 2)	●	SOCIAL SECURITY WAGE TAX (m, 3)	● ● ●	SOCIAL SECURITY WAGE TAX (m, n)

COMPANIES WEEKLY SEND "SOCIAL SECURITY TAXES" TO THE GOVERNMENT. "SOCIAL SECURITY TAXES" AND "SNOWBALL SOCIAL SECURITY TAXES" ARE ADDED TO COMPANY'S GROSS PROFITS. TO SECURE A PROFIT TO THEIR PRODUCTS, COMPANIES TRANSMIT "SOCIAL SECURITY TAXES" AND "SNOWBALL SOCIAL SECURITY TAXES" TO THE MARKET PLACE. "SOCIAL SECURITY TAXES" TURN OUT TO BE SALES' TAXES.

SNOWBALL SOCIAL SECURITY WAGE TAX

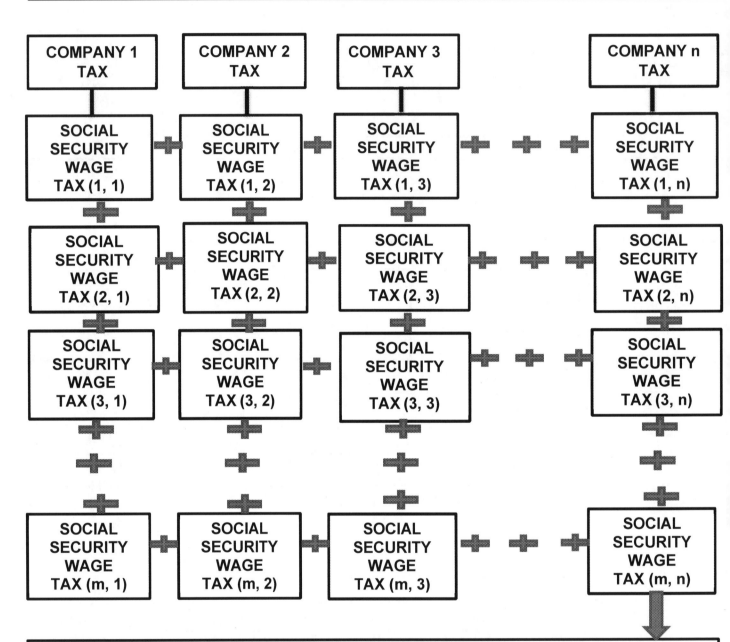

COMPANIES WEEKLY SEND "SOCIAL SECURITY TAX" TO THE GOVERNMENT. THE "SOCIAL SECURITY TAX" AND SNOWBALL SOCIAL SECURITY TAX" ARE ADDED TO COMPANYIES' GROSS PROFITS. TO SECURE A PROFIT TO THEIR PRODUCTS, COMPANIES TRANSMIT "SOCIAL SECURITY TAX" AND "SNOWBALL SOCIAL SECURITY TAX" TO THE MARKET PLACE. "SOCIAL SECURITY TAX" TURN'S OUT TO BE A SALE'S TAX.

SNOWBALL MEDICARE WAGE TAX
(NO COMPANY TAX)
SUIT (CLOTHING)
"MEDICARE WAGE TAX (1)"

PANTS* MEDICARE WAGE* TAX	PANTS* BUTTONS* MEDICARE WAGE* TAX	PANTS* WOOL* CLOTH MEDICARE WAGE* TAX	PANTS* ZIPPER* MEDICARE WAGE* TAX
JACKET* MEDICARE WAGE* TAX	JACKET* BUTTONS* MEDICARE WAGE* TAX	JACKET* SILK* CLOTH MEDICARE WAGE* TAX	JACKET* WOOL* CLOTH MEDICARE WAGE* TAX
VEST* MEDICARE WAGE* TAX	VEST* BUTTONS* MEDICARE WAGE* TAX	VEST* SILK* CLOTH MEDICARE WAGE* TAX	VEST* WOOL* CLOTH MEDICARE WAGE* TAX

"MEDICARE WAGE TAX (2)"

BUTTONS* MEDICARE WAGE* TAX	SILK* WEAVER MEDICARE WAGE* TAX	WOOL* WEAVER MEDICARE WAGE* TAX	METAL* MEDICARE WAGE* TAX

SIMPLE HYPTHETICAL CASE
"snowball medicare tax"="medicare wage tax (1)" +"medicare wage tax (2)"
ONE ITEM
ALGORITHM
MEDICARE WAGE SNOWBALL TAX!

k1, k2, k3,,,kn equals the number of workers whom manufactured or handled the item to be bought in 1,2,3,,,, n companies.

"snowball medicare wage tax (1)"=
    "medicare wage tax (1, 1)"
    +"medicare wage tax (1, 2)"
    +"medicare wage tax (1, 3)"
       +
       +
       +
    +"medicare wage tax (1, k1)"

> **k1 is the number of worker's medicare wage taxes in company (1) that are included in the "gross income" of the item. The k1 worker medicare wage taxes are delivered to the market place.**

"snowball medicare wage tax (2)"=
    "medicare wage tax (2, 1)"
    +"medicare wage tax (2, 2)"
    +"medicare wage tax (2, 3)"
       +
       +
       +
    +"medicare wage tax (2, k2)"

> **k2 is the number of worker's medicare wage taxes in company (2) that are included in the "gross income" of the item. The k2 worker medicare wage taxes are delivered to the market place.**

"snowball medicare wage tax (3)"=
    "medicare wage tax (3, 1)"
    +"medicare wage tax (3, 2)"
    +"medicare wage tax (3, 3)"
       +
       +
       +
    +"medicare wage tax (3, k3)"

> **k3 is the number of worker's medicare wage taxes in company (3) that are included in the "gross income" of the item. The k3 worker medicare wage taxes are delivered to the market place.**

       +
       +
       +

  "snowball medicare wage tax (n)"=
"medicare wage tax (n, 1)"
+"medicare wage tax (n, 2)"
+"medicare wage tax (n, 3)"
     +
     +
     +
+"medicare wage tax (n, kn)"

> **kn is the number of worker's medicare wage taxes in company (n) that are included in the "gross income" of the item. The kn worker medicare wage taxes are delivered to the market place.**

"snowball medicare wage tax"=
    "snowball medicare wage tax (1)"
    +"snowball medicare wage tax (2)"
    +"snowball medicare wage tax (3)"
        +
        +
        +
    +"snowball medicare wage tax (kn)"
"gross income"=
    "medicare tax"
    +"snowball medicare tax"
    +"company expenses"
    +"profit"

The total snowball worker's medicare wage taxes are included in the item's "gross income" and are delivered to the market place.

Since company's "gross income" includes the "medicare tax" and "snowball medicare tax," "gross income" increases!

- The "medicare tax" and "snowball medicare tax" will be passed to all consumers within the United States territories.
- For States Government, the "medicare tax" and "snowball medicare tax" will be passed to all consumers within the States Government's territory.
- For County Government, the "medicare tax" and "snowball medicare tax" will be passed to all consumers within the County Government's territory.
- For City Government, the "medicare tax" and "snowball medicare tax" consumers within the City Government's territory.
- For Town Government, the "medicare tax" and "snowball medicare tax" will be passed to all consumers within the Town Government's territory.
- Any increase to the "medicare wage tax" will increase the "gross income."
- Any decrease to the "medicare wage tax" will decrease the "gross income."

TRANSMIT MEDICARE WAGE TAX

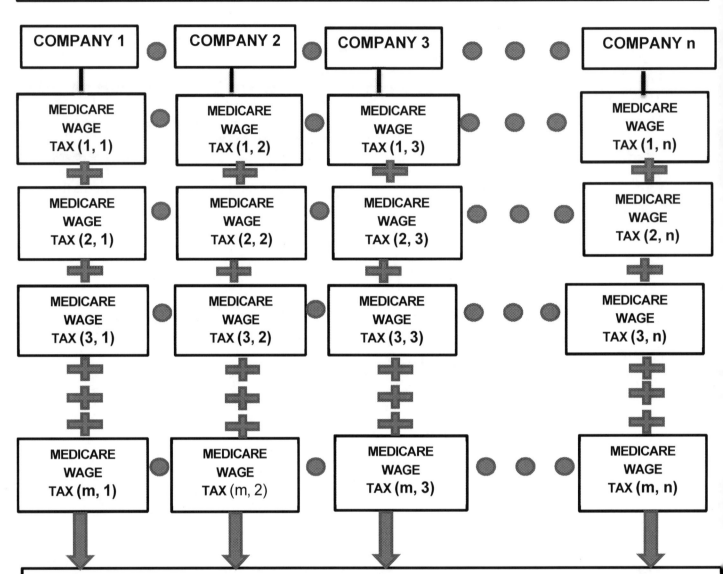

COMPANIES WEEKLY SEND "MEDICARE TAXES" TO THE GOVERNMENT. "MEDICARE TAXES" AND "SNOWBALL MEDICARE TAXES" ARE ADDED TO COMPANY'S GROSS PROFITS. TO SECURE A PROFIT TO THEIR PRODUCTS, COMPANIES TRANSMIT "MEDICARE TAXES" AND "SNOWBALL MEDICARE TAXES" TO THE MARKET PLACE. "MEDICARE TAXES" TURN OUT TO BE SALES' TAXES.

SNOWBALL MEDICARE WAGE TAX

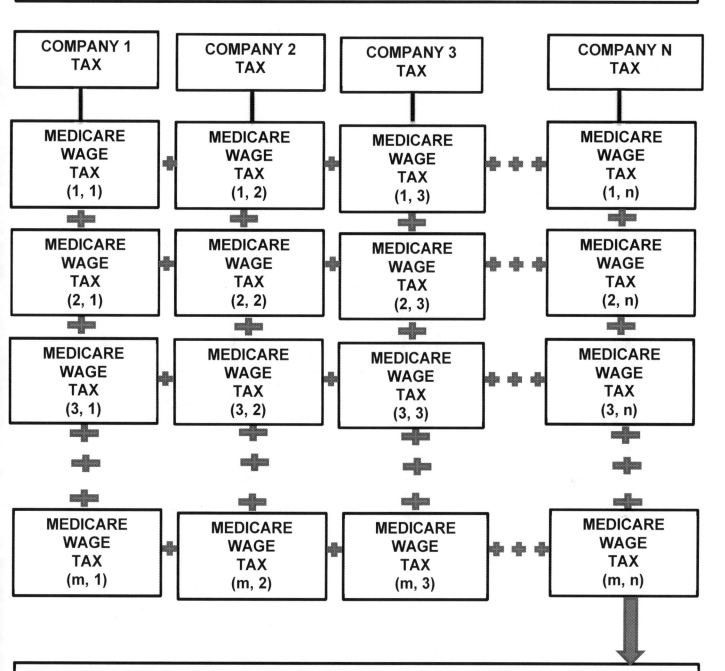

COMPANY 1 TAX	COMPANY 2 TAX	COMPANY 3 TAX	COMPANY N TAX
MEDICARE WAGE TAX (1, 1)	MEDICARE WAGE TAX (1, 2)	MEDICARE WAGE TAX (1, 3)	MEDICARE WAGE TAX (1, n)
MEDICARE WAGE TAX (2, 1)	MEDICARE WAGE TAX (2, 2)	MEDICARE WAGE TAX (2, 3)	MEDICARE WAGE TAX (2, n)
MEDICARE WAGE TAX (3, 1)	MEDICARE WAGE TAX (3, 2)	MEDICARE WAGE TAX (3, 3)	MEDICARE WAGE TAX (3, n)
MEDICARE WAGE TAX (m, 1)	MEDICARE WAGE TAX (m, 2)	MEDICARE WAGE TAX (m, 3)	MEDICARE WAGE TAX (m, n)

COMPANIES WEEKLY SEND "MEDICARE TAX" TO THE GOVERNMENT. THE "MEDICARE TAX" AND SNOWBALL MEDICARE TAX" ARE ADDED TO COMPANYIES' GROSS PROFITS. TO SECURE A PROFIT TO THEIR PRODUCTS, COMPANIES TRANSMIT "MEDICARE TAX" AND "SNOWBALL MEDICARE TAX" TO THE MARKET PLACE. "MEDICARE TAX" TURN'S OUT TO BE A SALE'S TAX.

SNOWBALL UNEMPLOYMENT WAGE TAX
(NO COMPANY TAX)
SUIT (CLOTHING)
"UNEMPLOYMENT WAGE TAX (1)"

PANTS* UNEMPLOYMENT WAGE* TAX	PANTS* BUTTONS* UNEMPLOYMENT WAGE* TAX	PANTS* WOOL* CLOTH UNEMPLOYMENT WAGE* TAX	PANTS* ZIPPER* UNEMPLOYMENT WAGE* TAX
JACKET* UNEMPLOYMENT WAGE* TAX	JACKET* BUTTONS* UNEMPLOYMENT WAGE* TAX	JACKET& SILK* CLOTH UNEMPLOYMENT WAGE* TAX	JACKET* WOOL* CLOTH UNEMPLOYMENT WAGE* TAX
VEST* UNEMPLOYMENT WAGE* TAX	VEST* BUTTONS* UNEMPLOYMENT WAGE* TAX	VEST* SILK* CLOTH UNEMPLOYMENT WAGE* TAX	VEST* WOOL* CLOTH UNEMPLOYMENT WAGE* TAX

"UNEMPLOYMENT WAGE TAX (2)"

BUTTONS* UNEMPLOYMENT WAGE* TAX	SILK* WEAVER UNEMPLOYMENT WAGE* TAX	WOOL* WEAVER UNEMPLOYMENT WAGE* TAX	METAL* UNEMPLOYMENT WAGE* TAX

ONE SUIT
SIMPLE HYPTHETICAL CASE

"snowball unemployment tax"="unemployment wage tax (1)" +"unemployment wage tax (2)"

ONE ITEM
ALGORITHM
UNEMPLOYMENT WAGE SNOWBALL TAX!

k1, k2, k3,,,kn equals the number of workers whom manufactured or handled the item to be bought in 1,2,3,,,, n companies.

"snowball unemployment wage tax (1)"=
    "unemployment wage tax (1, 1)"
    +"unemployment wage tax (1, 2)"
    +"unemployment wage tax (1, 3)"
        +
        +
        +
    +"unemployment wage tax (1, k1)"

k1 is the number of worker's unemployment wage taxes in company (1) that are included in the "gross income" of the item. The k1 worker unemployment wage taxes are delivered to the market place.

"snowball unemployment wage tax (2)"=
    "unemployment wage tax (2, 1)"
    +"unemployment wage tax (2, 2)"
    +"unemployment wage tax (2, 3)"
        +
        +
        +
    +"unemployment wage tax (2, k2)"

k2 is the number of worker's unemployment wage taxes in company (2) that are included in the "gross income" of the item. The k2 worker unemployment wage taxes are delivered to the market place.

"snowball unemployment wage tax (3)"=
    "unemployment wage tax (3, 1)"
    +"unemployment wage tax (3, 2)"
    +"unemployment wage tax (3, 3)"
        +
        +
        +
    +"unemployment wage tax (3, k3)"

k3 is the number of worker's unemployment wage taxes in company (3) that are included in the "gross income" of the item. The k3 worker unemployment wage taxes are delivered to the market place.

        +
        +
        +

 "snowball unemployment wage tax (n)"=
   "unemployment wage tax (n, 1)"
   +"unemployment wage tax (n, 2)"
   +"unemployment wage tax (n, 3)"
       +
       +
       +
   +"unemployment wage tax (n, kn)"

kn is the number of worker's unemployment wage taxes in company (n) that are included in the "gross income" of the item. The kn worker unemployment wage taxes are delivered to the market place.

"snowball unemployment wage tax"=
"snowball unemployment wage tax (1)"
+"snowball unemployment wage tax (2)"
+"snowball unemployment wage tax (3)"
+
+
+
+"snowball unemployment wage tax (kn)"
"gross income"=
"unemployment tax"
+"snowball unemployment tax"
+"company expenses"
+"profit"

> **The total snowball worker's unemployment wage taxes are included in the item's "gross income" and are delivered to the market place.**

> **Since company's "gross income" includes the "unemployment tax" and "snowball unemployment tax," "gross income" increases!**

- The "unemployment tax" and "snowball unemployment tax" will be passed to all consumers within the United States territories.
- For States Government, the "unemployment tax" and "snowball unemployment tax" will be passed to all consumers within the States Government's territory.
- For County Government, the "unemployment tax" and "snowball unemployment tax" will be passed to all consumers within the County Government's territory.
- For City Government, the "unemployment tax" and "snowball unemployment tax" will be passed to all consumers within the City Government's territory.
- For Town Government, the "unemployment tax" and "snowball unemployment tax" will be passed to all consumers within the Town Government's territory.
- Any increase to the "unemployment wage tax" will increase the "gross income."
- Any decrease to the "unemployment wage tax" will decrease the "gross income."

TRANSMIT UNEMPLOYMENT WAGE TAX

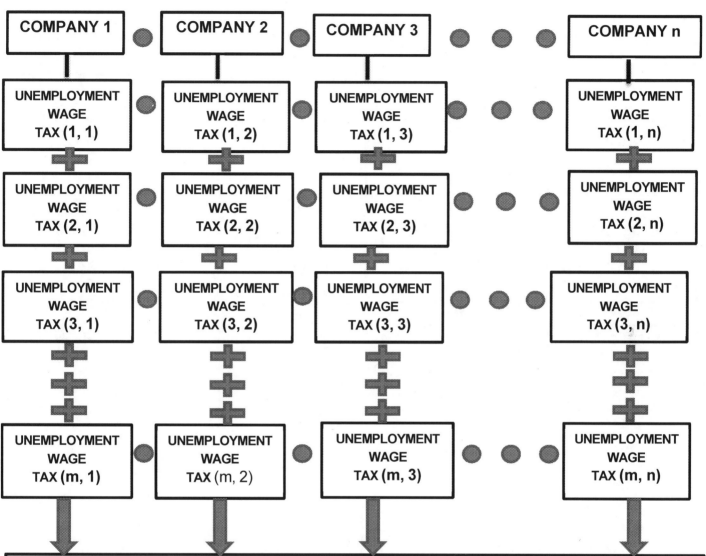

COMPANIES WEEKLY SEND "UNEMPLOYMENT TAXES" TO THE GOVERNMENT. "UNEMPLOYMENT TAXES" AND "SNOWBALL UNEMPLOYMENT TAXES" ARE ADDED TO COMPANY'S GROSS PROFITS. TO SECURE A PROFIT TO THEIR PRODUCTS, COMPANIES TRANSMIT "UNEMPLOYMENT TAXES" AND "SNOWBALL UNEMPLOYMENT TAXES" TO THE MARKET PLACE. "UNEMPLOYMENT TAXES" TURN OUT TO BE SALES' TAXES.

SNOWBALL UNEMPLOYMENT WAGE TAX

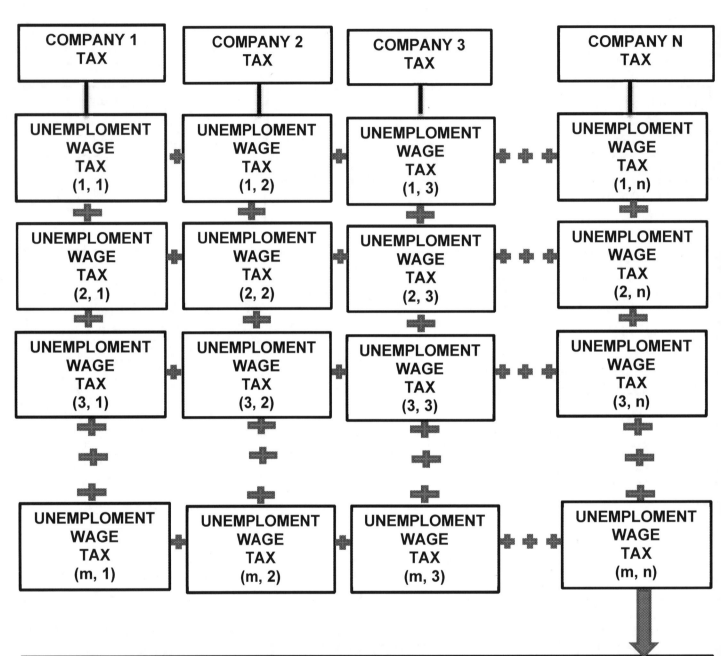

COMPANIES WEEKLY SEND "UNEMPLOYMENT TAX" TO THE GOVERNMENT. THE "UNEMPLOYMENT TAX" AND SNOWBALL UNEMPLOYMENT TAX" ARE ADDED TO COMPANYIES' GROSS PROFITS. TO SECURE A PROFIT TO THEIR PRODUCTS, COMPANIES TRANSMIT "UNEMPLOYMENT TAX" AND "SNOWBALL UNEMPLOYMENT TAX" TO THE MARKET PLACE. "UNEMPLOYMENT TAX" TURN'S OUT TO BE A SALE'S TAX.

SNOWBALL "16TH AMENDMENT," "SOCIAL SECURITY," "MEDICARE" AND "UNEMPLOYMENT" WAGE TAX (NO COMPANY TAX)

16TH AMENDMENT" "SOCIAL SECURITY" "MEDICARE" "UNEMPLOYMENT" WAGE TAX (1)"

16TH SOCIAL MED UNEMPLOY WAGE TAX (1)"

PANTS* 16TH AMENDMENT SOCIAL SECURITY MEDICARE UNEMPLOYMENT WAGE* TAX	PANTS* BUTTONS* 16TH AMENDMENT SOCIAL SECURITY MEDICARE UNEMPLOYMENT WAGE* TAX	PANTS* ZIPPER* 16TH AMENDMENT SOCIAL SECURITY MEDICARE UNEMPLOYMENT WAGE* TAX	PANTS* WOOL* CLOTH 16TH AMENDMENT SOCIAL SECURITY MEDICARE UNEMPLOYMENT WAGE* TAX
JACKET* 16TH AMENDMENT SOCIAL SECURITY MEDICARE UNEMPLOYMENT WAGE* TAX	JACKET* BUTTONS* 16TH AMENDMENT SOCIAL SECURITY MEDICARE UNEMPLOYMENT WAGE* TAX	JACKET* SILK* CLOTH 16TH AMENDMENT SOCIAL SECURITY MEDICARE UNEMPLOYMENT WAGE* TAX	JACKET* WOOL* CLOTH 16TH AMENDMENT SOCIAL SECURITY MEDICARE UNEMPLOYMENT WAGE* TAX
VEST* 16TH AMENDMENT SOCIAL SECURITY MEDICARE UNEMPLOYMENT WAGE% TAX	VEST* BUTTONS* 16TH AMENDMENT SOCIAL SECURITY MEDICARE UNEMPLOYMENT WAGE* TAX	VEST* SILK* CLOTH 16TH AMENDMENT SOCIAL SECURITY MEDICARE UNEMPLOYMENT WAGE* TAX	VEST* WOOL* CLOTH 16TH AMENDMENT SOCIAL SECURITY MEDICARE UNEMPLOYMENT WAGE* TAX
SUIT 16TH AMENDMENT SOCIAL SECURITY MEDICARE UNEMPLOYMENT WAGE* TAX			

"16TH AMENDMENT" "SOCIAL SECURITY" "MEDICARE" "UNEMPLOYMENT WAGE TAX
"16TH SOCIAL MED UNEMPLOY WAGE TAX (2)"

BUTTONS* 16TH AMENDMENT SOCIAL SECURITY MEDICARE UNEMPLOYMENT WAGE* TAX	SILK* WEAVER* 16TH AMENDMENT SOCIAL SECURITY MEDICARE UNEMPLOYMENT WAGE* TAX	WOOL* WEAVER* 16TH AMENDMENT SOCIAL SECURITY MEDICARE UNEMPLOYMENT WAGE* TAX	ZIPPER* METAL* 16TH AMENDMENT SOCIAL SECURITY MEDICARE UNEMPLOYMENT WAGE* TAX

ONE SUIT
SIMPLE HYPTHETICAL CASE

"snowball tax"="16th social med unemploy wage tax (1)"
+"16th social med unemploy wage tax (2)"

ONE ITEM
ALGORITHM
SNOWBALL COMPANY, 16TH AMENDMENT, SOCIAL SECURITY, MEDICARE AND WAGE UNEMPLOYMENT WAGE TAX!

k1, k2, k3,,,kn equals the number of workers whom manufactured or handled the item to be bought in 1,2,3,,,, n companies.

"snowball 16th amendment wage tax (1)"=
 "16th amendment wage tax (1, 1)"
 +"16th amendment wage tax (1, 2)"
 +"16th amendment wage tax (1, 3)"
 +
 +
 +
 +"16th amendment wage tax (1, k1)"
"snowball 16th amendment wage tax (2)"=
 "16th amendment wage tax (2, 1)"
 +"16th amendment wage tax (2, 2)"
 +"16th amendment wage tax (2, 3)"
 +
 +
 +
 +"16th amendment wage tax (2, k2)"

> **k1 is the number of worker's 16th amendment wage taxes in company (1) that are included in the "gross income" of the item. The k1 worker 16th amendment wage taxes are delivered to the market place.**

> **k2 is the number of worker's 16th amendment wage taxes in company (2) that are included in the "gross income" of the item. The k2 worker 16th amendment wage taxes are delivered to the market place.**

"snowball 16th amendment wage tax (3)"=
 "16th amendment wage tax (3, 1)"
 +"16th amendment wage tax (3, 2)"
 +"16th amendment wage tax (3, 3)"
  +
  +
  +
 +"16th amendment wage tax (3, k3)"
  +
  +
  +

> **k3 is the number of worker's 16th amendment wage taxes in company (3) that are included in the "gross income" of the item. The k3 worker 16th amendment wage taxes are delivered to the market place.**

"snowball 16th amendment wage tax (n)"=
 "16th amendment wage tax (n, 1)"
 +"16th amendment wage tax (n, 2)"
 +"16th amendment wage tax (n, 3)"
  +
  +
  +
 +"16th amendment wage tax (n, kn)"
"snowball 16th amendment wage tax"=
 "snowball 16th amendment wage tax (1)"
 +"snowball 16th amendment wage tax (2)"
 +"snowball 16th amendment wage tax (3)"
  +
  +
  +
 +"snowball 16th amendment wage tax (kn)"

> **kn is the number of worker's 16th amendment wage taxes in company (n) that are included in the "gross income" of the item. The kn worker 16th amendment wage taxes are delivered to the market place.**

> **The total snowball worker's 16th amendment wage taxes are included in the item's "gross income" and are delivered to the market place.**

"snowball social security tax (1)"=
 "social security wage tax (1, 1)"
 +"social security wage tax (1, 2)"
 +"social security wage tax (1, 3)"
  +
  +
  +
 +"social security wage tax (1, k1)"
"snowball social security tax (2)"=
 "social security wage tax (2, 1)"
 +"social security wage tax (2, 2)"
 +"social security wage tax (2, 3)"
  +
  +
  +
 +"social security wage tax (2, k2)"

> **k1 is the number of worker's social security wage taxes in company (1) that are included in the "gross income" of the item. The k1 worker social security wage taxes are delivered to the market place.**

> **k2 is the number of worker's social security wage taxes in company (2) that are included in the "gross income" of the item. The k2 worker social security wage taxes are delivered to the market place.**

"snowball social security tax (3)"=
    "social security wage tax (3, 1)"
    +"social security wage tax (3, 2)"
    +"social security wage tax (3, 3)"
        +
        +
        +
    +"social security wage tax (3, k3)"
        +
        +
        +

> k3 is the number of worker's social security wage taxes in company (3) that are included in the "gross income" of the item. The k3 worker social security wage taxes are delivered to the market place.

"snowball social security tax (n)"=
    "social security wage tax (n, 1)"
    +"social security wage tax (n, 2)"
    +"social security wage tax (n, 3)"
        +
        +
        +
    +"social security wage tax (n, kn)"

> kn is the number of worker's social security wage taxes in company (n) that are included in the "gross income" of the item. The kn worker social security wage taxes are delivered to the market place.

"snowball social security wage tax"=
    "snowball social security wage tax (1)"
    +"snowball social security wage tax (2)"
    +"snowball social security wage tax (3)"
        +
        +
        +
    +"snowball social security wage tax (kn)"

> The total snowball worker's social security wage taxes are included in the item's "gross income" and are delivered to the market place.

"snowball medicare tax (1)"=
    "medicare wage tax (1, 1)"
    +"medicare wage tax (1, 2)"
    +"medicare wage tax (1, 3)"
        +
        +
        +
    +"medicare wage tax (1, k1)"

> k1 is the number of worker's medicare wage taxes in company (1) that are included in the "gross income" of the item. The k1 worker medicare wage taxes are delivered to the market place.

"snowball medicare tax (2)"=
    "medicare wage tax (2, 1)"
    +"medicare wage tax (2, 2)"
    +"medicare wage tax (2, 3)"
        +
        +
        +
    +"medicare wage tax (2, k2)"

> k2 is the number of worker's medicare wage taxes in company (2) that are included in the "gross income" of the item. The k2 worker medicare wage taxes are delivered to the market place.

"snowball medicare tax (3)"=
"medicare wage tax (3, 1)"
+"medicare wage tax (3, 2)"
+"medicare wage tax (3, 3)"
+
+
+
+"medicare wage tax (3, k3)"
+
+
+

> **k3 is the number of worker's medicare wage taxes in company (3) that are included in the "gross income" of the item. The k3 worker medicare wage taxes are delivered to the market place.**

"snowball medicare tax (n)"=
"medicare wage tax (n,1)"
+"medicare wage tax (n, 2)"
+"medicare wage tax (n, 3)"
+
+
+
+"medicare wage tax (n, kn)"

> **kn is the number of worker's medicare wage taxes in company (n) that are included in the "gross income" of the item. The kn worker medicare wage taxes are delivered to the market place.**

"snowball medicare wage tax"=
"snowball medicare wage tax (1)"
+"snowball medicare wage tax (2)"
+"snowball medicare wage tax (3)"
+
+
+
+"snowball medicare wage tax (kn)"

> **The total snowball worker's medicare wage taxes are included in the item's "gross income" and are delivered to the market place.**

"snowball unemployment tax (1)"=
"unemployment wage tax (1, 1)"
+"unemployment wage tax (1, 2)"
+"unemployment wage tax (1, 3)"
+
+
+
+"unemployment wage tax (1,k1)"

> **k1 is the number of worker's unemployment wage taxes in company (1) that are included in the "gross income" of the item. The k1 worker unemployment wage taxes are delivered to the market place.**

"snowball unemployment tax (2)"=
"unemployment wage tax (2,1)"
+"unemployment wage tax (2, 2)"
+"unemployment wage tax (2,3)"
+
+
+
+"unemployment wage tax (2, k2)"

> **k2 is the number of worker's unemployment wage taxes in company (2) that are included in the "gross income" of the item. The k2 worker unemployment wage taxes are delivered to the market place.**

"snowball unemployment tax (3)"=
        "unemployment wage tax (3, 1)"
        +"unemployment wage tax (3, 2)"
        +"unemployment wage tax (3, 3)"
                        +
                        +
                        +
        +"unemployment wage tax (3, k3)"
                        +
                        +
                        +

k3 is the number of worker's unemployment wage taxes in company (3) that are included in the "gross income" of the item. The k3 worker unemployment wage taxes are delivered to the market place.

"snowball unemployment tax (n)"=
        "unemployment wage tax (n,1)"
        +"unemployment wage tax (n, 2)"
        +"unemployment wage tax (n, 3)"
                        +
                        +
                        +
        +"unemployment wage tax (n, kn)"

kn is the number of worker's unemployment wage taxes in company (n) that are included in the "gross income" of the item. The kn worker unemployment wage taxes are delivered to the market place.

"snowball unemployment wage tax"=
        "snowball unemployment wage tax (1)"
        +"snowball unemployment wage tax (2)"
        +"snowball unemployment wage tax (3)"
                        +
                        +
                        +
        +"snowball unemployment wage tax (kn)"

The total snowball worker's unemployment wage taxes are included in the item's "gross income" and are delivered to the market place.

"gross income"=
        "16th amendment wage tax"
        +"social security wage tax"
        +"medicare wage tax"
        +"unemployment wage tax"
        +"snowball 16th amendment wage tax"
        +"snowball social security wage tax"
        +"snowball medicare wage tax"
        +"snowball unemployment wage tax"
        +"company expenses"
        +"profit"

Since company's "gross income" includes the "16th amendment wage tax," "social security wage tax," "medicare wage tax," "unemployment wage tax," "snow ball 16th amendment wage tax," "snow ball social security wage tax," "snow ball medicare wage tax" and "snow ball unemployment wage tax" the "gross income" increases!

- The "16th amendment wage tax," "social security wage tax," "medicare wage tax" and "unemployment wage tax" will be passed to all consumers within the United States territories.
- For States Government, the "16th amendment wage tax," "social security wage tax," "medicare wage tax" and "unemployment wage tax" will be passed to all consumers within the States Government's territory.
- For County Government, the "16th amendment wage tax," "social security wage tax," "medicare wage tax" and "unemployment wage tax" will be passed to all consumers within the County Government's territory.
- For City Government, the "16th amendment wage tax," "social security wage tax," "medicare wage tax" and "unemployment wage tax" will be passed to all consumers within the City Government's territory.
- For Town Government, the "16th amendment wage tax," "social security wage tax," "medicare wage tax" and "unemployment wage tax" will be passed to all consumers within the Town Government's territory.
  - Any increase to the "16th amendment wage tax" will increase the "gross income."
  - Any increase to the "social security tax" will increase the "gross income."
  - Any increase to the "medicare wage tax" will increase the "gross income."
  - Any increase to the "unemployment wage tax" will increase the "gross income."
  - Any decrease to the "16th amendment wage tax" will decrease the "gross income."
  - Any decrease to the "social security tax" will decrease the "gross income."
  - Any decrease to the "medicare wage tax" will decrease the "gross income."
  - Any decrease to the "unemployment wage tax" will decrease the "gross income."

TRANSMIT 16TH AMENDMENT WAGE TAX

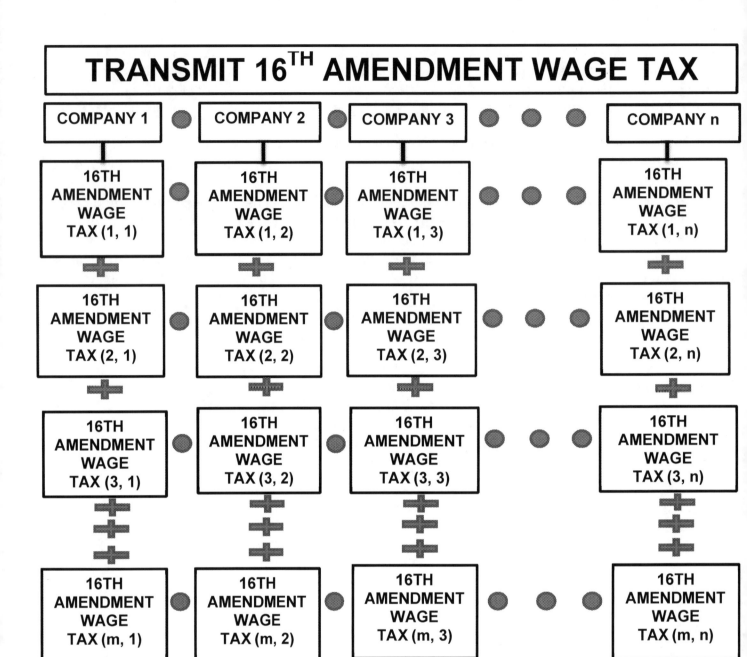

| COMPANY 1 | ● | COMPANY 2 | ● | COMPANY 3 | ● | ● | ● | COMPANY n |

16TH AMENDMENT WAGE TAX (1, 1) ● 16TH AMENDMENT WAGE TAX (1, 2) ● 16TH AMENDMENT WAGE TAX (1, 3) ● ● ● 16TH AMENDMENT WAGE TAX (1, n)

16TH AMENDMENT WAGE TAX (2, 1) ● 16TH AMENDMENT WAGE TAX (2, 2) ● 16TH AMENDMENT WAGE TAX (2, 3) ● ● ● 16TH AMENDMENT WAGE TAX (2, n)

16TH AMENDMENT WAGE TAX (3, 1) ● 16TH AMENDMENT WAGE TAX (3, 2) ● 16TH AMENDMENT WAGE TAX (3, 3) ● ● ● 16TH AMENDMENT WAGE TAX (3, n)

16TH AMENDMENT WAGE TAX (m, 1) ● 16TH AMENDMENT WAGE TAX (m, 2) ● 16TH AMENDMENT WAGE TAX (m, 3) ● ● ● 16TH AMENDMENT WAGE TAX (m, n)

COMPANIES WEEKLY SEND "16TH AMENDMENT TAXES" TO THE GOVERNMENT. "16TH AMENDMENT WAGE TAXES" AND "SNOWBALL 16TH AMENDMENT WAGE TAXES" ARE ADDED TO COMPANY'S GROSS PROFITS. TO SECURE A PROFIT TO THEIR PRODUCTS, COMPANIES TRANSMIT "16TH AMENDMENT TAXES" AND "SNOWBALL 16TH AMENDMENT TAXES" TO THE MARKET PLACE. "16TH AMENDMENT TAXES" TURN OUT TO BE SALES' TAXES.

TRANSMIT SOCIAL SECURITY WAGE TAX

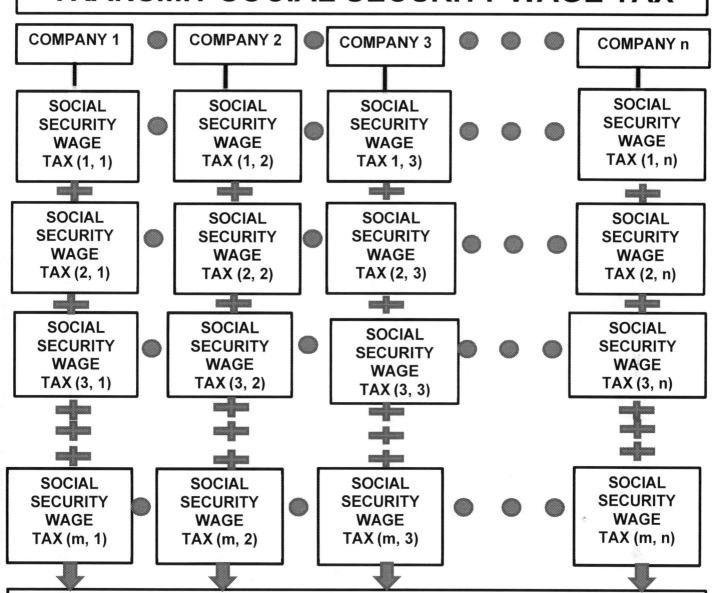

COMPANIES WEEKLY SEND "SOCIAL SECURITY TAXES" TO THE GOVERNMENT. "SOCIAL SECURITY TAXES" AND "SNOWBALL SOCIAL SECURITY TAXES" ARE ADDED TO COMPANY'S GROSS PROFITS. TO SECURE A PROFIT TO THEIR PRODUCTS, COMPANIES TRANSMIT "SOCIAL SECURITY TAXES" AND "SNOWBALL SOCIAL SECURITY TAXES" TO THE MARKET PLACE. "SOCIAL SECURITY TAXES" TURN OUT TO BE SALES' TAXES.

TRANSMIT MEDICARE WAGE TAX

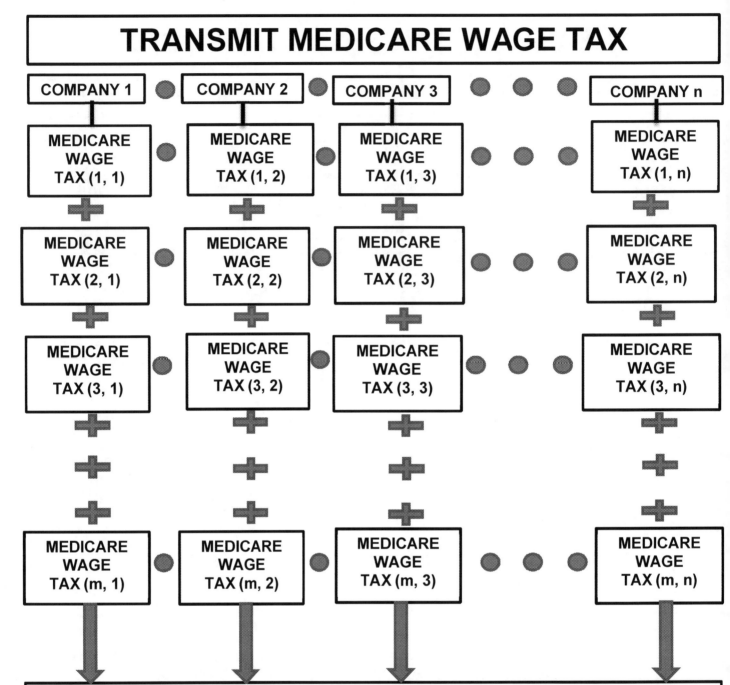

COMPANIES WEEKLY SEND "MEDICARE TAXES" TO THE GOVERNMENT. "MEDICARE TAXES" AND "SNOWBALL MEDICARE TAXES" ARE ADDED TO COMPANY'S GROSS PROFITS. TO SECURE A PROFIT TO THEIR PRODUCTS, COMPANIES TRANSMIT "MEDICARE TAXES" AND "SNOWBALL MEDICARE TAXES" TO THE MARKET PLACE. "MEDICARE TAXES" TURN OUT TO BE SALES' TAXES.

TRANSMIT UNEMPLOYMENT WAGE TAX

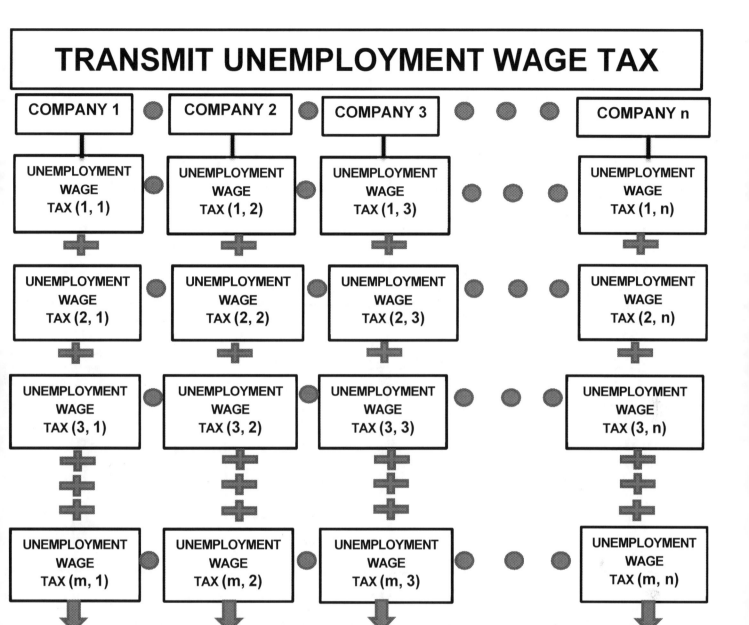

COMPANIES WEEKLY SEND "UNEMPLOYMENT TAXES" TO THE GOVERNMENT. "UNEMPLOYMENT TAXES" AND "SNOWBALL UNEMPLOYMENT TAXES" ARE ADDED TO COMPANY'S GROSS PROFITS. TO SECURE A PROFIT TO THEIR PRODUCTS, COMPANIES TRANSMIT "UNEMPLOYMENT TAXES" AND "SNOWBALL UNEMPLOYMENT TAXES" TO THE MARKET PLACE. "UNEMPLOYMENT TAXES" TURN OUT TO BE SALES' TAXES.

SNOWBALL 16TH AMENDMENT WAGE TAX

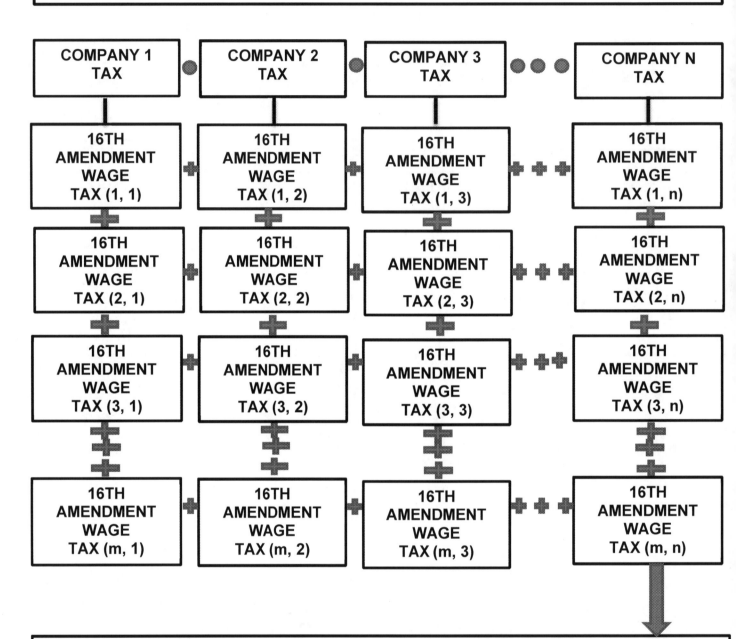

THE "16TH AMENDMENT TAX" AND "SNOWBALL 16TH AMENDMENT TAX" ARE INCLUDED IN THE PRICE OF THE ITEM PERMITTING THE ITEM'S COST TO INCREASE. THE COMPANY WEEKLY SENDS THE 16TH AMENDMENT TAX" TO THE GOVERNMENT.

THE "16TH AMENDMENT TAX" IS CONSIGNED TO THE MARKET PLACE. THE PAYMENT OF THE "16TH AMENDMENT TAX" IS LEFT TO THE CONSUMER INDICATING THAT THE 16TH AMENDMENT TAX" IS ACTUALLY A SALE'S TAX.

SNOWBALL SOCIAL SECURITY WAGE TAX

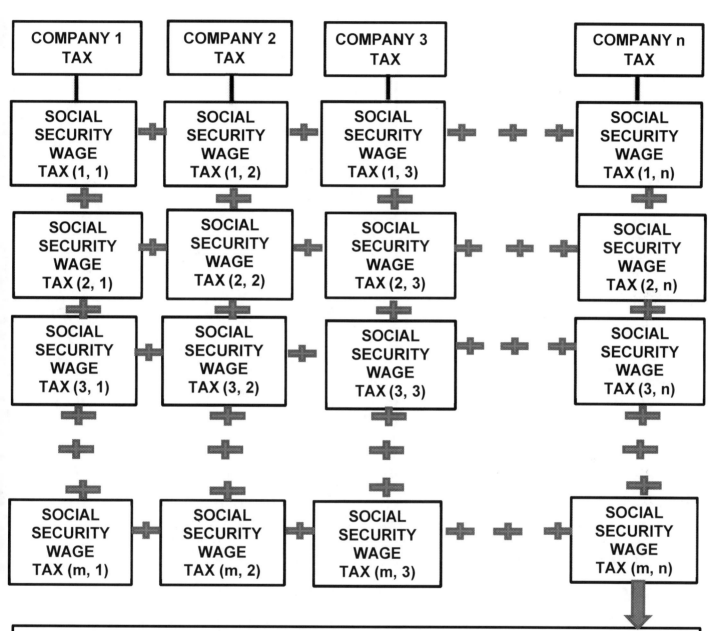

THE "SOCIAL SECURITY TAX" AND "SNOWBALL SOCIAL SECURITY TAX" ARE INCLUDED IN THE PRICE OF THE ITEM PERMITTING THE ITEM'S COST TO INCREASE.

THE COMPANY WEEKLY SENDS THE "SOCIAL SECURITY TAX" TO THE GOVERNMENT.

THE "SOCIAL SECURITY TAX" IS CONSIGNED TO THE MARKET PLACE.

SNOWBALL MEDICARE WAGE TAX

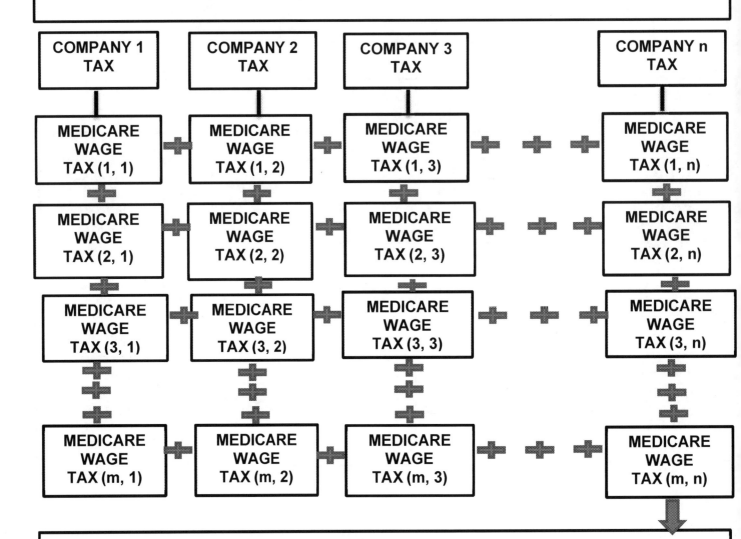

"MEDICARE TAX" AND "SNOWBALL MEDICARE TAX" ARE INCLUDED IN THE PRICE OF THE ITEM PERMITTING THE ITEM'S COST TO INCREASE.

THE COMPANY WEEKLY SENDS "MEDICARE TAX" TO THE GOVERNMENT.

"MEDICARE TAX" IS CONSIGNED TO THE MARKET PLACE.

THE PAYMENT OF THE "MEDICARE TAX" IS LEFT TO THE CONSUMER INDICATING THE "MEDICARE TAX" IS ACTUALLY A SALE'S TAX.

SNOWBALL UNEMPLOYMENT WAGE TAX

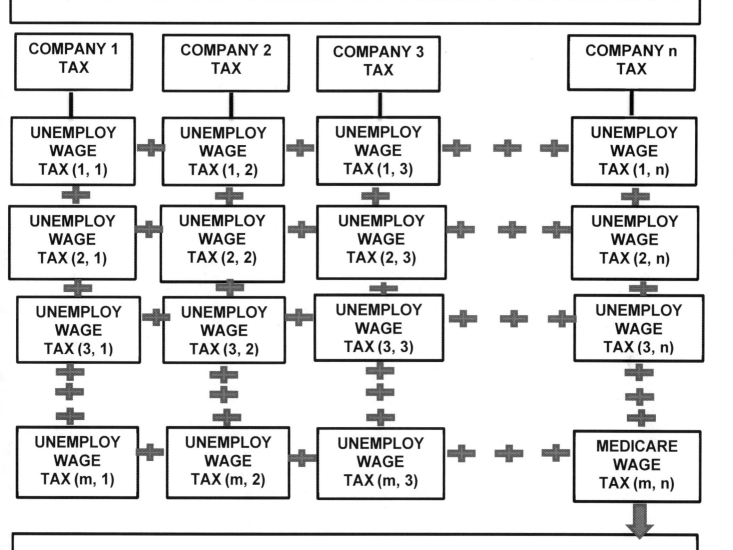

"UNEMPLOYMENT TAX" AND "SNOWBALL UNEMPLOYMENT TAX" ARE INCLUDED IN THE PRICE OF THE ITEM PERMITTING THE ITEM'S COST TO INCREASE.

THE COMPANY WEEKLY SENDS "UNEMPLOYMENT TAX" TO THE GOVERNMENT.

"UNEMPLOYMENT TAX" IS CONSIGNED TO THE MARKET PLACE.

THE PAYMENT OF THE "UNEMPLOYMENT TAX" IS LEFT TO THE CONSUMER INDICATING THE "UNEMPLOYMENT TAX" IS ACTUALLY A SALE'S TAX.

COAL MINER'S SYNDROME
THE COAL COMPANY OWNED THE HOUSES, SCHOOLS, CHURCHS AND STORES.

GOVERNMENT'S ITEM TAX SYNDROME
GOVERNMENT PLACES A TAX ON EVERY ITEM IN THE COUNTRY MARKET PLACE.

- "company tax"
- "16th amendment wage tax"
- "social security wage tax"
- "medicare wage tax"
- "unemployment wage tax"

n equals number of companies whom manufactured or handled the item to be bought.

"snowball company tax"=

    "company tax"
    +"company tax (1)"
    +"company tax (2)"
    +"company tax (3)"
       +
       +
       +
    +"company tax (n)"

> **Taxes of companies 1 thru n are added resulting in the production of an item through the delivering of a product or providing a service. All taxes are sent to the market place through the "gross income" as a "snowball company tax" that produced the item increasing the price of the item.**

k1, k2, k3,,,kn equals the number of workers whom manufactured or handled the item to be bought in 1,2,3,,,, n companies.

"snowball 16th amendment wage tax (1)"=

    "16th amendment wage tax (1, 1)"
    +"16th amendment wage tax (1, 2)"
    +"16th amendment wage tax (1, 3)"
       +
       +
       +
    +"16th amendment wage tax (1, k1)"

"snowball 16th amendment wage tax (2)"=

    "16th amendment wage tax (2, 1)"
    +"16th amendment wage tax (2, 2)"
    +"16th amendment wage tax (2, 3)"
       +
       +
       +
    +"16th amendment wage tax (2, k2)"

"snowball 16th amendment wage tax (3)"=

    "16th amendment wage tax (3, 1)"
    +"16th amendment wage tax (3, 2)"
    +"16th amendment wage tax (3, 3)"
       +
       +
       +
    +"16th amendment wage tax (3, k3)"

> **k1 is the number of worker's 16th amendment wage taxes in company (1) that are included in the cost of the item. The k1 worker 16th amendment wage taxes are delivered to the market place.**

> **k2 is the number of worker's 16th amendment wage taxes in company (2) that are included in the cost of the item. The k2 worker 16th amendment wage taxes are delivered to the market place.**

> **k3 is the number of worker's 16th amendment wage taxes in company (3) that are included in the cost of the item. The k3 worker 16th amendment wage taxes are delivered to the market place.**

```
        +
        +
        +
"snowball 16th amendment wage tax (n)"=
        "16th amendment wage tax (n, 1)"
        +"16th amendment wage tax (n, 2)"
        +"16th amendment wage tax (n, 3)"
                +
                +
                +
        +"16th amendment wage tax (n, kn)"
"snowball 16th amendment wage tax"=
        "snowball 16th amendment wage tax (1)"
        +"snowball 16th amendment wage tax (2)"
        +"snowball 16th amendment wage tax (3)"
                +
                +
                +
        +"snowball 16th amendment wage tax (kn)"
"snowball social security tax (1)"=
        "social security wage tax (1, 1)"
        +"social security wage tax (1, 2)"
        +"social security wage tax (1, 3)"
                +
                +
                +
        +"social security wage tax (1, k1)"
"snowball social security tax (2)"=
        "social security wage tax (2, 1)"
        +"social security wage tax (2, 2)"
        +"social security wage tax (2, 3)"
                +
                +
                +
        +"social security wage tax (2, k2)"
"snowball social security tax (3)"=
        "social security wage tax (3, 1)"
        +"social security wage tax (3, 2)"
        +"social security wage tax (3, 3)"
                +
                +
                +
        +"social security wage tax (3, k3)"
                +
                +
                +
```

kn is the number of worker's 16th amendment wage taxes in company (n) that are included in the cost of the item. The kn worker 16th amendment wage taxes are delivered to the market place.

The total snowball worker's 16th amendment wage taxes are included in the item's cost and are delivered to the market place.

k1 is the number of worker's social security wage taxes in company (1) that are included in the cost of the item. The k1 worker social security wage taxes are delivered to the market place.

k2 is the number of worker's social security wage taxes in company (2) that are included in the cost of the item. The k2 worker social security wage taxes are delivered to the market place.

k3 is the number of worker's social security wage taxes in company (3) that are included in the cost of the item. The k3 worker social security wage taxes are delivered to the market place.

"snowball social security tax (n)"=
    "social security wage tax (n,1)"
    +"social security wage tax (n, 2)"
    +"social security wage tax (n, 3)"
        +
        +
        +
    +"social security wage tax (n, kn)"
"snowball social security wage tax"=
    "snowball social security wage tax (1)"
    +"snowball social security wage tax (2)"
    +"snowball social security wage tax (3)"
        +
        +
        +
    +"snowball social security wage tax (kn)"
"snowball medicare tax (1)"=
    "medicare wage tax (1, 1)"
    +"medicare wage tax (1, 2)"
    +"medicare wage tax (1, 3)"
        +
        +
        +
    +"medicare wage tax (1, k1)"
"snowball medicare tax (2)"=
    "medicare wage tax (2, 1)"
    +"medicare wage tax (2, 2)"
    +"medicare wage tax (2, 3)"
        +
        +
        +
    +"medicare wage tax (2, k2)"
"snowball medicare tax (3)"=
    "medicare wage tax (3, 1)"
    +"medicare wage tax (3, 2)"
    +"medicare wage tax (3, 3)"
        +
        +
        +
    +"medicare wage tax (3, k3)"
        +
        +
        +

kn is the number of worker's social security wage taxes in company (n) that are included in the cost of the item. The kn worker social security wage taxes are delivered to the market place.

The total snowball worker's social security wage taxes are included in the item's cost and are delivered to the market place.

k1 is the number of worker's medicare wage taxes in company (1) that are included in the cost of the item. The k1 worker medicare wage taxes are delivered to the market place.

k2 is the number of worker's medicare wage taxes in company (2) that are included in the cost of the item. The k2 worker medicare wage taxes are delivered to the market place.

k3 is the number of worker's medicare wage taxes in company (3) that are included in the cost of the item. The k3 worker medicare wage taxes are delivered to the market place.

"snowball medicare tax (n)"=
    "medicare wage tax (n, 1)"
    +"medicare wage tax (n,2)"
    +"medicare wage tax (n, 3)"
      +
      +
      +
    +"medicare wage tax (n, kn)"
"snowball medicare wage tax"=
    "snowball medicare wage tax (1)"
    +"snowball medicare wage tax (2)"
    +"snowball medicare wage tax (3)"
      +
      +
      +
    +"snowball medicare wage tax (kn)"
"snowball unemployment tax (1)"=
    "unemployment wage tax (1, 1)"
    +"unemployment wage tax (1, 2)"
    +"unemployment wage tax (1, 3)"
      +
      +
      +
    +"unemployment wage tax (1, k1)"
"snowball unemployment tax (2)"=
    "unemployment wage tax (2,1)"
    +"unemployment wage tax (2, 2)"
    +"unemployment wage tax (2, 3)"
      +
      +
      +
    +"unemployment wage tax (2, k2)"
"snowball unemployment tax (3)"=
    "unemployment wage tax (3,1)"
    +"unemployment wage tax (3, 2)"
    +"unemployment wage tax (3, 3)"
      +
      +
      +
    +"unemployment wage tax (3, k3)"
      +
      +
      +

kn is the number of worker's medicare wage taxes in company (n) that are included in the cost of the item. The kn worker medicare wage taxes are delivered to the market place.

The total snowball worker's medicare wage taxes are included in the item's cost and are delivered to the market place.

k1 is the number of worker's unemployment wage taxes in company (1) that are included in the cost of the item. The k1 worker unemployment wage taxes are delivered to the market place.

k2 is the number of worker's unemployment wage taxes in company (2) that are included in the cost of the item. The k2 worker unemployment wage taxes are delivered to the market place.

k3 is the number of worker's unemployment wage taxes in company (3) that are included in the cost of the item. The k3 worker unemployment wage taxes are delivered to the market place.

"snowball unemployment tax (n)"=
      "unemployment wage tax (n,1)"
      +"unemployment wage tax (n, 2)"
      +"unemployment wage tax (n,3)"
          +
          +
          +
      +"unemployment wage tax (n, kn)"
"snowball unemployment wage tax"=
      "snowball unemployment wage tax (1)"
      +"snowball unemployment wage tax (2)"
      +"snowball unemployment wage tax (3)"
          +
          +
          +
      +"snowball unemployment wage tax (kn)"

kn is the number of worker's unemployment wage taxes in company (n) that are included in the cost of the item. The kn worker unemployment wage taxes are delivered to the market place.

The total snowball worker's unemployment wage taxes are included in the item's cost and are delivered to the market place.

SLAVE WAGE EARNER

The company sent the following item taxes to the government:
- "company tax"
- "16th amendment wage tax"
- "social security wage tax"
- "medicare wage tax"
- "unemployment wage tax"

The "slave gross wage earner" is reduced to a "slave net wage earner" who pays the following item taxes:
- "company tax"
- "16th amendment wage tax"
- "social security wage tax"
- "medicare wage tax"
- "unemployment wage tax"

The "slave net wage earner" pays the following item taxes of other companies whom handled the item:
- "company tax"
- "snowball company tax"
- "16th amendment wage tax"
- "snowball 16th amendment wage tax"
- "social security wage tax"
- "snowball social security wage tax"
- "medicare wage tax"
- "snowball medicare wage tax"
- "unemployment wage tax"
- "snowball unemployment wage tax"

ITEM TAXATION #1

ITEM TAXATION #2

ITEM TAXATION #3

COAL MINER'S SYNDROME

THE COAL COMPANY OWNED THE HOUSES, SCHOOLS, CHURCHS AND STORES.

16TH AMENDMENT ITEM TAX SYNDROME

GOVERNMENT PLACES A TAX ON EVERY ITEM IN THE COUNTRY MARKET PLACE.

"company tax"

"16th amendment wage tax"

n equals number of companies whom manufactured or handled the item to be bought.

"snowball company tax"=

+"company tax (1)"
+"company tax (2)"
+"company tax (3)"
+
+
+
+"company tax (n)"

Taxes of companies 1 thru n are added resulting in the production of an item through the delivering of a product or providing a service. All taxes are sent to the market place through the "gross income" as a "snowball company tax" that produced the item increasing the price of the item.

k1, k2, k3,,,kn equals the number of workers whom manufactured or handled the item to be bought in 1,2,3,,,, n companies.

"snowball 16th amendment wage tax (1)"=

"16th amendment wage tax (1, 1)"
+"16th amendment wage tax (1, 2)"
+"16th amendment wage tax (1, 3)"
+
+
+
+"16th amendment wage tax (1, k1)"

k1 is the number of worker's 16th amendment wage taxes in company (1) that are included in the cost of the item. The k1 worker 16th amendment wage taxes are delivered to the market place.

"snowball 16th amendment wage tax (2)"=

"16th amendment wage tax (2, 1)"
+"16th amendment wage tax (2, 2)"
+"16th amendment wage tax (2, 3)"
+
+
+
+"16th amendment wage tax (2, k2)"

k2 is the number of worker's 16th amendment wage taxes in company (2) that are included in the cost of the item. The k2 worker 16th amendment wage taxes are delivered to the market place.

"snowball 16th amendment wage tax (3)"=

"16th amendment wage tax (3, 1)"
+"16th amendment wage tax (3, 2)"
+"16th amendment wage tax (3, 3)"
+
+
+
+"16th amendment wage tax (3, k3)"

k3 is the number of worker's 16th amendment wage taxes in company (3) that are included in the cost of the item. The k3 worker 16th amendment wage taxes are delivered to the market place.

```
          +
          +
          +
"snowball 16th amendment wage tax (n)"=
     "16th amendment wage tax (n, 1)"
     +"16th amendment wage tax (n, 2)"
     +"16th amendment wage tax (n, 3)"
          +
          +
          +
     +"16th amendment wage tax (n, kn)"
"snowball 16th amendment wage tax"=
     "snowball 16th amendment wage tax (1)"
     +"snowball 16th amendment wage tax (2)"
     +"snowball 16th amendment wage tax (3)"
          +
          +
          +
     +"snowball 16th amendment wage tax (kn)"
```

kn is the number of worker's 16th amendment wage taxes in company (n) that are included in the cost of the item. The kn worker 16th amendment wage taxes are delivered to the market place.

The total snowball worker's 16th amendment wage taxes are included in the item's cost and are delivered to the market place.

SLAVE WAGE EARNER

The company sent the following item taxes to the government:
- "company tax"
- "16th amendment wage tax"

The "slave gross wage earner" is reduced to a "slave net wage earner" who pays the following item taxes:
- "company tax"
- "16th amendment wage tax"

The "slave net wage earner" pays the following Item taxes of other companies:
- "company tax"
- "snowball company tax"
- "16th amendment wage tax"
- "snowball 16th amendment wage tax"

ITEM TAXATION #1

ITEM TAXATION #2

ITEM TAXATION #3

COAL MINER'S SYNDROME

THE COAL COMPANY OWNED THE HOUSES, SCHOOLS, CHURCHS AND STORES.

SOCIAL SECURITY WAGE ITEM TAX SYNDROME

GOVERNMENT PLACES A TAX ON EVERY ITEM IN THE COUNTRY MARKET PLACE.

"company tax"

"social security wage tax"

n equals number of companies whom manufactured or handled the item to be bought.

"snowball company tax"=

+"company tax (1)"
+"company tax (2)"
+"company tax (3)"
+
+
+
+"company tax (n)"

> Taxes of companies 1 thru n are added resulting in the production of an item through the delivering of a product or providing a service. All taxes are sent to the market place through the "gross income" as a "snowball company tax" that produced the item increasing the price of the item.

k1, k2, k3,,,kn equals the number of workers whom manufactured or handled the item to be bought in 1,2,3,,,, n companies.

"snowball social security tax (1)"=

"social security wage tax (1, 1)"
+"social security wage tax (1, 2)"
+"social security wage tax (1, 3)"
+
+
+
+"social security wage tax (1, k1)"

"snowball social security tax (2)"=

"social security wage tax (2, 1)"
+"social security wage tax (2, 2)"
+"social security wage tax (2, 3)"
+
+
+
+"social security wage tax (2, k2)"

"snowball social security tax (3)"=

"social security wage tax (3, 1)"
+"social security wage tax (3, 2)"
+"social security wage tax (3, 3)"
+
+
+
+"social security wage tax (3, k3)"

> k1 is the number of worker's social security wage taxes in company (1) that are included in the cost of the item. The k1 worker social security wage taxes are delivered to the market place.

> k2 is the number of worker's social security wage taxes in company (2) that are included in the cost of the item. The k2 worker social security wage taxes are delivered to the market place.

> k3 is the number of worker's social security wage taxes in company (3) that are included in the cost of the item. The k3 worker social security wage taxes are delivered to the market place.

```
          +
          +
          +
"snowball social security tax (n)"=
        "social security wage tax (n,1)"
        +"social security wage tax (n, 2)"
        +"social security wage tax (n, 3)"
          +
          +
          +
        +"social security wage tax (n, kn)"
"snowball social security wage tax"=
        "snowball social security wage tax (1)"
        +"snowball social security wage tax (2)"
        +"snowball social security wage tax (3)"
          +
          +
          +
        +"snowball social security wage tax (kn)"
```

kn is the number of worker's social security wage taxes in company (n) that are included in the cost of the item. The kn worker social security wage taxes are delivered to the market place.

The total snowball worker's social security wage taxes are included in the item's cost and are delivered to the market place.

SLAVE WAGE EARNER

The company sent the following item taxes to the government:
- "company tax"
- "social security wage tax"

ITEM TAXATION #1

"slave gross wage earner" is reduced to a "slave net wage earner" who pays the following item taxes:
- "company tax"
- "social security wage tax"

ITEM TAXATION #2

The "slave net wage earner" pays the following item taxes of other companies:
- "company tax"
- "snowball company tax"
- "social security wage tax"
- "snowball social security wage tax"

ITEM TAXATION #3

COAL MINER'S SYNDROME

THE COAL COMPANY OWNED THE HOUSES, SCHOOLS, CHURCHS AND STORES.

MEDICARE ITEM TAX SYNDROME

GOVERNMENT PLACES A TAX ON EVERY ITEM IN THE COUNTRY MARKET PLACE.

"company tax"

"medicare wage tax"

n equals number of companies whom manufactured or handled the item to be bought.

"snowball company tax"=

+"company tax (1)"
+"company tax (2)"
+"company tax (3)"
+
+
+
+"company tax (n)"

> **Taxes of companies 1 thru n are added resulting in the production of an item through the delivering of a product or providing a service. All taxes are sent to the market place through the "gross income" as a "snowball company tax" that produced the item increasing the price of the item.**

k1, k2, k3,,,kn equals the number of workers whom manufactured or handled the item to be bought in 1,2,3,,,, n companies.

"snowball medicare wage tax (1)"=

"medicare wage tax (1, 1)"
+"medicare wage tax (1, 2)"
+"medicare wage tax (1, 3)"
+
+
+
+"medicare wage tax (1, k1)"

"snowball medicare wage tax (2)"=

"medicare wage tax (2, 1)"
+"medicare wage tax (2, 2)"
+"medicare wage tax (2, 3)"
+
+
+
+"medicare wage tax (2, k2)"

"snowball medicare wage tax (3)"=

"medicare wage tax (3, 1)"
+"medicare wage tax (3, 2)"
+"medicare wage tax (3, 3)"
+
+
+
+"medicare wage tax (3, k3)"

> **k1 is the number of worker's medicare wage taxes in company (1) that are included in the cost of the item. The k1 worker medicare wage taxes are delivered to the market place.**

> **k2 is the number of worker's medicare wage taxes in company (2) that are included in the cost of the item. The k2 worker medicare wage taxes are delivered to the market place.**

> **k3 is the number of worker's medicare wage taxes in company (3) that are included in the cost of the item. The k3 worker medicare wage taxes are delivered to the market place.**

```
        +
        +
        +
"snowball medicare tax (n)"=
        "medicare wage tax (n, 1)"
        +"medicare wage tax (n,2)"
        +"medicare wage tax (n, 3)"
            +
            +
            +
        +"medicare wage tax (n, kn)"
"snowball medicare wage tax"=
        "snowball medicare wage tax (1)"
        +"snowball medicare wage tax (2)"
        +"snowball medicare wage tax (3)"
            +
            +
            +
        +"snowball medicare wage tax (kn)"
```

kn is the number of worker's medicare wage taxes in company (n) that are included in the cost of the item. The kn worker medicare wage taxes are delivered to the market place.

The total snowball worker's medicare wage taxes are included in the item's cost and are delivered to the market place.

SLAVE WAGE EARNER

The company sent the following item taxes to the government:
- **"company tax"**
- **"medicare wage tax"**

The "slave gross wage earner" is reduced to a "slave net wage earner" who pays the following item taxes:
- **"company tax"**
- **"medicare wage tax"**

The "slave net wage earner" pays the following item taxes of other companies:
- **"company tax"**
- **"snowball company tax"**
- **"medicare wage tax"**
- **"snowball medicare wage tax"**

ITEM TAXATION #1

ITEM TAXATION #2

ITEM TAXATION #3

COAL MINER'S SYNDROME

THE COAL COMPANY OWNED THE HOUSES, SCHOOLS, CHURCHS AND STORES.

UNEMPLOYMENT WAGE TAX SYNDROME

GOVERNMENT PLACES A TAX ON EVERY ITEM IN THE COUNTRY MARKET PLACE.

"company tax"

"unemployment wage tax"

n equals number of companies whom manufactured or handled the item to be bought.

"snowball company tax"=

+"company tax (1)"

+"company tax (2)"

+"company tax (3)"

+

+

+

+"company tax (n)"

> **Taxes of companies 1 thru n are added resulting in the production of an item through the delivering of a product or providing a service. All taxes are sent to the market place through the "gross income" as a "snowball company tax" that produced the item increasing the price of the item.**

k1, k2, k3,,,kn equals the number of workers whom manufactured or handled the item to be bought in 1,2,3,,,, n companies.

"snowball unemployment tax (1)"=

"unemployment wage tax (1, 1)"

+"unemployment wage tax (1, 2)"

+"unemployment wage tax (1, 3)"

+

+

+

+"unemployment wage tax (1, k1)"

"snowball unemployment tax (2)"=

"unemployment wage tax (2,1)"

+"unemployment wage tax (2, 2)"

+"unemployment wage tax (2, 3)"

+

+

+

+"unemployment wage tax (2, k2)"

"snowball unemployment tax (3)"=

"unemployment wage tax (3,1)"

+"unemployment wage tax (3, 2)"

+"unemployment wage tax (3, 3)"

+

+

+

+"unemployment wage tax (3, k3)"

+

+

+

> **k1 is the number of worker's unemployment wage taxes in company (1) that are included in the cost of the item. The k1 worker unemployment wage taxes are delivered to the market place.**

> **k2 is the number of worker's unemployment wage taxes in company (2) that are included in the cost of the item. The k2 worker unemployment wage taxes are delivered to the market place.**

> **k3 is the number of worker's unemployment wage taxes in company (3) that are included in the cost of the item. The k3 worker unemployment wage taxes are delivered to the market place.**

"snowball unemployment tax (n)"=
   "unemployment wage tax (n,1)"
   +"unemployment wage tax (n, 2)"
   +"unemployment wage tax (n,3)"
      +
      +
      +
   +"unemployment wage tax (n, kn)"
"snowball unemployment wage tax"=
   "snowball unemployment wage tax (1)"
   +"snowball unemployment wage tax (2)"
   +"snowball unemployment wage tax (3)"
      +
      +
      +
   +"snowball unemployment wage tax (kn)"

kn is the number of worker's unemployment wage taxes in company (n) that are included in the cost of the item. The kn worker unemployment wage taxes are delivered to the market place.

The total snowball worker's unemployment wage taxes are included in the item's cost and are delivered to the market place.

SLAVE WAGE EARNER

The company sent the following item taxes to the government:
- "company tax"
- "unemployment wage tax" "

ITEM TAXATION #1

The "slave gross wage earner" is reduced to a "slave net wage earner" who pays the following item taxes:
- "company tax"
- "unemployment wage tax"

ITEM TAXATION #2

The "slave net wage earner" pays the following item taxes of other companies:
- "company tax"
- "snowball company tax"
- "unemployment wage tax"
- "snowball unemployment wage"

ITEM TAXATION #3

COAL MINER'S SYNDROME

THE COAL COMPANY OWNED THE HOUSES, SCHOOLS, CHURCHS AND STORES.
(NO COMPANY)

16TH AMENDMENT WAGE ITEM TAX SYNDROME

GOVERNMENT PLACES A TAX ON EVERY ITEM IN THE COUNTRY MARKET PLACE.

"16th amendment wage tax"
$k_1, k_2, k_3,,,k_n$ equals the number of workers whom manufactured or handled the item to be bought in $1, 2, 3,,,, n$ companies.

"snowball 16th amendment tax (1)"=
    "16th amendment wage tax (1, 1)"
    +"16th amendment wage tax (1, 2)"
    +"16th amendment wage tax (1, 3)"
       +
       +
       +
    +"16th amendment wage tax (1, k1)"

> k_1 is the number of worker's 16th amendment wage taxes in company (1) that are included in the cost of the item. The k1 worker 16th amendment wage taxes are delivered to the market place.

"snowball 16th amendment tax (2)"=
    "16th amendment wage tax (2, 1)"
    +"16th amendment wage tax (2, 2)"
    +"16th amendment wage tax (2, 3)"
       +
       +
       +
    +"16th amendment wage tax (2, k2)"

> k_2 is the number of worker's 16th amendment wage taxes in company (2) that are included in the cost of the item. The k2 worker 16th amendment wage taxes are delivered to the market place.

"snowball 16th amendment tax (3)"=
    "16th amendment wage tax (3, 1)"
    +"16th amendment wage tax (3, 2)"
    +"16th amendment wage tax (3, 3)"
       +
       +
       +
    +"16th amendment wage tax (3, k3)"
       +
       +
       +

> k_3 is the number of worker's 16th amendment 16th amendment wage taxes in company (3) that are included in the cost of the item. The k3 worker 16th amendment 16th amendment wage taxes are delivered to the market place.

"snowball 16th amendment tax (n)"=
    "16th amendment wage tax (n, 1)"
    +"16th amendment wage tax (n, 2)"
    +"16th amendment wage tax (n, 3)"
       +
       +
       +
    +"16th amendment wage tax (n, kn)"

> k_n is the number of worker's 16th amendment wage taxes in company (n) that are included in the cost of the item. The kn worker 16th amendment wage taxes are delivered to the market place.

"snowball 16th amendment wage tax"=

    "snowball 16th amendment wage tax (1)"

    +"snowball 16th amendment wage tax (2)"

    +"snowball 16th amendment wage tax (3)"

      +

      +

      +

    +"snowball 16th amendment wage tax (kn)"

> The total snowball worker's 16th amendment wage taxes are included in the item's cost and are delivered to the market place.

SLAVE WAGE EARNER

The company sent the item tax:
- "16th amendment wage tax"

ITEM TAXATION #1

The "slave gross wage earner" is reduced to a "slave net wage earner" who pays the following item tax:
- "16th amendment wage tax"

ITEM TAXATION #2

The "slave net wage earner" pays the following item taxes of other companies:
- "16th amendment wage tax"
- "snowball 16th amendment wage tax"

ITEM TAXATION #3

COAL MINER'S SYNDROME

THE COAL COMPANY OWNED THE HOUSES, SCHOOLS, CHURCHS AND STORES.
(NO COMPANY)

SOCIAL SECURITY WAGE ITEM TAX SYNDROME

GOVERNMENT PLACES A TAX ON EVERY ITEM IN THE COUNTRY MARKET PLACE.

"social security wage tax"

$k1, k2, k3,,,kn$ equals the number of workers whom manufactured or handled the item to be bought in $1,2,3,,,,n$ companies.

"snowball social security tax (1)"=

 "social security wage tax (1, 1)"
 +"social security wage tax (1, 2)"
 +"social security wage tax (1, 3)"
  +
  +
  +
 +"social security wage tax (1, k1)"

"snowball social security tax (2)"=

 "social security wage tax (2, 1)"
 +"social security wage tax (2, 2)"
 +"social security wage tax (2, 3)"
  +
  +
  +
 +"social security wage tax (2, k2)"

"snowball social security tax (3)"=

 "social security wage tax (3, 1)"
 +"social security wage tax (3, 2)"
 +"social security wage tax (3, 3)"
  +
  +
  +
 +"social security wage tax (3, k3)"
  +
  +
  +

"snowball social security tax (n)"=

 "social security wage tax (n,1)"
 +"social security wage tax (n, 2)"
 +"social security wage tax (n, 3)"
  +
  +
  +
 +"social security wage tax (n, kn)"

> **k1 is the number of worker's social security wage taxes in company (1) that are included in the cost of the item. The k1 worker social security wage taxes are delivered to the market place.**

> **k2 is the number of worker's social security wage taxes in company (2) that are included in the cost of the item. The k2 worker social security wage taxes are delivered to the market place.**

> **k3 is the number of worker's social security wage taxes in company (3) that are included in the cost of the item. The k3 worker social security wage taxes are delivered to the market place.**

> **kn is the number of worker's social security wage taxes in company (n) that are included in the cost of the item. The kn worker social security wage taxes are delivered to the market place.**

"snowball social security wage tax"=
 "snowball social security wage tax (1)"
 +"snowball social security wage tax (2)"
 +"snowball social security wage tax (3)"
  +
  +
  +
 +"snowball social security wage tax (kn)"

The total snowball worker's social security wage taxes are included in the item's cost and are delivered to the market place.

SLAVE WAGE EARNER

The company sent the item tax:
- "social security wage tax"

The "slave gross wage earner" is reduced to a "slave net wage earner" who pays the following item tax:
- "social security wage tax"

The "slave net wage earner" pays the following item taxes of other companies:
- "social security wage tax"
- "snowball social security wage tax"

ITEM TAXATION #1

ITEM TAXATION #2

ITEM TAXATION #3

COAL MINER'S SYNDROME

THE COAL COMPANY OWNED THE HOUSES, SCHOOLS, CHURCHS AND STORES.
(NO COMPANY)

MEDICARE WAGE ITEM TAX SYNDROME

GOVERNMENT PLACES A TAX ON EVERY ITEM IN THE COUNTRY MARKET PLACE.

"medicare wage tax"
k1, k2, k3,,,kn equals the number of workers whom manufactured or handled the item to be bought in 1,2,3,,,, n companies.

"snowball medicare tax (1)"=
    "medicare wage tax (1, 1)"
    +"medicare wage tax (1, 2)"
    +"medicare wage tax (1, 3)"
        +
        +
        +
    +"medicare wage tax (1, k1)"
"snowball medicare tax (2)"=
    "medicare wage tax (2, 1)"
    +"medicare wage tax (2, 2)"
    +"medicare wage tax (2, 3)"
        +
        +
        +
    +"medicare wage tax (2, k2)"
"snowball medicare tax (3)"=
    "medicare wage tax (3, 1)"
    +"medicare wage tax (3, 2)"
    +"medicare wage tax (3, 3)"
        +
        +
        +
    +"medicare wage tax (3, k3)"
        +
        +
        +
"snowball medicare tax (n)"=
    "medicare wage tax (n,1)"
    +"medicare wage tax (n, 2)"
    +"medicare wage tax (n, 3)"
        +
        +
        +
    +"medicare wage tax (n, kn)"

k1 is the number of worker's medicare wage taxes in company (1) that are included in the cost of the item. The k1 worker medicare wage taxes are delivered to the market place.

k2 is the number of worker's medicare wage taxes in company (2) that are included in the cost of the item. The k2 worker medicare wage taxes are delivered to the market place.

k3 is the number of worker's medicare wage taxes in company (3) that are included in the cost of the item. The k3 worker medicare wage taxes are delivered to the market place.

kn is the number of worker's medicare wage taxes in company (n) that are included in the cost of the item. The kn worker medicare wage taxes are delivered to the market place.

"snowball medicare wage tax"=
 "snowball medicare wage tax (1)"
 +"snowball medicare wage tax (2)"
 +"snowball medicare wage tax (3)"
   +
   +
   +
 +"snowball medicare wage tax (kn)"

The total snowball worker's medicare wage taxes are included in the item's cost and are delivered to the market place.

SLAVE WAGE EARNER

The company sent the item taxes:
- "medicare wage tax"

The "slave gross wage earner" is reduced to a "slave net wage earner" who pays the following item taxes:
- "medicare wage tax"

The "slave net wage earner" pays the following item taxes of other companies:
- "medicare wage tax"
- "snowball medicare wage tax"

ITEM TAXATION #1

ITEM TAXATION #2

ITEM TAXATION #3

COAL MINER'S SYNDROME

THE COAL COMPANY OWNED THE HOUSES, SCHOOLS, CHURCHS AND STORES.
(NO COMPANY)

UNEMPLOYMENT WAGE TAX SYNDROME

GOVERNMENT PLACES A TAX ON EVERY ITEM IN THE COUNTRY MARKET PLACE.

"unemployment wage tax"

k1, k2, k3,,,kn equals the number of workers whom manufactured or handled the item to be bought in 1,2,3,,,, n companies.

"snowball unemployment tax (1)"=
    "unemployment wage tax (1, 1)"
    +"unemployment wage tax (1, 2)"
    +"unemployment wage tax (1, 3)"
    +
    +
    +
    +"unemployment wage tax (1, k1)"

k1 is the number of worker's unemployment wage taxes in company (1) that are included in the cost of the item. The k1 worker unemployment wage taxes are delivered to the market place.

"snowball unemployment tax (2)"=
    "unemployment wage tax (2,1)"
    +"unemployment wage tax (2, 2)"
    +"unemployment wage tax (2, 3)"
    +
    +
    +
    +"unemployment wage tax (2, k2)"

k2 is the number of worker's unemployment wage taxes in company (2) that are included in the cost of the item. The k2 worker unemployment wage taxes are delivered to the market place.

"snowball unemployment tax (3)"=
    "unemployment wage tax (3,1)"
    +"unemployment wage tax (3, 2)"
    +"unemployment wage tax (3, 3)"
    +
    +
    +
    +"unemployment wage tax (3, k3)"
    +
    +
    +

k3 is the number of worker's unemployment wage taxes in company (3) that are included in the cost of the item. The k3 worker unemployment wage taxes are delivered to the market place.

"snowball unemployment tax (n)"=
    "unemployment wage tax (n,1)"
    +"unemployment wage tax (n, 2)"
    +"unemployment wage tax (n,3)"
    +
    +
    +
    +"unemployment wage tax (n, kn)"

kn is the number of worker's unemployment wage taxes in company (n) that are included in the cost of the item. The kn worker unemployment wage taxes are delivered to the market place.

"snowball unemployment wage tax"=
"snowball unemployment wage tax (1)"
+"snowball unemployment wage tax (2)"
+"snowball unemployment wage tax (3)"
+
+
+
+"snowball unemployment wage tax (kn)"

The total snowball worker's unemployment wage taxes are included in the item's cost and are delivered to the market place.

SLAVE WAGE EARNER

The company sent the item tax:
- "unemployment wage tax"

ITEM TAXATION #1

The "slave gross wage earner" is reduced to a "slave net wage earner" who pays the following item tax:
- "unemployment wage tax"

ITEM TAXATION #2

The "slave net wage earner" pays the following item taxes of other companies:
- "unemployment wage tax"
- "snowball unemployment wage"

ITEM TAXATION #3

FUNCTIONAL
EQUATIONS
SYMBOLS
REPRESENT
MATHEMATICAL
FUNCTIONAL
EQUATION
TO
SIMPLIFY
FUNCTIONAL
TAXATIONAL
EXAMPLES

CIVIL WAR FUNCTION4

"civil war company tax"
"snowball civil war company tax"
"civil war wage tax"
"snowball civil war wage tax"

CIVIL WAR FUNCTION2

"civil war wage tax"
"snowball civil war wage tax"

FUNCTIONCS16S10

"company tax"
"snowball company tax"
"16th amendment wage tax"
"snowball 16th amendment wage tax"
"social security wage tax"
"snowball social security wage tax"
"medicare wage tax"
"snowball medicare wage tax"
"unemployment wage tax"
"snowball unemployment wage tax"

FUNCTIONC16S9

"company tax"
"16th amendment wage tax"
"snowball 16th amendment wage tax"
"social security wage tax"
"snowball social security wage tax"
"medicare wage tax"
"snowball medicare wage tax"
"unemployment wage tax"
"snowball unemployment wage tax"

FUNCTION16S8

"16th amendment wage tax"
"snowball 16th amendment wage tax"
"social security wage tax"
"snowball social security wage tax"
"medicare wage tax"
"snowball medicare wage tax"
"unemployment wage tax"
"snowball unemployment wage tax"

FUNCTIONCS16S4

"company tax"
"snowball company tax"
"16th amendment wage tax"
"snowball 16th amendment wage tax"

FUNCTIONCSSS4

"company tax"
"snowball company tax"
"social security wage tax"
"snowball social security wage tax"

FUNCTIONCSMS4

"company tax"
"snowball company tax"
"medicare wage tax"
"snowball medicare wage tax"

FUNCTIONCSUS4

"company tax"
"snowball company tax"
"unemployment wage tax"
"snowball unemployment wage tax"

FUNCTIONCSSSN4

"state company tax"
"snowball state company tax"
"state wage tax"
"snowball state wage tax"

FUNCTIONCSCS4

"city company tax"
"snowball city company tax"
"city wage tax"
"snowball city wage tax"

FUNCTIONC16S3

"company tax"
"16th amendment wage tax"
"snowball 16th amendment wage tax"

FUNCTIONCSS3

"company tax"
"social security wage tax"
"snowball social security wage tax"

FUNCTIONCMS3

"company tax"
"medicare wage tax"
"snowball medicare wage tax"

FUNCTIONCUS3

"company tax"
"unempolyment wage tax"
"snowball unempolyment wage tax"

FUNCTION162

"16th amendment wage tax"
"snowball 16th amendment wage tax"

FUNCTIONSS2

"social security wage tax"
"snowball social security wage tax"

FUNCTIONMS2

"medicare wage tax"
"snowball medicare wage tax"

FUNCTIONUS2

"unemployment wage tax"
"snowball unemployment wage tax"

FUNCTION161

"16th amendment wage tax"

FUNCTIONS1

"social security wage tax"

FUNCTIONM1

"medicare wage tax"

FUNCTIONU1

"unemployment wage tax"

EQUATIONS

REPRESENTATING

MATHEMATICAL

ALGORITHMIC

MODEL

PER

ITEM

CIVIL WAR

The Civil War income tax was the first tax paid on individual incomes by residents of the United States. Abraham Lincoln instituted America's first income tax in 1862, as he searched for money that would enable the union to wage and win the war. As Northern losses mounted, the war would be long, bloody, and expensive. The income tax was certainly the largest single tax source.

The Revenue Act increased taxes dramatically; and, soaked up much of the inflationary pressure produced by Greenbacks. The Revenue Act lasted a decade being repealed in 1872 seven years after the end of the war. Revenue Act set the precedent for the income tax in 1894 (declared unconstitutional) and the current income tax provisions beginning in 1913 after the passage of the war.

It was a "progressive" tax in that it initially levied a tax any income over $10,000. In 1864 the rates increased and the ceiling dropped so that incomes between $600 and $5,000 were taxed. Passed as an emergency measure to finance the Union cause in the Civil War, the first income tax generated approximately $55 million in government revenues during the war. Paying the taxes was viewed as part of the patriotic war effort, and the whole country was proud when the merchant prince A. T. Stewart paid $400,000 in taxes on an income of $4 million.

Taxes were levied on residents of all states and territories not in rebellion. In the South, some states operated under reconstruction governments while the war went on. Virginia, for example, the site of the Confederate capital, was largely controlled by federal forces, and northern and western Virginians were subject to the income tax from the beginning. States that seceded were included in the tax base as soon as Union troops established control. Georgians paid income taxes in 1865 even though their state was not officially readmitted to the Union until 1870.

The Civil War taxes were not immediately repealed at the end of the war but continued in force until 1872, when the Grant administration sponsored the repeal of most of the "emergency" taxes.

Fifteen years later the Populists attempted to revive the income tax and Congress passed a law providing for a new 2 percent tax on incomes over $4,000. But the Supreme Court surprised the nation, reversing its earlier decision and declaring the law unconstitutional in 1895. This ruling declaring that an income tax is a direct tax and therefore unconstitutional led to the ratification of the sixteenth amendment in 1913.

More significantly, the Internal Revenue Act of 1861, the first federal income tax in American history, assured the financial community that the government would have a reliable source of income to pay the interest on war bonds. Subsequent Revenue Acts of 1862 and 1864 created moderately progressive tax brackets and set rates at 5, 7.5, and 10 percent. By the end of the war nearly one in ten American households (mostly in the affluent states in the industrial Northeast, the section of the country that held most of the wealth) paid an income tax.

CIVIL WAR FUNCTION4

> "civil war company tax"
> "snowball civil war company tax"
> "civil war wage tax"
> "snowball civil war wage tax"

- civil war company tax
- civil war wage tax

n equals number of companies whom manufactured or handled the item to be bought.

"snowball civil war company tax"=

    "civil war company tax"
    +"civil war company tax (1)"
    +"civil war company tax (2)"
    +"civil war company tax (3)"
        +
        +
        +
    +"civil war company tax (n)"

> **Taxes of companies 1 thru n are added resulting in the production of an item through the delivering of a product or providing a service. All taxes are sent to the market place through the "gross income" as a "snowball war company tax" that produced the item increasing the price of the item.**

k1, k2, k3,,,kn equals the number of workers whom manufactured or handled the item to be bought in 1,2,3,,,, n companies.

"snowball civil war wage tax (1)"=

    "civil war wage tax (1, 1)"
    +"civil war wage tax (1, 2)"
    +"civil war wage tax (1, 3)"
        +
        +
        +
    +"civil war wage tax (1, k1)"

"snowball civil war wage tax (2)"=

    "civil war wage tax (2, 1)"
    +"civil war wage tax (2, 2)"
    +"civil war wage tax (2, 3)"
        +
        +
        +
    +"civil war wage tax (2, k2)"

"snowball civil war wage tax (3)"=

    "civil war wage tax (3, 1)"
    +"civil war wage tax (3, 2)"
    +"civil war wage tax (3, 3)"
        +
        +
        +
    +"civil war wage tax (3, k3)"

> **k1 is the number of worker's wage taxes in war company (1) that are included in the cost of the item. The k1 worker wage taxes are delivered to the market place.**

> **k2 is the number of worker's wage taxes in war company (2) that are included in the cost of the item. The k2 worker wage taxes are delivered to the market place.**

> **k3 is the number of worker's wage taxes in war company (3) that are included in the cost of the item. The k3 worker wage taxes are delivered to the market place.**

```
                    +
                    +
                    +
"snowball civil war wage tax (n)"=
        "civil war wage tax (n, 1)"
        +"civil war wage tax (n, 2)"
        +"civil war wage tax (n, 3)"
                    +
                    +
                    +
        +"civil war wage tax (n, kn)"
"snowball civil war wage tax"=
        "snowball civil war wage tax (1)"
        +"snowball civil war wage tax (2)"
        +"snowball civil war wage tax (3)"
                    +
                    +
                    +
        +"snowball civil war wage tax (kn)"
"gross income"=
        "civil war company tax"
        +"snowball civil war company tax"
        +"civil war wage tax"
        +"snowball civil war wage tax"
        +civil war company expenses
        +"item profit"
```

> kn is the number of worker's wage taxes in war company (n) that are included in the cost of the item. The kn worker wage taxes are delivered to the market place.

> The total snowball worker's wage taxes are included in the item's cost and are delivered to the market place.

The war company transmits the following to the government and the market place:
   "war company tax"
   "war wage tax"
"gross wage earner" becomes "net wage earner."
Other companies transmit the following to the government:
   "war company tax"   "war wage tax"
The following develops:
   "war company tax" becomes "snowball war company tax"
   "war wage tax" becomes "snowball war wage tax"
The other companies add the following to the "war company's tax:
   "war company tax"   "snowball war company tax"
   "war wage tax"   "snowball war wage tax"
The war company transmits the following to the market place:
   "war company tax,"   "snowball war company tax"
   "war wage tax"   "snowball war wage tax"
A "net wage earner" who buys any product in the market place ends up paying a "triple tax."
Any "non-net wage earner" or "consumer" who buys any product in the market place pays a "double tax."

"war company tax"
"war wage tax"

TAXATION #1
Taxes are sent to government!
Taxes are sent to market place too!
"gross wage earner" becomes "net wage earner"

"war company tax"
"war wage tax"

TAXATION #2
"net wage earner" and consumer pay these taxes in the market place.

"war company tax"
"snowball war company tax"
"war wage tax"
"snowball war wage tax"

TAXATION #3
Companies' whom handled or produce the item of both snowball and regular taxes had been sent to the government. "net wage earner" and consumer pay these taxes in the market place!

Note! "net wage earners" and consumers pay war company taxes in the market place!

FUNCTION END

CIVIL WAR FUNCTION2

> "civil war wage tax"
> "snowball civil war wage tax"

- civil war wage tax

k1, k2, k3,,,kn equals the number of workers whom manufactured or handled the item to be bought in 1,2,3,,,, n companies.

"snowball civil war wage tax (1)"=
    "civil war wage tax (1, 1)"
    +"civil war wage tax (1, 2)"
    +"civil war wage tax (1, 3)"
       +
       +
       +
    +"civil war wage tax (1, k1)"

"snowball civil war wage tax (2)"=
    "civil war wage tax (2, 1)"
    +"civil war wage tax (2, 2)"
    +"civil war wage tax (2, 3)"
       +
       +
       +
    +"civil war wage tax (2, k2)"

"snowball civil war wage tax (3)"=
    "civil war wage tax (3, 1)"
    +"civil war wage tax (3, 2)"
    +"civil war wage tax (3, 3)"
       +
       +
       +
    +"civil war wage tax (3, k3)"
       +
       +
       +

"snowball civil war wage tax (n)"=
    "civil war wage tax (n, 1)"
    +"civil war wage tax (n, 2)"
    +"civil war wage tax (n, 3)"
       +
       +
       +
    +"civil war wage tax (n, kn)"

> k1 is the number of worker's wage taxes in war company (1) that are included in the cost of the item. The k1 worker wage taxes are delivered to the market place.

> k2 is the number of worker's wage taxes in war company (2) that are included in the cost of the item. The k2 worker wage taxes are delivered to the market place.

> k3 is the number of worker's wage taxes in war company (3) that are included in the cost of the item. The k3 worker wage taxes are delivered to the market place.

> kn is the number of worker's wage taxes in war company (n) that are included in the cost of the item. The kn worker wage taxes are delivered to the market place.

"snowball civil war wage tax"=
    "snowball civil war wage tax (1)"
    +"snowball civil war wage tax (2)"
    +"snowball civil war wage tax (3)"
        +
        +
        +
    +"snowball civil war wage tax (kn)"
"gross income"=
    +"civil war wage tax"
    +"snowball civil war wage tax"
    +civil war company expenses
    +"item profit"

The total snowball worker's wage taxes are included in the item's cost and are delivered to the market place.

The civil war company transmits the following to the government and the market place:
    "civil war wage tax"
"gross wage earner" becomes "net wage earner."
Other companies transmit the following to the government:
    "civil war wage tax"
The following develops:
    "civil war wage tax" becomes "snowball civil war wage tax"
The other companies add the following to the "civil war company's tax:
    "civil war wage tax"   "snowball civil war wage tax"
The civil war company transmits the following to the market place:
    "civil war wage tax"   "snowball civil war wage tax"
A "net wage earner" who buys any product in the market place ends up paying a "triple tax."
Any "non-net wage earner" or "consumer" who buys any product in the market place pays a "double tax."

"civil war wage tax"

TAXATION #1
Taxes are sent to government!
Taxes are sent to market place too!
"gross wage earner" becomes "net wage earner"

"civil war wage tax"

TAXATION #2
"net wage earner" and consumer pay this tax in the market place.

"civil war wage tax"
"snowball civil war wage tax"

TAXATION #3
Companies' whom handled or produce the item of both snowball and regular taxes had been sent to the government. "net wage earner" and consumer pay these taxes in the market place!

FUNCTION END

FUNCTIONCS16S10

"company tax"
"snowball company tax"
"16th amendment wage tax"
"snowball 16th amendment wage tax"
"social security wage tax"
"snowball social security wage tax"
"medicare wage tax"
"snowball medicare wage tax"
"unemployment wage tax"
"snowball unemployment wage tax"

- "company tax"
- "16th amendment wage tax"
- "social security wage tax"
- "medicare wage tax"
- "unemployment wage tax"

n equals number of companies whom manufactured or handled the item to be bought.

"snowball company tax"=
    +"company tax (1)"
    +"company tax (2)"
    +"company tax (3)"
        +
        +
        +
    +"company tax (n)"

> **Taxes of companies 1 thru n are added resulting in the production of an item through the delivering of a product or providing a service. All taxes are sent to the market place through the "gross income" as a "snowball company tax" that produced the item increasing the price of the item.**

k1, k2, k3,,,kn equals the number of workers whom manufactured or handled the item to be bought in 1,2,3,,,, n companies.

"snowball 16th amendment wage tax (1)"=
    "16th amendment wage tax (1, 1)"
    +"16th amendment wage tax (1, 2)"
    +"16th amendment wage tax (1, 3)"
        +
        +
        +
    +"16th amendment wage tax (1, k1)"

> **k1 is the number of worker's 16th amendment wage taxes in company (1) that are included in the cost of the item. The k1 worker 16th amendment wage taxes are delivered to the market place.**

"snowball 16th amendment wage tax (2)"=
    "16th amendment wage tax (2, 1)"
    +"16th amendment wage tax (2, 2)"
    +"16th amendment wage tax (2, 3)"
        +
        +
        +
    +"16th amendment wage tax (2, k2)"

> **k2 is the number of worker's 16th amendment wage taxes in company (2) that are included in the cost of the item. The k2 worker 16th amendment wage taxes are delivered to the market place.**

"snowball 16th amendment tax (3)"=
    "16th amendment wage tax (3, 1)"
    +"16th amendment wage tax (3, 2)"
    +"16th amendment wage tax (3, 3)"
        +
        +
        +
    +"16th amendment wage tax (3, k3)"
        +
        +
        +

> **k3 is the number of worker's 16th amendment wage taxes in company (3) that are included in the cost of the item. The k3 worker 16th amendment wage taxes are delivered to the market place.**

"snowball 16th amendment tax (n)"=
    "16th amendment wage tax (n,1)"
    +"16th amendment wage tax (n, 2)"
    +"16th amendment wage tax (n, 3)"
        +
        +
        +
    +"16th amendment wage tax (n, kn)"

> **kn is the number of worker's 16th amendment wage taxes in company (n) that are included in the cost of the item. The kn worker 16th amendment wage taxes are delivered to the market place.**

"snowball 16th amendment wage tax"=
    "snowball 16th amendment wage tax (1)"
    +"snowball 16th amendment wage tax (2)"
    +"snowball 16th amendment wage tax (3)"
        +
        +
        +
    +"snowball 16th amendment wage tax (kn)"

> **The total snowball worker's 16th amendment wage taxes are included in the item's cost and are delivered to the market place.**

"snowball social security tax (1)"=
    "social security wage tax (1, 1)"
    +"social security wage tax (1, 2)"
    +"social security wage tax (1, 3)"
        +
        +
        +
    +"social security wage tax (1, k1)"

> **k1 is the number of worker's social security wage taxes in company (1) that are included in the cost of the item. The k1 worker social security wage taxes are delivered to the market place.**

"snowball social security tax (2)"=
    "social security wage tax (2, 1)"
    +"social security wage tax (2, 2)"
    +"social security wage tax (2, 3)"
        +
        +
        +
    +"social security wage tax (2, k2)"

> **k2 is the number of worker's social security wage taxes in company (2) that are included in the cost of the item. The k2 worker social security wage taxes are delivered to the market place.**

"snowball social security tax (3)"=
   "social security wage tax (3, 1)"
   +"social security wage tax (3, 2)"
   +"social security wage tax (3, 3)"
      +
      +
      +
   +"social security wage tax (3, k3)"

> **k3 is the number of worker's social security wage taxes in company (3) that are included in the cost of the item. The k3 worker social security wage taxes are delivered to the market place.**

      +
      +
      +

"snowball social security tax (n)"=
   "social security wage tax (n, 1)"
   +"social security wage tax (n,2)"
   +"social security wage tax (n, 3)"
      +
      +
      +
   +"social security wage tax (n, kn)"

> **kn is the number of worker's social security wage taxes in company (n) that are included in the cost of the item. The kn worker social security wage taxes are delivered to the market place.**

"snowball social security wage tax"=
   "snowball social security wage tax (1)"
   +"snowball social security wage tax (2)"
   +"snowball social security wage tax (3)"
      +
      +
      +
   +"snowball social security wage tax (kn)"

> **The total snowball worker's social security wage taxes are included in the item's cost and are delivered to the market place.**

"snowball medicare tax (1)"=
   "medicare wage tax (1, 1)"
   +"medicare wage tax (1, 2)"
   +"medicare wage tax (1, 3)"
      +
      +
      +
   +"medicare wage tax (1, k1)"

> **k1 is the number of worker's medicare wage taxes in company (1) that are included in the cost of the item. The k1 worker medicare wage taxes are delivered to the market place.**

"snowball medicare tax (2)"=
   "medicare wage tax (2, 1)"
   +"medicare wage tax (2, 2)"
   +"medicare wage tax (2, 3)"
      +
      +
      +
   +"medicare wage tax (2, k2)"

> **k2 is the number of worker's medicare wage taxes in company (2) that are included in the cost of the item. The k2 worker medicare wage taxes are delivered to the market place.**

"snowball medicare tax (3)"=
    "medicare wage tax (3, 1)"
    +"medicare wage tax (3, 2)"
    +"medicare wage tax (3, 3)"
        +
        +
        +
    +"medicare wage tax (3, k3)"
        +
        +
        +

k3 is the number of worker's medicare wage taxes in company (3) that are included in the cost of the item. The k3 worker medicare wage taxes are delivered to the market place.

"snowball medicare tax (n)"=
    "medicare wage tax (n, 1)"
    +"medicare wage tax (n,2)"
    +"medicare wage tax (n, 3)"
        +
        +
        +

kn is the number of worker's medicare wage taxes in company (n) that are included in the cost of the item. The kn worker medicare wage taxes are delivered to the market place.

    +"medicare wage tax (n, kn)"
"snowball medicare wage tax"=
    "snowball medicare wage tax (1)"
    +"snowball medicare wage tax (2)"
    +"snowball medicare wage tax (3)"
        +
        +
        +

The total snowball worker's medicare wage taxes are included in the item's cost and are delivered to the market place.

    +"snowball medicare wage tax (kn)"
"snowball unemployment tax (1)"=
    "unemployment wage tax (1, 1)"
    +"unemployment wage tax (1, 2)"
    +"unemployment wage tax (1, 3)"
        +
        +
        +

k1 is the number of worker's unemployment wage taxes in company (1) that are included in the cost of the item. The k1 worker unemployment wage taxes are delivered to the market place.

    +"unemployment wage tax (1, k1)"
"snowball unemployment tax (2)"=
    "unemployment wage tax (2,1)"
    +"unemployment wage tax (2, 2)"
    +"unemployment wage tax (2, 3)"
        +
        +
        +

k2 is the number of worker's unemployment wage taxes in company (2) that are included in the cost of the item. The k2 worker unemployment wage taxes are delivered to the market place.

    +"unemployment wage tax (2, k2)"

"snowball unemployment tax (3)"=
  "unemployment wage tax (3,1)"
  +"unemployment wage tax (3, 2)"
  +"unemployment wage tax (3, 3)"
    +
    +
    +
  +"unemployment wage tax (3, k3)"
    +
    +
    +

k3 is the number of worker's unemployment wage taxes in company (3) that are included in the cost of the item. The k3 worker unemployment wage taxes are delivered to the market place.

"snowball unemployment tax (n)"=
  "unemployment wage tax (n,1)"
  +"unemployment wage tax (n, 2)"
  +"unemployment wage tax (n,3)"
    +
    +
    +
  +"unemployment wage tax (n, kn)"

kn is the number of worker's unemployment wage taxes in company (n) that are included in the cost of the item. The kn worker unemployment wage taxes are delivered to the market place.

"snowball unemployment wage tax"=
  "snowball unemployment wage tax (1)"
  +"snowball unemployment wage tax (2)"
  +"snowball unemployment wage tax (3)"
    +
    +
    +
  +"snowball unemployment wage tax (kn)"

The total snowball worker's unemployment wage taxes are included in the item's cost and are delivered to the market place.

"company gross income"=
  "company tax"
  +"snowball company tax"
  +"16th amendment wage tax"
  +"social security wage tax"
  +"medicare wage tax"
  +"unemployment wage tax"
  +"snowball 16th amendment wage tax"
  +"snowball social security wage tax"
  +"snowball medicare wage tax"
  +"snowball unemployment wage tax"
  +"item profit"
  +company expenses

These taxes are placed on items being sold throughout the country's market place indicating that the company does not pay taxes leaving the paying of taxes to the people in the market place producing "multi taxation."
A "net wage earner" who purchases in the market place would be subject to a "triple taxation" and any other person would be subjected to a "double taxation."

"multi tax"=
> "company tax"
> +"snowball company tax"
> +"16th amendment wage tax"
> +"social security wage tax"
> +"medicare wage tax"
> +"unemployment wage tax"
> +"snowball 16th amendment wage tax"
> +"snowball social security wage tax"
> +"snowball medicare wage tax"
> +"snowball unemployment wage tax"

Upon substitution,

"company gross income"="multi tax"+"item profit "+company expenses

FEDERAL GOVERNMENT TAX BONANZA

The government has already been compensated the following taxes:
- "company tax"
- "16th amendment wage tax"
- "social security wage tax"
- "medicare wage tax"
- "unemployment wage tax"

Company's yearly **"GROSS INCOME"** includes the:
- "multi tax"
- "item profit"
- company expenses

The following are included in the government's next tax appraisal of the "company tax" cycling back into the government's "company tax" calculation:
- "multi tax"
- "item profit"
- company expenses

Through the "company gross income" and a "graduated tax table", the government receives a percentage of the "company gross income."

Since the following United States (USA) Corporate Tax Rates are fix, the new "company tax" could move up or down a tax bracket permitting the new "company tax" to snow ball.

TAX YEAR 2010 2009 2008 2007 2006 2005 2004 AND 2003 FEDERAL UNITED STATES (USA) CORPORATE TAX RATES PERSONAL SERVICE CORPORATIONS PAY A FLAT RATE OF 35%			
TAXABLE INCOME OVER	BUT NOT OVER	YOUR TAX IS	
$0	$50,000		15%
$50,000	$75,000	7,500	25%
$75,000	$100,000	13,750	34%
$100,000	$335,000	22,250	39%
$335,000	$10,000,000	113,900	34%
$10,000,000	$15,000,000	3,400,000	35%
$15,000,000	$18,333,333	5,150,000	38%
$18,333,333		FLAT RATE 35%	

TAXABLE INCOME IS GROSS INCOME.

The following represent possible "government tax income":
"company gross income"= "multi tax" +"item profit" +company expenses
   government tax possible income is:

$$0<\text{"company gross income"}<50,000$$
"government tax income"=15% x "multi tax"+15% x "item profit"
$$50,000<\text{"company gross income"}<75,000$$
"government tax income"=25% x "multi tax"+25% x "item profit"
$$75,000<\text{"company gross income"}<100,000$$
"government tax income"=34% x "multi tax"+34% x "item profit"
$$100,000<\text{"company gross income"}<335,000$$
"government tax income"=39% x "multi tax"+39% x "item profit"
$$335,000<\text{"company gross income"}<10,000,000$$
"government tax income"=34% x "multi tax"+34% x "item profit"
$$10,000,000<\text{"company gross income"}<15,000,000$$
"government tax income"=35% x "multi tax"+35% x "item profit"
$$15,000,000<\text{"company gross income"}<18,333,333$$
"government tax income"=38% x "multi tax"+38% x "item profit"
$$18,000,000<\text{"company gross income"}$$
"government tax income"=35% x "multi tax"+35% x "item profit"

"company tax"
"16th amendment wage tax"
"social security wage tax"
"medicare wage tax"
"unemployment wage tax"

TAXATION #1
Taxes are sent to government!
Taxes are sent to market place too!
"gross wage earner" becomes "net wage earner"

"company tax"
"16th amendment wage tax"
"social security wage tax"
"medicare wage tax"
"unemployment wage tax"

TAXATION #2
"net wage earner" and consumer pay these taxes in the market place.

"company tax"
"snowball company tax"
"16th amendment wage tax"
"snowball 16th amendment wage tax"
"social security wage tax"
"snowball social security wage tax"
"medicare wage tax"
"snowball medicare wage tax"
"unemployment wage tax"
"snowball unemployment wage tax"

TAXATION #3
Companies' whom handled or produce the item of both snowball and regular taxes had been sent to the government. "net wage earner" and consumer pay these taxes in the market place!

Note! "net wage earners" and consumers pay company taxes in the market place!

FUNCTION END

FUNCTIONC16S9

"company tax"
 "16th amendment wage tax"
"snowball 16th amendment wage tax"
"social security wage tax"
"snowball social security wage tax"
"medicare wage tax"
"snowball medicare wage tax"
"unemployment wage tax"
"snowball unemployment wage tax"

- "company tax"
- "16th amendment wage tax"
- "social security wage tax"
- "medicare wage tax"
- "unemployment wage tax"

n equals number of companies whom manufactured or handled the item to be bought.
k1, k2, k3,,,kn equals the number of workers whom manufactured or handled the item to be bought in 1,2,3,,,, n companies.

"snowball 16th amendment wage tax (1)"=
        "16th amendment wage tax (1, 1)"
        +"16th amendment wage tax (1, 2)"
        +"16th amendment wage tax (1, 3)"
                +
                +
                +
        +"16th amendment wage tax (1, k1)"

"snowball 16th amendment wage tax (2)"=
        "16th amendment wage tax (2, 1)"
        +"16th amendment wage tax (2, 2)"
        +"16th amendment wage tax (2, 3)"
                +
                +
                +
        +"16th amendment wage tax (2, k2)"

"snowball 16th amendment tax (3)"=
        "16th amendment wage tax (3, 1)"
        +"16th amendment wage tax (3, 2)"
        +"16th amendment wage tax (3, 3)"
                +
                +
                +
        +"16th amendment wage tax (3, k3)"

k1 is the number of worker's 16th amendment wage taxes in company (1) that are included in the cost of the item. The k1 worker 16th amendment wage taxes are delivered to the market place.

k2 is the number of worker's 16th amendment wage taxes in company (2) that are included in the cost of the item. The k2 worker 16th amendment wage taxes are delivered to the market place.

k3 is the number of worker's 16th amendment wage taxes in company (3) that are included in the cost of the item. The k3 worker 16th amendment wage taxes are delivered to the market place.

+
+
+

"snowball 16th amendment tax (n)"=
    "16th amendment wage tax (n,1)"
    +"16th amendment wage tax (n, 2)"
    +"16th amendment wage tax (n, 3)"
      +
      +
      +
    +"16th amendment wage tax (n, kn)"

> **kn is the number of worker's 16th amendment wage taxes in company (n) that are included in the cost of the item. The kn worker 16th amendment wage taxes are delivered to the market place.**

"snowball 16th amendment wage tax"=
    "snowball 16th amendment wage tax (1)"
    +"snowball 16th amendment wage tax (2)"
    +"snowball 16th amendment wage tax (3)"
      +
      +
      +
    +"snowball 16th amendment wage tax (kn)"

> **The total snowball worker's 16th amendment wage taxes are included in the item's cost and are delivered to the market place.**

"snowball social security tax (1)"=
    "social security wage tax (1, 1)"
    +"social security wage tax (1, 2)"
    +"social security wage tax (1, 3)"
      +
      +
      +
    +"social security wage tax (1, k1)"

> **k1 is the number of worker's social security wage taxes in company (1) that are included in the cost of the item. The k1 worker social security wage taxes are delivered to the market place.**

"snowball social security tax (2)"=
    "social security wage tax (2, 1)"
    +"social security wage tax (2, 2)"
    +"social security wage tax (2, 3)"
      +
      +
      +
    +"social security wage tax (2, k2)"

> **k2 is the number of worker's social security wage taxes in company (2) that are included in the cost of the item. The k2 worker social security wage taxes are delivered to the market place.**

"snowball social security tax (3)"=
    "social security wage tax (3, 1)"
    +"social security wage tax (3, 2)"
    +"social security wage tax (3, 3)"
      +
      +
      +
    +"social security wage tax (3, k3)"

> **k3 is the number of worker's social security wage taxes in company (3) that are included in the cost of the item. The k3 worker social security wage taxes are delivered to the market place.**

      +
      +
      +

"snowball social security tax (n)"=
  "social security wage tax (n, 1)"
  +"social security wage tax (n,2)"
  +"social security wage tax (n, 3)"
   +
   +
   +
  +"social security wage tax (n, kn)"

kn is the number of worker's social security wage taxes in company (n) that are included in the cost of the item. The kn worker social security wage taxes are delivered to the market place.

"snowball social security wage tax"=
  "snowball social security wage tax (1)"
  +"snowball social security wage tax (2)"
  +"snowball social security wage tax (3)"
   +
   +
   +
  +"snowball social security wage tax (kn)"

The total snowball worker's social security wage taxes are included in the item's cost and are delivered to the market place.

"snowball medicare tax (1)"=
  "medicare wage tax (1, 1)"
  +"medicare wage tax (1, 2)"
  +"medicare wage tax (1, 3)"
   +
   +
   +
  +"medicare wage tax (1, k1)"

k1 is the number of worker's medicare wage taxes in company (1) that are included in the cost of the item. The k1 worker medicare wage taxes are delivered to the market place.

"snowball medicare tax (2)"=
  "medicare wage tax (2, 1)"
  +"medicare wage tax (2, 2)"
  +"medicare wage tax (2, 3)"
   +
   +
   +
  +"medicare wage tax (2, k2)"

k2 is the number of worker's medicare wage taxes in company (2) that are included in the cost of the item. The k2 worker medicare wage taxes are delivered to the market place.

"snowball medicare tax (3)"=
  "medicare wage tax (3, 1)"
  +"medicare wage tax (3, 2)"
  +"medicare wage tax (3, 3)"
   +
   +
   +
  +"medicare wage tax (3, k3)"
   +
   +
   +

k3 is the number of worker's medicare wage taxes in company (3) that are included in the cost of the item. The k3 worker medicare wage taxes are delivered to the market place.

"snowball medicare tax (n)"=
  "medicare wage tax (n, 1)"
  +"medicare wage tax (n,2)"
  +"medicare wage tax (n, 3)"
  +
  +
  +
  +"medicare wage tax (n, kn)"
"snowball medicare wage tax"=
  "snowball medicare wage tax (1)"
  +"snowball medicare wage tax (2)"
  +"snowball medicare wage tax (3)"
  +
  +
  +
  +"snowball medicare wage tax (kn)"
"snowball unemployment tax (1)"=
  "unemployment wage tax (1, 1)"
  +"unemployment wage tax (1, 2)"
  +"unemployment wage tax (1, 3)"
  +
  +
  +
  +"unemployment wage tax (1, k1)"
"snowball unemployment tax (2)"=
  "unemployment wage tax (2,1)"
  +"unemployment wage tax (2, 2)"
  +"unemployment wage tax (2, 3)"
  +
  +
  +
  +"unemployment wage tax (2, k2)"
"snowball unemployment tax (3)"=
  "unemployment wage tax (3,1)"
  +"unemployment wage tax (3, 2)"
  +"unemployment wage tax (3, 3)"
  +
  +
  +
  +"unemployment wage tax (3, k3)"
  +
  +
  +

kn is the number of worker's medicare wage taxes in company (n) that are included in the cost of the item. The kn worker medicare wage taxes are delivered to the market place.

The total snowball worker's medicare wage taxes are included in the item's cost and are delivered to the market place.

k1 is the number of worker's unemployment wage taxes in company (1) that are included in the cost of the item. The k1 worker unemployment wage taxes are delivered to the market place.

k2 is the number of worker's unemployment wage taxes in company (2) that are included in the cost of the item. The k2 worker unemployment wage taxes are delivered to the market place.

k3 is the number of worker's unemployment wage taxes in company (3) that are included in the cost of the item. The k3 worker unemployment wage taxes are delivered to the market place.

"snowball unemployment tax (n)"=
  "unemployment wage tax (n,1)"
  +"unemployment wage tax (n, 2)"
  +"unemployment wage tax (n,3)"
      +
      +
      +
  +"unemployment wage tax (n, kn)"
"snowball unemployment wage tax"=
  "snowball unemployment wage tax (1)"
  +"snowball unemployment wage tax (2)"
  +"snowball unemployment wage tax (3)"
      +
      +
      +
  +"snowball unemployment wage tax (kn)"
"company gross income"=
  "company tax"
  +"16th amendment wage tax"
  +"social security wage tax"
  +"medicare wage tax"
  +"unemployment wage tax"
  +"snowball 16th amendment wage tax"
  +"snowball social security wage tax"
  +"snowball medicare wage tax"
  +"snowball unemployment wage tax"
  +"item profit"
  +company expenses

kn is the number of worker's unemployment wage taxes in company (n) that are included in the cost of the item. The kn worker unemployment wage taxes are delivered to the market place.

The total snowball worker's unemployment wage taxes are included in the item's cost and are delivered to the market place.

These taxes are placed on items being sold throughout the country's market place indicating that the company does not pay taxes leaving the paying of taxes to the people in the market place producing "multi taxation."
A "net wage earner" who purchases in the market place would be subject to a "triple taxation" and any other person would be subjected to a "double taxation."

"multi tax"=
  "company tax"
  +"16th amendment wage tax"
  +"social security wage tax"
  +"medicare wage tax"
  +"unemployment wage tax"
  +"snowball 16th amendment wage tax"
  +"snowball social security wage tax"
  +"snowball medicare wage tax"
  +"snowball unemployment wage tax"
Upon substitution,
"company gross income"="multi tax "+"item profit "+company expenses

FEDERAL GOVERNMENT TAX BONANZA

The government has already been compensated the following taxes:

- "company tax"
- "16th amendment wage tax"
- "social security wage tax"
- "medicare wage tax"
- "unemployment wage tax"

Company's yearly "**GROSS INCOME**" includes the:

- "multi tax"
- "item profit"
- company expenses

The following are included in the government's next tax appraisal of the "company tax" cycling back into the government's "company tax" calculation:

- "multi tax"
- "item profit"
- company expenses

Through the "company gross income" and a "graduated tax table", the government receives a percentage of the "company gross income."

Since the following United States (USA) Corporate Tax Rates are fix, the new "company tax" could move up or down a tax bracket permitting the new "company tax" to snow ball.

TAX YEAR 2010 2009 2008 2007 2006 2005 2004 AND 2003 FEDERAL UNITED STATES (USA) CORPORATE TAX RATES PERSONAL SERVICE CORPORATIONS PAY A FLAT RATE OF 35%			
TAXABLE INCOME OVER	BUT NOT OVER	YOUR TAX IS	
$0	$50,000		15%
$50,000	$75,000	7,500	25%
$75,000	$100,000	13,750	34%
$100,000	$335,000	22,250	39%
$335,000	$10,000,000	113,900	34%
$10,000,000	$15,000,000	3,400,000	35%
$15,000,000	$18,333,333	5,150,000	38%
$18,333,333		FLAT RATE 35%	

TAXABLE INCOME IS GROSS INCOME

The following represent possible "government tax income":

"company gross income"= "multi tax" +"item profit" +company expenses
government tax possible income is:

$$0<\text{"company gross income"}<50,000$$

"government tax income"=15% x "multi tax"+15% x "item profit"

$$50,000<\text{"company gross income"}<75,000$$

"government tax income"=25% x "multi tax"+25% x "item profit"

$$75,000<\text{"company gross income"}<100,000$$

"government tax income"=34% x "multi tax"+34% x "item profit"

$$100,000<\text{"company gross income"}<335,000$$

"government tax income"=39% x "multi tax"+39% x "item profit"

$$335,000<\text{"company gross income"}<10,000,000$$

"government tax income"=34% x "multi tax"+34% x "item profit"

$$10,000,000<\text{"company gross income"}<15,000,000$$

"government tax income"=35% x "multi tax"+35% x "item profit"
                15,000,000<"company gross income"<18,333,333
"government tax income"=38% x "multi tax"+38% x "item profit"
                18,000,000<"company gross income"
"government tax income"=35% x "multi tax"+35% x "item profit"

"company tax"
"16th amendment wage tax"
"social security wage tax"
"medicare wage tax"
"unemployment wage tax"

TAXATION #1
Taxes are sent to government!
Taxes are sent to market place too!
"gross wage earner" becomes "net wage earner"

"company tax"
"16th amendment wage tax"
"social security wage tax"
"medicare wage tax"
"unemployment wage tax"

TAXATION #2
"net wage earner" and consumer pay these taxes in the market place.

"company tax"
"16th amendment wage tax"
"snowball 16th amendment wage tax"
"social security wage tax"
"snowball social security wage tax"
"medicare wage tax"
"snowball medicare wage tax"
"unemployment wage tax"
"snowball unemployment wage tax"

TAXATION #3
Companies' whom handled or produce the item of both snowball and regular taxes had been sent to the government. "net wage earner" and consumer pay these taxes in the market place!

Note! "net wage earners" and consumers pay company taxes in the market place!

FUNCTION END

FUNCTION16S8

> "16th amendment wage tax"
> "snowball 16th amendment wage tax"
> "social security wage tax"
> "snowball social security wage tax"
> "medicare wage tax"
> "snowball medicare wage tax"
> "unemployment wage tax"
> "snowball unemployment wage tax"

=

- "16th amendment wage tax"
- "social security wage tax"
- "medicare wage tax"
- "unemployment wage tax"

k1, k2, k3,,,kn equals the number of workers whom manufactured or handled the item to be bought in 1,2,3,,,, n companies.

"snowball 16th amendment wage tax (1)"=
    "16th amendment wage tax (1, 1)"
    +"16th amendment wage tax (1, 2)"
    +"16th amendment wage tax (1, 3)"
        +
        +
        +
    +"16th amendment wage tax (1, k1)"
"snowball 16th amendment wage tax (2)"=
    "16th amendment wage tax (2, 1)"
    +"16th amendment wage tax (2, 2)"
    +"16th amendment wage tax (2, 3)"
        +
        +
        +
    +"16th amendment wage tax (2, k2)"
"snowball 16th amendment wage tax (3)"=
    "16th amendment wage tax (3, 1)"
    +"16th amendment wage tax (3, 2)"
    +"16th amendment wage tax (3, 3)"
        +
        +
        +
    +"16th amendment wage tax (3, k3)"

> k1 is the number of worker's 16th amendment wage taxes in company (1) that are included in the cost of the item. The k1 worker 16th amendment wage taxes are delivered to the market place.

> k2 is the number of worker's 16th amendment wage taxes in company (2) that are included in the cost of the item. The k2 worker 16th amendment wage taxes are delivered to the market place.

> k3 is the number of worker's 16th amendment wage taxes in company (3) that are included in the cost of the item. The k3 worker 16th amendment wage taxes are delivered to the market place.

```
                +
                +
                +
"snowball 16th amendment wage tax (n)"=
        "16th amendment wage tax (n, 1)"
        +"16th amendment wage tax (n, 2)"
        +"16th amendment wage tax (n, 3)"
                +
                +
                +
        +"16th amendment wage tax (n, kn)"
"snowball 16th amendment wage tax"=
        "snowball 16th amendment wage tax (1)"
        +"snowball 16th amendment wage tax (2)"
        +"snowball 16th amendment wage tax (3)"
                +
                +
                +
        +"snowball 16th amendment wage tax (kn)"
"snowball social security tax (1)"=
        "social security wage tax (1, 1)"
        +"social security wage tax (1, 2)"
        +"social security wage tax (1, 3)"
                +
                +
                +
        +"social security wage tax (1, k1)"
"snowball social security tax (2)"=
        "social security wage tax (2, 1)"
        +"social security wage tax (2, 2)"
        +"social security wage tax (2, 3)"
                +
                +
                +
        +"social security wage tax (2, k2)"
"snowball social security tax (3)"=
        "social security wage tax (3, 1)"
        +"social security wage tax (3, 2)"
        +"social security wage tax (3, 3)"
                +
                +
                +
        +"social security wage tax (3, k3)"
                +
                +
                +
```

kn is the number of worker's 16th amendment wage taxes in company (n) that are included in the cost of the item. The kn worker 16th amendment wage taxes are delivered to the market place.

The total snowball worker's 16th amendment wage taxes are included in the item's cost and are delivered to the market place.

k1 is the number of worker's social security wage taxes in company (1) that are included in the cost of the item. The k1 worker social security wage taxes are delivered to the market place.

k2 is the number of worker's social security wage taxes in company (2) that are included in the cost of the item. The k2 worker social security wage taxes are delivered to the market place.

k3 is the number of worker's social security wage taxes in company (3) that are included in the cost of the item. The k3 worker social security wage taxes are delivered to the market place.

"snowball social security tax (n)"=
 "social security wage tax (n,1)"
 +"social security wage tax (n, 2)"
 +"social security wage tax (n, 3)"
  +
  +
  +
 +"social security wage tax (n, kn)"
"snowball social security wage tax"=
 "snowball social security wage tax (1)"
 +"snowball social security wage tax (2)"
 +"snowball social security wage tax (3)"
  +
  +
  +
 +"snowball social security wage tax (kn)"
"snowball medicare tax (1)"=
 "medicare wage tax (1, 1)"
 +"medicare wage tax (1, 2)"
 +"medicare wage tax (1, 3)"
  +
  +
  +
 +"medicare wage tax (1, k1)"
"snowball medicare tax (2)"=
 "medicare wage tax (2, 1)"
 +"medicare wage tax (2, 2)"
 +"medicare wage tax (2, 3)"
  +
  +
  +
 +"medicare wage tax (2, k2)"
"snowball medicare tax (3)"=
 "medicare wage tax (3, 1)"
 +"medicare wage tax (3, 2)"
 +"medicare wage tax (3, 3)"
  +
  +
  +
 +"medicare wage tax (3, k3)"
  +
  +
  +

kn is the number of worker's social security wage taxes in company (n) that are included in the cost of the item. The kn worker social security wage taxes are delivered to the market place.

The total snowball worker's social security wage taxes are included in the item's cost and are delivered to the market place.

k1 is the number of worker's medicare wage taxes in company (1) that are included in the cost of the item. The k1 worker medicare wage taxes are delivered to the market place.

k2 is the number of worker's medicare wage taxes in company (2) that are included in the cost of the item. The k2 worker medicare wage taxes are delivered to the market place.

k3 is the number of worker's medicare wage taxes in company (3) that are included in the cost of the item. The k3 worker medicare wage taxes are delivered to the market place.

"snowball medicare tax (n)"=
        "medicare wage tax (n, 1)"
        +"medicare wage tax (n,2)"
        +"medicare wage tax (n, 3)"
                +
                +
                +
        +"medicare wage tax (n, kn)"
"snowball medicare wage tax"=
        "snowball medicare wage tax (1)"
        +"snowball medicare wage tax (2)"
        +"snowball medicare wage tax (3)"
                +
                +
                +
        +"snowball medicare wage tax (kn)"
"snowball unemployment tax (1)"=
        "unemployment wage tax (1, 1)"
        +"unemployment wage tax (1, 2)"
        +"unemployment wage tax (1, 3)"
                +
                +
                +
        +"unemployment wage tax (1, k1)"
"snowball unemployment tax (2)"=
        "unemployment wage tax (2,1)"
        +"unemployment wage tax (2, 2)"
        +"unemployment wage tax (2, 3)"
                +
                +
                +
        +"unemployment wage tax (2, k2)"
"snowball unemployment tax (3)"=
        "unemployment wage tax (3,1)"
        +"unemployment wage tax (3, 2)"
        +"unemployment wage tax (3, 3)"
                +
                +
                +
        +"unemployment wage tax (3, k3)"
                +
                +
                +

kn is the number of worker's medicare wage taxes in company (n) that are included in the cost of the item. The kn worker medicare wage taxes are delivered to the market place.

The total snowball worker's medicare wage taxes are included in the item's cost and are delivered to the market place.

k1 is the number of worker's unemployment wage taxes in company (1) that are included in the cost of the item. The k1 worker unemployment wage taxes are delivered to the market place.

k2 is the number of worker's unemployment wage taxes in company (2) that are included in the cost of the item. The k2 worker unemployment wage taxes are delivered to the market place.

k3 is the number of worker's unemployment wage taxes in company (3) that are included in the cost of the item. The k3 worker unemployment wage taxes are delivered to the market place.

"snowball unemployment tax (n)"=
  "unemployment wage tax (n,1)"
  +"unemployment wage tax (n, 2)"
  +"unemployment wage tax (n,3)"
    +
    +
    +
  +"unemployment wage tax (n, kn)"
"snowball unemployment wage tax"=
  "snowball unemployment wage tax (1)"
  +"snowball unemployment wage tax (2)"
  +"snowball unemployment wage tax (3)"
    +
    +
    +
  +"snowball unemployment wage tax (kn)"

kn is the number of worker's unemployment wage taxes in company (n) that are included in the cost of the item. The kn worker unemployment wage taxes are delivered to the market place.

The total snowball worker's unemployment wage taxes are included in the item's cost and are delivered to the market place.

The company transmits the following to the government and the market place:
    "16th amendment wage tax"
    "social security wage tax"
    "medicare wage tax"
    "unemployment wage tax"
"gross wage earner" becomes "net wage earner."
Other companies transmit the following to the government:
    "16th amendment wage tax"
    "social security wage tax"
    "medicare wage tax"
    "unemployment wage tax"
The following develops:
    "16th amendment wage tax" becomes "snowball 16th amendment wage tax"
    "social security wage tax" becomes "snowball social security wage tax"
    "medicare wage tax" becomes "snowball medicare wage tax"
    "unemployment wage tax" becomes "snowball unemployment wage tax"
The "snowballs" are added in the following to the transmitted taxes:
    "16th amendment wage tax"
    "social security wage tax"
    "medicare wage tax"
    "unemployment wage tax"
    "snowball 16th amendment wage tax"
    "snowball social security wage tax"
    "snowball medicare wage tax"
    "snowball unemployment wage tax"
The company transmits the following to the market place:
    "16th amendment wage tax"
    "social security wage tax"
    "medicare wage tax"
    "unemployment wage tax"
    "snowball 16th amendment wage tax"
    "snowball social security wage tax"
    "snowball medicare wage tax"
    "snowball unemployment wage tax"
A "net wage earner" who buys any product in the market place ends up paying a "triple tax."
Any "non-net wage earner" or "consumer" who buys any product in the market place pays a "double tax."

"16th amendment wage tax"
"social security wage tax"
"medicare wage tax"
"unemployment wage tax"

TAXATION #1
Taxes are sent to government!
Taxes are sent to market place too!
"gross wage earner" becomes "net wage earner"

"16th amendment wage tax"
"social security wage tax"
"medicare wage tax"
"unemployment wage tax"

TAXATION #2
"net wage earner" and consumer pay these taxes in the market place.

"16th amendment wage tax"
"snowball 16th amendment wage tax"
"social security wage tax"
"snowball social security wage tax"
"medicare wage tax"
"snowball medicare wage tax"
"unemployment wage tax"
"snowball unemployment wage tax"

TAXATION #3
Companies' whom handled or produce the item of both snowball and regular taxes had been sent to the government. "net wage earner" and consumer pay these taxes in the market place!

FUNCTION END

FUNCTIONCS16S4

> "company tax"
> "snowball company tax"
> "16th amendment wage tax"
> "snowball 16th amendment wage tax"

- "company tax"
- "16th amendment wage tax"

n equals number of companies whom manufactured or handled the item to be bought.

"snowball company tax"=
+"company tax (1)"
+"company tax (2)"
+"company tax (3)"
+
+
+
+"company tax (n)"

> **Taxes of companies 1 thru n are added resulting in the production of an item through the delivering of a product or providing a service. All taxes are sent to the market place through the "GROSS INCOME" as a "snowball company tax" that produced the item increasing the price of the item.**

k1, k2, k3,,,kn equals the number of workers whom manufactured or handled the item to be bought in 1,2,3,,,, n companies.

"snowball 16th amendment wage tax (1)"=
"16th amendment wage tax (1, 1)"
+"16th amendment wage tax (1, 2)"
+"16th amendment wage tax (1, 3)"
+
+
+
+"16th amendment wage tax (1, k1)"

> **k1 is the number of worker's 16th amendment wage taxes in company (1) that are included in the cost of the item. The k1 worker 16th amendment wage taxes are delivered to the market place.**

"snowball 16th amendment wage tax (2)"=
"16th amendment wage tax (2, 1)"
+"16th amendment wage tax (2, 2)"
+"16th amendment wage tax (2, 3)"
+
+
+
+"16th amendment wage tax (2, k2)"

> **k2 is the number of worker's 16th amendment wage taxes in company (2) that are included in the cost of the item. The k2 worker 16th amendment wage taxes are delivered to the market place.**

"snowball 16th amendment wage tax (3)"=
"16th amendment wage tax (3, 1)"
+"16th amendment wage tax (3, 2)"
+"16th amendment wage tax (3, 3)"
+
+
+
+"16th amendment wage tax (3, k3)"

> **k3 is the number of worker's 16th amendment wage taxes in company (3) that are included in the cost of the item. The k3 worker 16th amendment wage taxes are delivered to the market place.**

```
        +
        +
        +
```
"snowball 16th amendment wage tax (n)"=
     "16th amendment wage tax (n, 1)"
     +"16th amendment wage tax (n, 2)"
     +"16th amendment wage tax (n, 3)"
```
            +
            +
            +
```
     +"16th amendment wage tax (n, kn)"
"snowball 16th amendment wage tax"=
     "snowball 16th amendment wage tax (1)"
     +"snowball 16th amendment wage tax (2)"
     +"snowball 16th amendment wage tax (3)"
```
            +
            +
            +
```
     +"snowball 16th amendment wage tax (kn)"
"company gross income"=
     "company tax"
     +"snowball company tax"
     +"16th amendment wage tax"
     +"snowball 16th amendment wage tax"
     +"item profit"
     +company expenses

> kn is the number of worker's 16th amendment wage taxes in company (n) that are included in the cost of the item. The kn worker 16th amendment wage taxes are delivered to the market place.

> The total snowball worker's 16th amendment wage taxes are included in the item's cost and are delivered to the market place.

> These taxes are placed on items being sold throughout the country's market place indicating that the company does not pay taxes leaving the paying of taxes to the people in the market place producing "multi taxation."
> A "net wage earner" who purchases in the market place would be subject to a "triple taxation" and any other person would be subjected to a "double taxation."

"multi tax"=
     "company tax"
     +"snowball company tax"
     +"16th amendment wage tax"
     +"snowball 16th amendment wage tax"
Upon substitution,
"company gross income"="multi tax "+"item profit "+company expenses

FEDERAL GOVERNMENT TAX BONANZA

The government has already been compensated the following taxes:
- "company tax"
- "16th amendment wage tax"

Company's yearly "gross income" includes the:
- "multi tax"
- "item profit"
- company expenses

The following are included in the government's next tax appraisal of the "company tax" cycling back into the government's "company tax" calculation:
- "multi tax"
- "item profit"
- company expenses

Through the "company gross income" and a "graduated tax table", the government receives a percentage of the "company gross income."

Since the following United States (USA) Corporate Tax Rates are fix, the new "company tax" could move up or down a tax bracket permitting the new "company tax" to snow ball.

TAX YEAR 2010 2009 2008 2007 2006 2005 2004 AND 2003 FEDERAL UNITED STATES (USA) CORPORATE TAX RATES PERSONAL SERVICE CORPORATIONS PAY A FLAT RATE OF 35%		
TAXABLE INCOME OVER	BUT NOT OVER	YOUR TAX IS
$0	$50,000	15%
$50,000	$75,000	7,500 25%
$75,000	$100,000	13,750 34%
$100,000	$335,000	22,250 39%
$335,000	$10,000,000	113,900 34%
$10,000,000	$15,000,000	3,400,000 35%
$15,000,000	$18,333,333	5,150,000 38%
$18,333,333		FLAT RATE 35%

TAXABLE INCOME IS GROSS INCOME.

The following represent possible "government tax income":

"company gross income"= "multi tax" +"item profit" +company expenses
government tax possible income is:

0<"company gross income"<50,000

"government tax income"=15% x "multi tax"+15% x "item profit"

50,000<"company gross income"<75,000

"government tax income"=25% x "multi tax"+25% x "item profit"

75,000<"company gross income"<100,000

"government tax income"=34% x "multi tax"+34% x "item profit"

100,000<"company gross income"<335,000

"government tax income"=39% x "multi tax"+39% x "item profit"

335,000<"company gross income"<10,000,000

"company tax
"16th amendment wage tax"

TAXATION #1
Taxes are sent to government!
Taxes are sent to market place too!
"gross wage earner" becomes "net wage earner"

"company tax"
"16th amendment wage tax"

TAXATION #2
"net wage earner" and consumer pay these taxes in the market place.

"company tax"
"snowball company tax"
"16th amendment wage tax"
"snowball 16th amendment wage tax"

TAXATION #3
Companies' whom handled or produce the item of both snowball and regular taxes had been sent to the government. "net wage earner" and consumer pay these taxes in the market place!

Note! "net wage earners" and consumers pay company taxes in the market place!

FUNCTION END

FUNCTIONCSSS4

> "company tax"
> "snowball company tax"
> "social security wage tax"
> "snowball social security wage tax"

- "company tax"
- "social security wage tax"

n equals number of companies whom manufactured or handled the item to be bought.

"snowball company tax"=

+"company tax (1)"
+"company tax (2)"
+"company tax (3)"
+
+
+
+"company tax (n)"

> **Taxes of companies 1 thru n are added resulting in the production of an item through the delivering of a product or providing a service. All taxes are sent to the market place through the "GROSS INCOME" as a "snowball company tax" that produced the item increasing the price of the item.**

k1, k2, k3,,,kn equals the number of workers whom manufactured or handled the item to be bought in 1,2,3,,,, n companies.

"snowball social security wage tax (1)"=

"social security wage tax (1, 1)"
+"social security wage tax (1, 2)"
+"social security wage tax (1, 3)"
+
+
+
+"social security wage tax (1, k1)"

> **k1 is the number of worker's social security wage taxes in company (1) that are included in the cost of the item. The k1 worker social security wage taxes are delivered to the market place.**

"snowball social security wage tax (2)"=

"social security wage tax (2, 1)"
+"social security wage tax (2, 2)"
+"social security wage tax (2, 3)"
+
+
+
+"social security wage tax (2, k2)"

> **k2 is the number of worker's social security wage taxes in company (2) that are included in the cost of the item. The k2 worker social security wage taxes are delivered to the market place.**

"snowball social security wage tax (3)"=

"social security wage tax (3, 1)"
+"social security wage tax (3, 2)"
+"social security wage tax (3, 3)"
+
+
+
+"social security wage tax (3, k3)"

> **k3 is the number of worker's social security wage taxes in company (3) that are included in the cost of the item. The k3 worker social security wage taxes are delivered to the market place.**

```
                +
                +
                +
"snowball social security wage tax (n)"=
        "social security wage tax (n, 1)"
        +"social security wage tax (n, 2)"
        +"social security wage tax (n, 3)"
                +
                +
                +
        +"social security wage tax (n, kn)"
"snowball social security wage tax"=
        "snowball social security wage tax (1)"
        +"snowball social security wage tax (2)"
        +"snowball social security wage tax (3)"
                +
                +
                +
        +"snowball social security wage tax (kn)"
"company gross income"=
        "company tax"
        +"snowball company tax"
        +"social security wage tax"
        +"snowball social security wage tax"
        +"item profit"
        +company expenses
```

kn is the number of worker's social security wage taxes in company (n) that are included in the cost of the item. The kn worker social security wage taxes are delivered to the market place.

The total snowball worker's social security wage taxes are included in the item's cost and are delivered to the market place.

These taxes are placed on items being sold throughout the country's market place indicating that the company does not pay taxes leaving the paying of taxes to the people in the market place producing "multi taxation."
A "net wage earner" who purchases in the market place would be subject to a "triple taxation" and any other person would be subjected to a "double taxation."

```
"multi tax"=
        "company tax"
        +"snowball company tax"
        +"social security wage tax"
        +"snowball social security wage tax"
Upon substitution,
"company gross income"="multi tax "+"item profit "+company expenses
```

FEDERAL GOVERNMENT TAX BONANZA

The government has already been compensated the following taxes:
- "company tax"
- "social security wage tax"

Company's yearly "gross income" includes the:
- "multi tax"
- "item profit"
- company expenses

The following are included in the government's next tax appraisal of the "company tax" cycling back into the government's "company tax" calculation:
- "multi tax"
- "item profit"
- company expenses

Through the "company gross income" and a "graduated tax table", the government receives a percentage of the "company gross income."

Since the following United States (USA) Corporate Tax Rates are fix, the new "company tax" could move up or down a tax bracket permitting the new "company tax" to snow ball.

TAX YEAR 2010 2009 2008 2007 2006 2005 2004 AND 2003 FEDERAL UNITED STATES (USA) CORPORATE TAX RATES PERSONAL SERVICE CORPORATIONS PAY A FLAT RATE OF 35%			
TAXABLE INCOME OVER	BUT NOT OVER	YOUR TAX IS	
$0	$50,000		15%
$50,000	$75,000	7,500	25%
$75,000	$100,000	13,750	34%
$100,000	$335,000	22,250	39%
$335,000	$10,000,000	113,900	34%
$10,000,000	$15,000,000	3,400,000	35%
$15,000,000	$18,333,333	5,150,000	38%
$18,333,333		FLAT RATE 35%	

TAXABLE INCOME IS GROSS INCOME.

The following represent possible "government tax income":

"company gross income"= "multi tax" +"item profit" +company expenses

Government tax possible income is:

$$0<\text{"company gross income"}<50,000$$

"government tax income"=15% x "multi tax"+15% x "item profit"

$$50,000<\text{"company gross income"}<75,000$$

"government tax income"=25% x "multi tax"+25% x "item profit"

$$75,000<\text{"company gross income"}<100,000$$

"government tax income"=34% x "multi tax"+34% x "item profit"

$$100,000<\text{"company gross income"}<335,000$$

"government tax income"=39% x "multi tax"+39% x "item profit"

$$335,000<\text{"company gross income"}<10,000,000$$

"government tax income"=34% x "multi tax"+34% x "item profit"

$$10,000,000<\text{"company gross income"}<15,000,000$$

"government tax income"=35% x "multi tax"+35% x "item profit"

$$15,000,000<\text{"company gross income"}<18,333,333$$

"government tax income"=38% x "multi tax"+38% x "item profit"

$$18,000,000<\text{"company gross income"}$$

"government tax income"=35% x "multi tax"+35% x "item profit"

The company transmits the following to the government and the market place:
   "company tax"
   "social security wage tax"
 "gross wage earner" becomes "net wage earner."
Other companies transmit the following to the government:
   "company tax"
   "social security wage tax"
The following develops:
   "company' tax" becomes "snowball company tax"
   "social security wage tax" becomes "snowball social security wage tax"
The "snowballs" are added in the following to the transmitted taxes:
   "company tax"
   "social security wage tax"
   "snowball company tax"
   "snowball social security wage tax"
The company transmits the following to the market place:
   "company tax"
   "social security wage tax"
   "snowball company tax"
   "snowball social security wage tax"
A "net wage earner" who buys any product in the market place ends up paying a "triple tax."
Any "non-net wage earner" or "consumer" who buys any product in the market place pays a "double tax."

"company tax" "social security wage tax"	**TAXATION #1** Taxes are sent to government! Taxes are sent to market place too! "gross wage earner" becomes "net wage earner"
"company tax" "social security wage tax"	**TAXATION #2** "net wage earner" and consumer pay these taxes in the market place.
"company tax" "snowball company tax" "social security wage tax" "snowball social security wage tax" Note! "net wage earner" and consumer pay company taxes in the market place!	**TAXATION #3** Companies' whom handled or produce the item of both snowball and regular taxes had been sent to the government. "net wage earner" and consumer pay these taxes in the market place!

FUNCTION END

FUNCTIONCSMS4

> "company tax"
> "snowball company tax"
> "medicare wage tax"
> "snowball medicare wage tax"

- "company tax"
- "medicare wage tax"

n equals number of companies whom manufactured or handled the item to be bought.

"snowball company tax"=
   +"company tax (1)"
   +"company tax (2)"
   +"company tax (3)"
       +
       +
       +
   +"company tax (n)"

> **Taxes of companies 1 thru n are added resulting in the production of an item through the delivering of a product or providing a service. All taxes are sent to the market place through the "GROSS INCOME" as a "snowball company tax" that produced the item increasing the price of the item.**

k1, k2, k3,,,kn equals the number of workers whom manufactured or handled the item to be bought in 1,2,3,,,, n companies.

"snowball medicare wage tax (1)"=
   "medicare wage tax (1, 1)"
   +"medicare wage tax (1, 2)"
   +"medicare wage tax (1, 3)"
       +
       +
       +
   +"medicare wage tax (1, k1)"

"snowball medicare wage tax (2)"=
   "medicare wage tax (2, 1)"
   +"medicare wage tax (2, 2)"
   +"medicare wage tax (2, 3)"
       +
       +
       +
   +"medicare wage tax (2, k2)"

"snowball medicare wage tax (3)"=
   "medicare wage tax (3, 1)"
   +"medicare wage tax (3, 2)"
   +"medicare wage tax (3, 3)"
       +
       +
       +
   +"medicare wage tax (3, k3)"

> **k1 is the number of worker's medicare wage taxes in company (1) that are included in the cost of the item. The k1 worker medicare wage taxes are delivered to the market place.**

> **k2 is the number of worker's medicare wage taxes in company (2) that are included in the cost of the item. The k2 worker medicare wage taxes are delivered to the market place.**

> **k3 is the number of worker's medicare wage taxes in company (3) that are included in the cost of the item. The k3 worker medicare wage taxes are delivered to the market place.**

```
        +
        +
        +
"snowball medicare wage tax (n)"=
        "medicare wage tax (n, 1)"
        +"medicare wage tax (n, 2)"
        +"medicare wage tax (n, 3)"
        +
        +
        +
        +"medicare wage tax (n, kn)"
"snowball medicare wage tax"=
        "snowball medicare wage tax (1)"
        +"snowball medicare wage tax (2)"
        +"snowball medicare wage tax (3)"
        +
        +
        +
        +"snowball medicare wage tax (kn)"
"company gross income"=
        "company tax"
        +"snowball company tax"
        +"medicare wage tax"
        +"snowball medicare wage tax"
        +"item profit"
        +company expenses
```

kn is the number of worker's medicare wage taxes in company (n) that are included in the cost of the item. The kn worker medicare wage taxes are delivered to the market place.

The total snowball worker's medicare wage taxes are included in the item's cost and are delivered to the market place.

These taxes are placed on items being sold throughout the country's market place indicating that the company does not pay taxes leaving the paying of taxes to the people in the market place producing "multi taxation."
A "net wage earner" who purchases in the market place would be subject to a "triple taxation" and any other person would be subjected to a "double taxation."

```
"multi tax"=
        "company tax"
        +"snowball company tax"
        +"medicare wage tax"
        +"snowball medicare wage tax"
Upon substitution,
"company gross income"="multi tax "+"item profit "+company expenses
```

FEDERAL GOVERNMENT TAX BONANZA

The government has already been compensated the following taxes:

- "company tax"
- "medicare wage tax"

Company's yearly "gross income" includes the:

- "multi tax"
- "item profit"
- company expenses

The following are included in the government's next tax appraisal of the "company tax" cycling back into the government's "company tax" calculation:

- "multi tax"
- "item profit"
- company expenses

Through the "company gross income" and a "graduated tax table", the government receives a percentage of the "company gross income."

Since the following United States (USA) Corporate Tax Rates are fix, the new "company tax" could move up or down a tax bracket permitting the new "company tax" to snow ball.

TAX YEAR 2010 2009 2008 2007 2006 2005 2004 AND 2003 FEDERAL UNITED STATES (USA) CORPORATE TAX RATES PERSONAL SERVICE CORPORATIONS PAY A FLAT RATE OF 35%			
TAXABLE INCOME OVER	BUT NOT OVER	YOUR TAX IS	
$0	$50,000		15%
$50,000	$75,000	7,500	25%
$75,000	$100,000	13,750	34%
$100,000	$335,000	22,250	39%
$335,000	$10,000,000	113,900	34%
$10,000,000	$15,000,000	3,400,000	35%
$15,000,000	$18,333,333	5,150,000	38%
$18,333,333		FLAT RATE 35%	

TAXABLE INCOME IS GROSS INCOME.

The following represent possible "government tax income":
"company gross income"= "multi tax" +"item profit" +company expenses
   Government tax possible income is:
$$0<\text{"company gross income"}<50,000$$
"government tax income"=15% x "multi tax"+15% x "item profit"
$$50,000<\text{"company gross income"}<75,000$$
"government tax income"=25% x "multi tax"+25% x "item profit"
$$75,000<\text{"company gross income"}<100,000$$
"government tax income"=34% x "multi tax"+34% x "item profit"
$$100,000<\text{"company gross income"}<335,000$$
"government tax income"=39% x "multi tax"+39% x "item profit"
$$335,000<\text{"company gross income"}<10,000,000$$
"government tax income"=34% x "multi tax"+34% x "item profit"
$$10,000,000<\text{"company gross income"}<15,000,000$$
"government tax income"=35% x "multi tax"+35% x "item profit"
$$15,000,000<\text{"company gross income"}<18,333,333$$
"government tax income"=38% x "multi tax"+38% x "item profit"
$$18,000,000<\text{"company gross income"}$$
"government tax income"=35% x "multi tax"+35% x "item profit"

The company transmits the following to the government and the market place:
   "company tax"
   "medicare wage tax"
 "gross wage earner" becomes "net wage earner."
Other companies transmit the following to the government:
   "company tax"
   "medicare wage tax"
The following develops:
   "company' tax" becomes "snowball company tax"
   "medicare wage tax" becomes "snowball medicare wage tax"
The "snowballs" are added in the following to the transmitted taxes:
   "company tax"
   "medicare wage tax"
   "snowball company tax"
   "snowball medicare wage tax"
The company transmits the following to the market place:
   "company tax"
   "medicare wage tax"
   "snowball company tax"
   "snowball medicare wage tax"
A "net wage earner" who buys any product in the market place ends up paying a "triple tax."
Any "non-net wage earner" or "consumer" who buys any product in the market place pays a "double tax."

"company tax"
"medicare wage tax"

TAXATION #1
Taxes are sent to government!
Taxes are sent to market place too!
"gross wage earner" becomes "net wage earner."

"company tax"
"medicare wage tax"

TAXATION #2
"net wage earner" and consumer pay these taxes in the market place.

"company tax"
"snowball company tax"
"medicare wage tax"
"snowball medicare wage tax"

Note! "net wage earner" and consumer pay company taxes in the market place!

TAXATION #3
Companies' whom handled or produce the item of both snowball and regular taxes had been sent to the government. "net wage earner" and consumer pay these taxes in the market place!

FUNCTION END

FUNCTIONCSUS4

"company tax"
"snowball company tax"
"unemployment wage tax"
"snowball unemployment wage tax"

- "company tax"
- "unemployment wage tax"

n equals number of companies whom manufactured or handled the item to be bought.

"snowball company tax"=
+"company tax (1)"
+"company tax (2)"
+"company tax (3)"
+
+
+
+"company tax (n)"

> Taxes of companies 1 thru n are added resulting in the production of an item through the delivering of a product or providing a service. All taxes are sent to the market place through the "GROSS INCOME" as a "snowball company tax" that produced the item increasing the price of the item.

k1, k2, k3,,,kn equals the number of workers whom manufactured or handled the item to be bought in 1,2,3,,,, n companies.

"snowball unemployment wage tax (1)"=
"unemployment wage tax (1, 1)"
+"unemployment wage tax (1, 2)"
+"unemployment wage tax (1, 3)"
+
+
+
+"unemployment wage tax (1, k1)"

"snowball unemployment wage tax (2)"=
"unemployment wage tax (2, 1)"
+"unemployment wage tax (2, 2)"
+"unemployment wage tax (2, 3)"
+
+
+
+"unemployment wage tax (2, k2)"

"snowball unemployment wage tax (3)"=
"unemployment wage tax (3, 1)"
+"unemployment wage tax (3, 2)"
+"unemployment wage tax (3, 3)"
+
+
+
+"unemployment wage tax (3, k3)"

> k1 is the number of worker's unemployment wage taxes in company (1) that are included in the cost of the item. The k1 worker unemployment wage taxes are delivered to the market place.

> k2 is the number of worker's unemployment wage taxes in company (2) that are included in the cost of the item. The k2 worker unemployment wage taxes are delivered to the market place.

> k3 is the number of worker's unemployment wage taxes in company (3) that are included in the cost of the item. The k3 worker unemployment wage taxes are delivered to the market place.

+
+
+
"snowball unemployment wage tax (n)"=
    "unemployment wage tax (n, 1)"
    +"unemployment wage tax (n, 2)"
    +"unemployment wage tax (n, 3)"
        +
        +
        +
    +"unemployment wage tax (n, kn)"
"snowball unemployment wage tax"=
    "snowball unemployment wage tax (1)"
    +"snowball unemployment wage tax (2)"
    +"snowball unemployment wage tax (3)"
        +
        +
        +
    +"snowball unemployment wage tax (kn)"
"company gross income"=
    "company tax"
    +"snowball company tax"
    +"unemployment wage tax"
    +"snowball unemployment wage tax"
    +"item profit"
    +company expenses

> kn is the number of worker's unemployment wage taxes in company (n) that are included in the cost of the item. The kn worker unemployment wage taxes are delivered to the market place.

> The total snowball worker's unemployment wage taxes are included in the item's cost and are delivered to the market place.

> These taxes are placed on items being sold throughout the country's market place indicating that the company does not pay taxes leaving the paying of taxes to the people in the market place producing "multi taxation."
> A "net wage earner" who purchases in the market place would be subject to a "triple taxation" and any other person would be subjected to a "double taxation."

"multi tax"=
    "company tax"
    +"snowball company tax"
    +"unemployment wage tax"
    +"snowball unemployment wage tax"
Upon substitution,
"company gross income"="multi tax "+"item profit "+company expenses

FEDERAL GOVERNMENT TAX BONANZA

The government has already been compensated the following taxes:
- "company tax"
- "unemployment wage tax"

Company's yearly "gross income" includes the:
- "multi tax"
- "item profit"
- company expenses

The following are included in the government's next tax appraisal of the "company tax" cycling back into the government's "company tax" calculation:
- "multi tax"
- "item profit"
- company expenses

Through the "company gross income" and a "graduated tax table", the government receives a percentage of the "company gross income."

Since the following United States (USA) Corporate Tax Rates are fix, the new "company tax" could move up or down a tax bracket permitting the new "company tax" to snow ball.

TAX YEAR 2010 2009 2008 2007 2006 2005 2004 AND 2003 FEDERAL UNITED STATES (USA) CORPORATE TAX RATES PERSONAL SERVICE CORPORATIONS PAY A FLAT RATE OF 35%			
TAXABLE INCOME OVER	BUT NOT OVER	YOUR TAX IS	
$0	$50,000		15%
$50,000	$75,000	7,500	25%
$75,000	$100,000	13,750	34%
$100,000	$335,000	22,250	39%
$335,000	$10,000,000	113,900	34%
$10,000,000	$15,000,000	3,400,000	35%
$15,000,000	$18,333,333	5,150,000	38%
$18,333,333		FLAT RATE 35%	

TAXABLE INCOME IS GROSS INCOME.

The following represent possible "government tax income":

"company gross income"= "multi tax" +"item profit" +company expenses

Government tax possible income is:

0<"company gross income"<50,000

"government tax income"=15% x "multi tax"+15% x "item profit"

50,000<"company gross income"<75,000

"government tax income"=25% x "multi tax"+25% x "item profit"

75,000<"company gross income"<100,000

"government tax income"=34% x "multi tax"+34% x "item profit"

100,000<"company gross income"<335,000

"government tax income"=39% x "multi tax"+39% x "item profit"

335,000<"company gross income"<10,000,000

"government tax income"=34% x "multi tax"+34% x "item profit"

10,000,000<"company gross income"<15,000,000

"government tax income"=35% x "multi tax"+35% x "item profit"

15,000,000<"company gross income"<18,333,333

"company tax"
"unemployment wage tax"

TAXATION #1
Taxes are sent to government!
Taxes are sent to market place too!
"gross wage earner" becomes "net wage earner."

"company tax"
 "unemployment wage tax"

TAXATION #2
"net wage earner" and consumer pay these taxes in the market place.

"company tax"
"snowball company tax"
"unemployment wage tax"
"snowball unemployment wage tax"

TAXATION #3
Companies' whom handled or produce the item of both snowball and regular taxes had been sent to the government. "net wage earner" and consumer pay these taxes in the market place!

Note! "net wage earner" and consumer pay company taxes in the market place!

FUNCTION END

FUNCTIONCSSSN4

> "state company tax"
> "snowball state company tax"
> "state wage tax"
> "snowball state wage tax"

- "state company tax"
- "state wage tax"

n equals number of companies whom manufactured or handled the item to be bought.

"snowball state company tax"=

 "state company tax"
 +"state company tax (1)"
 +"state company tax (2)"
 +"state company tax (3)"
  +
  +
  +
 +"state company tax (n)"

> **Taxes of companies 1 thru n are added resulting in the production of an item through the delivering of a product or providing a service. All taxes are sent to the market place through the "GROSS INCOME" as a "snowball company tax" that produced the item increasing the price of the item.**

k1, k2, k3,,,kn equals the number of workers whom manufactured or handled the item to be bought in 1,2,3,,,, n companies.

"snowball state wage tax (1)"=

 "state wage tax (1, 1)"
 +"state wage tax (1, 2)"
 +"state wage tax (1, 3)"
  +
  +
  +
 +"state wage tax (1, k1)"

> **k1 is the number of worker's state wage taxes in company (1) that are included in the cost of the item. The k1 worker state wage taxes are delivered to the market place.**

"snowball state wage tax (2)"=

 "state wage tax (2, 1)"
 +"state wage tax (2, 2)"
 +"state wage tax (2, 3)"
  +
  +
  +
 +"state wage tax (2, k2)"

> **k2 is the number of worker's state wage taxes in company (2) that are included in the cost of the item. The k2 worker state wage taxes are delivered to the market place.**

"snowball state wage tax (3)"=

 "state wage tax (3, 1)"
 +"state wage tax (3, 2)"
 +"state wage tax (3, 3)"
  +
  +
  +
 +"state wage tax (3, k3)"

> **k3 is the number of worker's state wage taxes in company (3) that are included in the cost of the item. The k3 worker state wage taxes are delivered to the market place.**

```
        +
        +
        +
"snowball state wage tax (n)"=
        "state wage tax (n, 1)"
        +"state wage tax (n, 2)"
        +"state wage tax (n, 3)"
                +
                +
                +
        +"state wage tax (n, kn)"
"snowball state wage tax"=
        "snowball state wage tax (1)"
        +"snowball state wage tax (2)"
        +"snowball state wage tax (3)"
                +
                +
                +
        +"snowball state wage tax (kn)"
"gross income"=
        "state company tax"
        +"snowball state company tax"
        +"state wage tax"
        +"snowball state wage tax"
        +state company expenses
        +"item profit"
```

kn is the number of worker's state wage taxes in company (n) that are included in the cost of the item. The kn worker state wage taxes are delivered to the market place.

The total snowball worker's state wage taxes are included in the item's cost and are delivered to the market place.

The state company transmits the following to the government and the state market place:
    "state company tax"
    "state wage tax"
 "gross state wage earner" becomes "net state wage earner."
Other state companies transmit the following to the state government:
    "state company tax"
    "state wage tax"
The following develops:
    "state company' tax" becomes "snowball state company tax"
    "state wage tax" becomes "snowball state wage tax"
The "snowballs" are added in the following to the transmitted taxes:
    "state company tax"
    "state wage tax"
    "snowball state company tax"
    "snowball state wage tax"
The state company transmits the following to the state market place:
    "state company tax"
    "state wage tax"
    "snowball state company tax"
    "snowball state wage tax"
A "net state wage earner" who buys any product in the state market place ends up paying a "triple tax."
Any "non-net state wage earner" or "consumer" who buys any product in the state market place pays a "double tax."

"state company tax"
"state wage tax"

TAXATION #1
Taxes are sent to city government!
Taxes are sent to city market place too!
"gross wage earner" becomes "net wage earner"

"state company tax"
 "state wage tax"

TAXATION #2
"net wage earner" and consumer pay these taxes in the state market place.

"state company tax"
"snowball state company tax"
"state wage tax"
"snowball state wage tax"

Note! "net wage earner" and consumer pay state company taxe in the state market place!

TAXATION #3
Companies' whom handled or produce the item of both snowball and regular taxes had been sent to the government. "net wage earner" and consumer pay these taxes in the market place!

FUNCTION END

FUNCTIONCSCS4

> "city company tax"
> "snowball city company tax"
> "city wage tax"
> "snowball city wage tax"

- "city company tax"
- "city wage tax"

n equals number of companies whom manufactured or handled the item to be bought.

"snowball city company tax"=
    +"city company tax (1)"
    +"city company tax (2)"
    +"city company tax (3)"
        +
        +
        +
    +"city company tax (n)"

> Taxes of companies 1 thru n are added resulting in the production of an item through the delivering of a product or providing a service. All taxes are sent to the market place through the "GROSS INCOME" as a "snowball company tax" that produced the item increasing the price

k1, k2, k3,,,kn equals the number of workers whom manufactured or handled the item to be bought in 1,2,3,,,, n companies.

"snowball city wage tax (1)"=
    "city wage tax (1, 1)"
    +"city wage tax (1, 2)"
    +"city wage tax (1, 3)"
        +
        +
        +
    +"city wage tax (1, k1)"

"snowball city wage tax (2)"=
    "city wage tax (2, 1)"
    +"city wage tax (2, 2)"
    +"city wage tax (2, 3)"
        +
        +
        +
    +"city wage tax (2, k2)"

"snowball city wage tax (3)"=
    "city wage tax (3, 1)"
    +"city wage tax (3, 2)"
    +"city wage tax (3, 3)"
        +
        +
        +
    +"city wage tax (3, k3)"

> k1 is the number of worker's city wage taxes in company (1) that are included in the cost of the item. The k1 worker city wage taxes are delivered to the market place.

> k2 is the number of worker's city wage taxes in company (2) that are included in the cost of the item. The k2 worker city wage taxes are delivered to the market place.

> k3 is the number of worker's city wage taxes in company (3) that are included in the cost of the item. The k3 worker city wage taxes are delivered to the market place.

```
        +
        +
        +
"snowball city wage tax (n)"=
        "city wage tax (n, 1)"
        +"city wage tax (n, 2)"
        +"city wage tax (n, 3)"
                +
                +
                +
        +"city wage tax (n, kn)"
"snowball city wage tax"=
        "snowball city wage tax (1)"
        +"snowball city wage tax (2)"
        +"snowball city wage tax (3)"
                +
                +
                +
        +"snowball city wage tax (kn)"
"gross income"=
        "city company tax"
        +"snowball city company tax"
        +"city wage tax"
        +"snowball city wage tax"
        +city company expenses
        +"item profit"
```

kn is the number of worker's city wage taxes in company (n) that are included in the cost of the item. The kn worker city wage taxes are delivered to the market place.

The total snowball worker's city wage taxes are included in the item's cost and are delivered to the market place.

The city company transmits the following to the city government and the city market place:
"city company tax"
"city wage tax"
"gross city wage earner" becomes "net city wage earner."
Other companies transmit the following to the city government:
"city company tax"
"city wage tax"
The following develops:
"city company' tax" becomes "snowball city company tax"
"city wage tax" becomes "snowball city wage tax"
The "snowballs" are added in the following to the transmitted taxes:
"city company tax"
"city wage tax"
"snowball city company tax"
"snowball city wage tax"
The city company transmits the following to the city market place:
"city company tax"
"city wage tax"
"snowball city company tax"
"snowball city wage tax"
A "net city wage earner" who buys any product in the city market place ends up paying a "triple tax."
Any "non-net city wage earner" or "consumer" who buys any product in the city market place pays a "double tax."

"city company tax"
"city wage tax"

TAXATION #1
Taxes are sent to city government!
Taxes are sent to city market place too!
"gross wage earner" becomes "net wage earner"

"city company tax"
"city wage tax"

TAXATION #2
"net wage earner" and consumer pay these taxes in the city market place.

"city company tax"
"snowball city company tax"
"city wage tax"
"snowball city wage tax"

Note! "net wage earner" and consumer pay city company tax in the city market place!

TAXATION #3
Companies' whom handled or produce the item of both snowball and regular taxes had been sent to the government. "net wage earner" and consumer pay these taxes in the market place!

FUNCTION END

FUNCTIONC16S3

> **"company tax"**
> **"16th amendment wage tax"**
> **"snowball 16th amendment wage tax"**

- "company tax"
- "16th amendment wage tax"

k1, k2, k3,,,kn equals the number of workers whom manufactured or handled the item to be bought in 1,2,3,,,, n companies.

"snowball 16th amendment wage tax (1)"=
    "16th amendment wage tax (1, 1)"
    +"16th amendment wage tax (1, 2)"
    +"16th amendment wage tax (1, 3)"
        +
        +
        +
    +"16th amendment wage tax (1, k1)"

> **k1 is the number of worker's 16th amendment wage taxes in company (1) that are included in the cost of the item. The k1 worker 16th amendment wage taxes are delivered to the market place.**

"snowball 16th amendment wage tax (2)"=
    "16th amendment wage tax (2, 1)"
    +"16th amendment wage tax (2, 2)"
    +"16th amendment wage tax (2, 3)"
        +
        +
        +
    +"16th amendment wage tax (2, k2)"

> **k2 is the number of worker's 16th amendment wage taxes in company (2) that are included in the cost of the item. The k2 worker 16th amendment wage taxes are delivered to the market place.**

"snowball 16th amendment wage tax (3)"=
    "16th amendment wage tax (3, 1)"
    +"16th amendment wage tax (3, 2)"
    +"16th amendment wage tax (3, 3)"
        +
        +
        +
    +"16th amendment wage tax (3, k3)"
        +
        +
        +

> **k3 is the number of worker's 16th amendment wage taxes in company (3) that are included in the cost of the item. The k3 worker 16th amendment wage taxes are delivered to the market place.**

"snowball 16th amendment wage tax (n)"=
    "16th amendment wage tax (n, 1)"
    +"16th amendment wage tax (n, 2)"
    +"16th amendment wage tax (n, 3)"
        +
        +
        +
    +"16th amendment wage tax (n, kn)"

> **kn is the number of worker's 16th amendment wage taxes in company (n) that are included in the cost of the item. The kn worker 16th amendment wage taxes are delivered to the market place.**

"snowball 16th amendment wage tax"=
"snowball 16th amendment wage tax (1)"
+"snowball 16th amendment wage tax (2)"
+"snowball 16th amendment wage tax (3)"
+
+
+
+"snowball 16th amendment wage tax (kn)"
"company gross income"=
"company tax"
+"16th amendment wage tax"
+"snowball 16th amendment wage tax"
+"item profit"
+company expenses

> **The total snowball worker's 16th amendment wage taxes are included in the item's cost and are delivered to the market place.**

> **These taxes are placed on items being sold throughout the country's market place indicating that the company does not pay taxes leaving the paying of taxes to the people in the market place producing "multi taxation."**
> **A "net wage earner" who purchases in the market place would be subject to a "triple taxation" and any other person would be subjected to a "double taxation."**

"multi tax"=
"company tax"
+"16th amendment wage tax"
+"snowball 16th amendment wage tax"
Upon substitution,
"company gross income"="multi tax "+"item profit "+company expenses

FEDERAL GOVERNMENT TAX BONANZA

The government has already been compensated the following taxes:
- "company tax"
- "16th amendment wage tax"

Company's yearly "gross income" includes the:
- "multi tax"
- "item profit"
- company expenses

The following are included in the government's next tax appraisal of the "company tax" cycling back into the government's "company tax" calculation:
- "multi tax"
- "item profit"
- company expenses

Through the "company gross income" and a "graduated tax table", the government receives a percentage of the "company gross income."

Since the following United States (USA) Corporate Tax Rates are fix, the new "company tax" could move up or down a tax bracket permitting the new "company tax" to snow ball.

TAX YEAR 2010 2009 2008 2007 2006 2005 2004 AND 2003 FEDERAL UNITED STATES (USA) CORPORATE TAX RATES PERSONAL SERVICE CORPORATIONS PAY A FLAT RATE OF 35%			
TAXABLE INCOME OVER	BUT NOT OVER	YOUR TAX IS	
$0	$50,000		15%
$50,000	$75,000	7,500	25%
$75,000	$100,000	13,750	34%
$100,000	$335,000	22,250	39%
$335,000	$10,000,000	113,900	34%
$10,000,000	$15,000,000	3,400,000	35%
$15,000,000	$18,333,333	5,150,000	38%
$18,333,333		FLAT RATE 35%	

TAXABLE INCOME IS GROSS INCOME.

The following represent possible "government tax income":

"company gross income"= "multi tax" +"item profit" +company expenses

Government tax possible income is:

0<"company gross income"<50,000

"government tax income"=15% x "multi tax"+15% x "item profit"

50,000<"company gross income"<75,000

"government tax income"=25% x "multi tax"+25% x "item profit"

75,000<"company gross income"<100,000

"government tax income"=34% x "multi tax"+34% x "item profit"

100,000<"company gross income"<335,000

"government tax income"=39% x "multi tax"+39% x "item profit"

335,000<"company gross income"<10,000,000

"government tax income"=34% x "multi tax"+34% x "item profit"

10,000,000<"company gross income"<15,000,000

"government tax income"=35% x "multi tax"+35% x "item profit"

15,000,000<"company gross income"<18,333,333

"government tax income"=38% x "multi tax"+38% x "item profit"

18,000,000<"company gross income"

"government tax income"=35% x "multi tax"+35% x "item profit"

The company transmits the following to the government and the market place:

"company tax"

"16th amendment wage tax"

 "gross wage earner" becomes "net wage earner."

Other companies transmit the following to the government:

"16th amendment wage tax"

The following develops:

"16th amendment wage tax" becomes "snowball 16th amendment wage tax"

The "snowball" is added in the following to the transmitted taxes:

"company tax"

"16th amendment wage tax"

"snowball 16th amendment wage tax"

The company transmits the following to the market place:

"company tax"

"16th amendment wage tax"

"snowball 16th amendment wage tax"

A "net wage earner" who buys any product in the market place ends up paying a "triple tax."

Any "non-net wage earner" or "consumer" who buys any product in the market place pays a "double tax."

"company tax"
"16th amendment wage tax"

TAXATION #1
Taxes are sent to government!
taxes are sent to market place too!
"gross wage earner" becomes "net wage earner"

"company tax"
"16th amendment wage tax"

TAXATION #2
"net wage earner" and consumer pay these taxes in the market place.

"company tax"
"16th amendment wage tax"
"snowball 16th amendment wage tax"

TAXATION #3
Companies' whom handled or produce the item of both snowball and regular taxes had been sent to the government. "net wage earner" and consumer pay these taxes in the market place!

Note! "net wage earners" and consumers pay company tax in the market place!

FUNCTION END

FUNCTIONCSS3

> **"company tax"**
> **"social security wage tax"**
> **"snowball social security wage tax"**

- "company tax"
- "social security wage tax"

k1, k2, k3,,,kn equals the number of workers whom manufactured or handled the item to be bought in 1,2,3,,,, n companies.

"snowball social security wage tax (1)"=
> "social security wage tax (1, 1)"
> +"social security wage tax (1, 2)"
> +"social security wage tax (1, 3)"
> +
> +
> +
> +"social security wage tax (1, k1)"

"snowball social security wage tax (2)"=
> "social security wage tax (2, 1)"
> +"social security wage tax (2, 2)"
> +"social security wage tax (2, 3)"
> +
> +
> +
> +"social security wage tax (2, k2)"

"snowball social security wage tax (3)"=
> "social security wage tax (3, 1)"
> +"social security wage tax (3, 2)"
> +"social security wage tax (3, 3)"
> +
> +
> +
> +"social security wage tax (3, k3)"
> +
> +
> +

"snowball social security wage tax (n)"=
> "social security wage tax (n, 1)"
> +"social security wage tax (n, 2)"
> +"social security wage tax (n, 3)"
> +
> +
> +

k1 is the number of worker's social security wage taxes in company (1) that are included in the cost of the item. The k1 worker social security wage taxes are delivered to the market place.

k2 is the number of worker's social security wage taxes in company (2) that are included in the cost of the item. The k2 worker social security wage taxes are delivered to the market place.

k3 is the number of worker's social security wage taxes in company (3) that are included in the cost of the item. The k3 worker social security wage taxes are delivered to the market place.

kn is the number of worker's social security wage taxes in company (n) that are included in the cost of the item. The kn worker social security wage taxes are delivered to the market place.

+"social security wage tax (n, kn)"
"snowball social security wage tax"=
    "snowball social security wage tax (1)"
    +"snowball social security wage tax (2)"
    +"snowball social security wage tax (3)"
        +
        +
        +
    +"snowball social security wage tax (kn)"
"company gross income"=
    "company tax"
    +"social security wage tax"
    +"snowball social security wage tax"
    +"item profit"
    +company expenses

> **The total snowball worker's social security wage taxes are included in the item's cost and are delivered to the market place.**

> **These taxes are placed on items being sold throughout the country's market place indicating that the company does not pay taxes leaving the paying of taxes to the people in the market place producing "multi taxation."**
> **A "net wage earner" who purchases in the market place would be subject to a "triple taxation" and any other person would be subjected to a "double taxation."**

"multi tax"=
    "company tax"
    +"social security wage tax"
    +"snowball social security wage tax"
Upon substitution,
"company gross income"="multi tax "+"item profit "+company expenses

FEDERAL GOVERNMENT TAX BONANZA

The government has already been compensated the following taxes:
- "company tax"
- "social security wage tax"

Company's yearly "gross income" includes the:
- "multi tax"
- "item profit"
- company expenses

The following are included in the government's next tax appraisal of the "company tax" cycling back into the government's "company tax" calculation:
- "multi tax"
- "item profit"
- company expenses

Through the "company gross income" and a "graduated tax table", the government receives a percentage of the "company gross income."
Since the following United States (USA) Corporate Tax Rates are fix, the new "company tax" could move up or down a tax bracket permitting the new "company tax" to snow ball.

TAX YEAR 2010 2009 2008 2007 2006 2005 2004 AND 2003 FEDERAL UNITED STATES (USA) CORPORATE TAX RATES PERSONAL SERVICE CORPORATIONS PAY A FLAT RATE OF 35%			
TAXABLE INCOME OVER	BUT NOT OVER	YOUR TAX IS	
$0	$50,000		15%
$50,000	$75,000	7,500	25%
$75,000	$100,000	13,750	34%
$100,000	$335,000	22,250	39%
$335,000	$10,000,000	113,900	34%
$10,000,000	$15,000,000	3,400,000	35%
$15,000,000	$18,333,333	5,150,000	38%
$18,333,333		FLAT RATE 35%	

TAXABLE INCOME IS GROSS INCOME.

The following represent possible "government tax income":
"company gross income"= "multi tax" +"item profit" +company expenses
Government tax possible income is:

0<"company gross income"<50,000
"government tax income"=15% x "multi tax"+15% x "item profit"
50,000<"company gross income"<75,000
"government tax income"=25% x "multi tax"+25% x "item profit"
75,000<"company gross income"<100,000
"government tax income"=34% x "multi tax"+34% x "item profit"
100,000<"company gross income"<335,000
"government tax income"=39% x "multi tax"+39% x "item profit"
335,000<"company gross income"<10,000,000
"government tax income"=34% x "multi tax"+34% x "item profit"
10,000,000<"company gross income"<15,000,000
"government tax income"=35% x "multi tax"+35% x "item profit"
15,000,000<"company gross income"<18,333,333
"government tax income"=38% x "multi tax"+38% x "item profit"
18,000,000<"company gross income"
"government tax income"=35% x "multi tax"+35% x "item profit"

The company transmits the following to the government and the market place:
  "company tax"
  "social security wage tax"
 "gross wage earner" becomes "net wage earner."
Other companies transmit the following to the government:
  "social security wage tax"
The following develops:
  "social security wage tax" becomes "snowball social security wage tax"
The "snowball" is added in the following to the transmitted taxes:
  "company tax"
  "social security wage tax"
  "snowball social security wage tax"
The company transmits the following to the market place:
  "company tax"
  "social security wage tax"
  "snowball social security wage tax"
A "net wage earner" who buys any product in the market place ends up paying a "triple tax."
Any "non-net wage earner" or "consumer" who buys any product in the market place pays a "double tax."

"company tax"
"social security wage tax"

TAXATION #1
Taxes are sent to government!
taxes are sent to market place too!
"gross wage earner" becomes "net wage earner"

"company tax"
 "social security wage tax"

TAXATION #2
"net wage earner" and consumer pay these taxes in the market place.

"company tax"
"social security wage tax"
"snowball social security wage tax"

TAXATION #3
Companies' whom handled or produce the item of both snowball and regular taxes had been sent to the government. "net wage earner" and consumer pay these taxes in the market place!

Note! "net wage earners" and consumers pay company taxes in the market place!

FUNCTION END

FUNCTIONCMS3

> **"company tax"**
> **"medicare wage tax"**
> **"snowball medicare wage tax"**

- "company tax"
- "medicare wage tax"

k1, k2, k3,,,kn equals the number of workers whom manufactured or handled the item to be bought in 1,2,3,,,, n companies.

"snowball medicare wage tax (1)"=
    "medicare wage tax (1, 1)"
    +"medicare wage tax (1, 2)"
    +"medicare wage tax (1, 3)"
       +
       +
       +
    +"medicare wage tax (1, k1)"

"snowball medicare wage tax (2)"=
    "medicare wage tax (2, 1)"
    +"medicare wage tax (2, 2)"
    +"medicare wage tax (2, 3)"
       +
       +
       +
    +"medicare wage tax (2, k2)"

"snowball medicare wage tax (3)"=
    "medicare wage tax (3, 1)"
    +"medicare wage tax (3, 2)"
    +"medicare wage tax (3, 3)"
       +
       +
       +
    +"medicare wage tax (3, k3)"
       +
       +
       +

"snowball medicare wage tax (n)"=
    "medicare wage tax (n, 1)"
    +"medicare wage tax (n, 2)"
    +"medicare wage tax (n, 3)"
       +
       +

k1 is the number of worker's medicare wage taxes in company (1) that are included in the cost of the item. The k1 worker medicare wage taxes are delivered to the market place.

k2 is the number of worker's medicare wage taxes in company (2) that are included in the cost of the item. The k2 worker medicare wage taxes are delivered to the market place.

k3 is the number of worker's medicare wage taxes in company (3) that are included in the cost of the item. The k3 worker medicare wage taxes are delivered to the market place.

kn is the number of worker's medicare wage taxes in company (n) that are included in the cost of the item. The kn worker medicare wage taxes are delivered to the market place.

        +
    +"medicare wage tax (n, kn)"
"snowball medicare wage tax"=
    "snowball medicare wage tax (1)"
    +"snowball medicare wage tax (2)"
    +"snowball medicare wage tax (3)"
        +
        +
        +
    +"snowball medicare wage tax (kn)"
"company gross income"=
    "company tax"
    +"medicare wage tax"
    +"snowball medicare wage tax"
    +"item profit"
    +company expenses

> The total snowball worker's medicare wage taxes are included in the item's cost and are delivered to the market place.

> These taxes are placed on items being sold throughout the country's market place indicating that the company does not pay taxes leaving the paying of taxes to the people in the market place producing "multi taxation."
> A "net wage earner" who purchases in the market place would be subject to a "triple taxation" and any other person would be subjected to a "double taxation."

"multi tax"=
    "company tax"
    +"medicare wage tax"
    +"snowball medicare wage tax"
Upon substitution,
"company gross income"="multi tax "+"item profit "+company expenses

FEDERAL GOVERNMENT TAX BONANZA

The government has already been compensated the following taxes:
- "company tax"
- "medicare wage tax"

Company's yearly "gross income" includes the:
- "multi tax"
- "item profit"
- company expenses

The following are included in the government's next tax appraisal of the "company tax" cycling back into the government's "company tax" calculation:
- "multi tax"
- "item profit"
- company expenses

Through the "company gross income" and a "graduated tax table", the government receives a percentage of the "company gross income."
Since the following United States (USA) Corporate Tax Rates are fix, the new "company tax" could move up or down a tax bracket permitting the new "company tax" to snow ball.

TAX YEAR 2010 2009 2008 2007 2006 2005 2004 AND 2003 FEDERAL UNITED STATES (USA) CORPORATE TAX RATES PERSONAL SERVICE CORPORATIONS PAY A FLAT RATE OF 35%			
TAXABLE INCOME OVER	BUT NOT OVER	YOUR TAX IS	
$0	$50,000		15%
$50,000	$75,000	7,500	25%
$75,000	$100,000	13,750	34%
$100,000	$335,000	22,250	39%
$335,000	$10,000,000	113,900	34%
$10,000,000	$15,000,000	3,400,000	35%
$15,000,000	$18,333,333	5,150,000	38%
$18,333,333		FLAT RATE 35%	

TAXABLE INCOME IS GROSS INCOME.

The following represent possible "government tax income":
"company gross income"= "multi tax" +"item profit" +company expenses
Government tax possible income is:
0<"company gross income"<50,000
"government tax income"=15% x "multi tax"+15% x "item profit"
50,000<"company gross income"<75,000
"government tax income"=25% x "multi tax"+25% x "item profit"
75,000<"company gross income"<100,000
"government tax income"=34% x "multi tax"+34% x "item profit"
100,000<"company gross income"<335,000
"government tax income"=39% x "multi tax"+39% x "item profit"
335,000<"company gross income"<10,000,000
"government tax income"=34% x "multi tax"+34% x "item profit"
10,000,000<"company gross income"<15,000,000
"government tax income"=35% x "multi tax"+35% x "item profit"
15,000,000<"company gross income"<18,333,333
"government tax income"=38% x "multi tax"+38% x "item profit"
18,000,000<"company gross income"
"government tax income"=35% x "multi tax"+35% x "item profit"

The company transmits the following to the government and the market place:
    "company tax"
    "medicare wage tax"
 "gross wage earner" becomes "net wage earner."
Other companies transmit the following to the government:
    "medicare wage tax"
The following develops:
    "medicare wage tax" becomes "snowball medicare wage tax"
The "snowball" is added in the following to the transmitted taxes:
    "company tax"
    "medicare wage tax"
    "snowball medicare wage tax"
The company transmits the following to the market place:
    "company tax"
    "medicare wage tax"
    "snowball medicare wage tax"
A "net wage earner" who buys any product in the market place ends up paying a "triple tax."
Any "non-net wage earner" or "consumer" who buys any product in the market place pays a "double tax."

"company tax"
"medicare wage tax"

TAXATION #1
Taxes are sent to government!
Taxes are sent to market place too!
"gross wage earner" becomes "net wage earner"

"company tax"
 "medicare wage tax"

TAXATION #2
"net wage earner" and consumer pay these taxes in the market place.

"company tax"
"medicare wage tax"
"snowball medicare wage tax"

TAXATION #3
Companies' whom handled or produce the item of both snowball and regular taxes had been sent to the government. "net wage earner" and consumer pay these taxes in the market place!

Note! "net wage earners" and consumers pay company taxes in the market place!

FUNCTION END

FUNCTIONCUS3

> **"company tax"**
> **"unemployment wage tax"**
> **"snowball unemployment wage tax"**

- "company tax"
- "unemployment wage tax"

k1, k2, k3,,,kn equals the number of workers whom manufactured or handled the item to be bought in 1,2,3,,,, n companies.

"snowball unemployment wage tax (1)"=
    "unemployment wage tax (1, 1)"
    +"unemployment wage tax (1, 2)"
    +"unemployment wage tax (1, 3)"
        +
        +
        +
    +"unemployment wage tax (1, k1)"

"snowball unemployment wage tax (2)"=
    "unemployment wage tax (2, 1)"
    +"unemployment wage tax (2, 2)"
    +"unemployment wage tax (2, 3)"
        +
        +
        +
    +"unemployment wage tax (2, k2)"

"snowball unemployment wage tax (3)"=
    "unemployment wage tax (3, 1)"
    +"unemployment wage tax (3, 2)"
    +"unemployment wage tax (3, 3)"
        +
        +
        +
    +"unemployment wage tax (3, k3)"
        +
        +
        +

> **k1 is the number of worker's unemployment wage taxes in company (1) that are included in the cost of the item. The k1 worker unemployment wage taxes are delivered to the market place.**

> **k2 is the number of worker's unemployment wage taxes in company (2) that are included in the cost of the item. The k2 worker unemployment wage taxes are delivered to the market place.**

> **k3 is the number of worker's unemployment wage taxes in company (3) that are included in the cost of the item. The k3 worker unemployment wage taxes are delivered to the market place.**

"snowball unemployment wage tax (n)"=
    "unemployment wage tax (n, 1)"
    +"unemployment wage tax (n, 2)"
    +"unemployment wage tax (n, 3)"
      +
      +
      +
    +"unemployment wage tax (n, kn)"
"snowball unemployment wage tax"=
    "snowball unemployment wage tax (1)"
    +"snowball unemployment wage tax (2)"
    +"snowball unemployment wage tax (3)"
      +
      +
      +
    +"snowball unemployment wage tax (kn)"
"company gross income"=
    "company tax"
    +"unemployment wage tax"
    +"snowball unemployment wage tax"
    +"item profit"
    +company expenses

> kn is the number of worker's unemployment wage taxes in company (n) that are included in the cost of the item. The kn worker unemployment wage taxes are delivered to the market place.

> The total snowball worker's unemployment wage taxes are included in the item's cost and are delivered to the market place.

> These taxes are placed on items being sold throughout the country's market place indicating that the company does not pay taxes leaving the paying of taxes to the people in the market place producing "multi taxation."
> A "net wage earner" who purchases in the market place would be subject to a "triple taxation" and any other person would be subjected to a "double taxation."

"multi tax"=
    "company tax"
    +"unemployment wage tax"
    +"snowball unemployment wage tax"
Upon substitution,
"company gross income"="multi tax "+"item profit "+company expenses

FEDERAL GOVERNMENT TAX BONANZA

The government has already been compensated the following taxes:
- "company tax"
- "unemployment wage tax"

Company's yearly "gross income" includes the:
- "multi tax"
- "item profit"
- company expenses

The following are included in the government's next tax appraisal of the "company tax" cycling back into the government's "company tax" calculation:
    "multi tax"
    "item profit"
    company expenses

Through the "company gross income" and a "graduated tax table", the government receives a percentage of the "company gross income."
Since the following United States (USA) Corporate Tax Rates are fix, the new "company tax" could move up or down a tax bracket permitting the new "company tax" to snow ball.

Tax Year 2010 2009 2008 2007 2006 2005 2004 and 2003 Federal United States (USA) Corporate Tax Rates Personal service corporations pay a flat rate of 35%			
Taxable income over	**But not over**	**Your tax is**	
$0	$50,000		15%
$50,000	$75,000	7,500	25%
$75,000	$100,000	13,750	34%
$100,000	$335,000	22,250	39%
$335,000	$10,000,000	113,900	34%
$10,000,000	$15,000,000	3,400,000	35%
$15,000,000	$18,333,333	5,150,000	38%
$18,333,333		Flat rate 35%	

TAXABLE INCOME IS GROSS INCOME.

The following represent possible "government tax income":

"company gross income"= "multi tax" +"item profit" +company expenses

Government tax possible income is:

0<"company gross income"<50,000

"government tax income"=15% x "multi tax"+15% x "item profit"

50,000<"company gross income"<75,000

"government tax income"=25% x "multi tax"+25% x "item profit"

75,000<"company gross income"<100,000

"government tax income"=34% x "multi tax"+34% x "item profit"

100,000<"company gross income"<335,000

"government tax income"=39% x "multi tax"+39% x "item profit"

335,000<"company gross income"<10,000,000

"government tax income"=34% x "multi tax"+34% x "item profit"

10,000,000<"company gross income"<15,000,000

"government tax income"=35% x "multi tax"+35% x "item profit"

15,000,000<"company gross income"<18,333,333

"government tax income"=38% x "multi tax"+38% x "item profit"

18,000,000<"company gross income"

"government tax income"=35% x "multi tax"+35% x "item profit"

The company transmits the following to the government and the market place:
"company tax"
"unemployment wage tax"
"gross wage earner" becomes "net wage earner."
Other companies transmit the following to the government:
"unemployment wage tax"
The following develops:
"unemployment wage tax" becomes "snowball unemployment wage tax"
The "snowball" is added in the following to the transmitted taxes:
"company tax"
"unemployment wage tax"
"snowball unemployment wage tax"
The company transmits the following to the market place:
"company tax"
"unemployment wage tax"
"snowball unemployment wage tax"
A "net wage earner" who buys any product in the market place ends up paying a "triple tax."
Any "non-net wage earner" or "consumer" who buys any product in the market place pays a "double tax."

"company tax"
"unemployment wage tax"

TAXATION #1
Taxes are sent to government!
taxes are sent to market place too!
"gross wage earner" becomes "net wage earner"

"company tax"
"unemployment wage tax"

TAXATION #2
"net wage earner" and consumer pay these taxes in the market place.

"company tax"
"unemployment wage tax"
"snowball unemployment wage tax"

TAXATION #3
Companies' whom handled or produce the item of both snowball and regular taxes had been sent to the government. "net wage earner" and consumer pay these taxes in the market place!

Note! "net wage earners" and consumers pay company taxes in the market place!

FUNCTION END

FUNCTION162

"16th amendment wage tax"
"snowball 16th amendment wage tax"

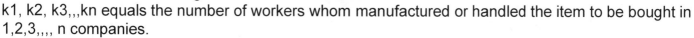

- "16th amendment wage tax"

k1, k2, k3,,,kn equals the number of workers whom manufactured or handled the item to be bought in 1,2,3,,,, n companies.

"snowball 16th amendment tax (1)"=

 "16th amendment wage tax (1, 1)"
 +"16th amendment wage tax (1, 2)"
 +"16th amendment wage tax (1, 3)"
  +
  +
  +
 +"16th amendment wage tax (1, k1)"

> **k1 is the number of worker's 16th amendment wage taxes in company (1) that are included in the cost of the item. The k1 worker 16th amendment wage taxes are delivered to the market place.**

"snowball 16th amendment tax (2)"=

 "16th amendment wage tax (2,1)"
 +"16th amendment wage tax (2, 2)"
 +"16th amendment wage tax (2, 3)"
  +
  +
  +
 +"16th amendment wage tax (2, k2)"

> **k2 is the number of worker's 16th amendment wage taxes in company (2) that are included in the cost of the item. The k2 worker 16th amendment wage taxes are delivered to the market place.**

"snowball 16th amendment tax (3)"=

 "16th amendment wage tax (3,1)"
 +"16th amendment wage tax (3, 2)"
 +"16th amendment wage tax (3, 3)"
  +
  +
  +
 +"16th amendment wage tax (3, k3)"
  +
  +
  +

> **k3 is the number of worker's 16th amendment wage taxes in company (3) that are included in the cost of the item. The k3 worker medicare wage taxes are delivered to the market place.**

"snowball 16th amendment tax (n)"=

 "16th amendment wage tax (n,1)"
 +"16th amendment wage tax (n, 2)"
 +"16th amendment wage tax (n,3)"
  +
  +
  +
 +"16th amendment wage tax (n, kn)"

> **kn is the number of worker's 16th amendment wage taxes in company (n) that are included in the cost of the item. The kn worker 16th amendment wage taxes are delivered to the market place.**

"snowball 16th amendment wage tax"=
    "snowball 16th amendment wage tax (1)"
    +"snowball 16th amendment wage tax (2)"
    +"snowball 16th amendment wage tax (3)"
        +
        +
        +
    +"snowball 16th amendment wage tax (kn)"

The total snowball worker's 16th amendment 16th amendment wage taxes are included in the item's cost and are delivered to the market place.

The company transmits the following to the government and the market place:
    "16th amendment wage tax"
"gross wage earner" becomes "net wage earner."
Other companies transmit the following to the government:
    "16th amendment wage tax"
The following develops:
    "16th amendment wage tax" becomes "snowball 16th amendment wage tax"
The "snowball" is added in the following to the transmitted tax:
    "16th amendment wage tax"
    "snowball 16th amendment wage tax"
The company transmits the following to the market place:
    "16th amendment wage tax"
    "snowball 16th amendment wage tax"
A "net wage earner" who buys any product in the market place ends up paying a "triple tax."
Any "non-net wage earner" or "consumer" who buys any product in the market place pays a "double tax."

"16th amendment wage tax"	**TAXATION #1** Tax is sent to government! Tax is sent to market place too! "gross wage earner" becomes "net wage earner"
"16th amendment wage tax"	**TAXATION #2** "net wage earner" and consumer pay this tax in the market place.
"16th amendment wage tax" "snowball 16th amendment wage tax"	**TAXATION #3** Companies' whom handled or produce the item of both snowball and regular taxes had been sent to the government. "net wage earner" and consumer pay these taxes in the market place!

FUNCTION END

FUNCTIONSS2

> **"social security wage tax"**
> **"snowball social security wage tax"**

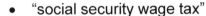

- "social security wage tax"

k1, k2, k3,,,kn equals the number of workers whom manufactured or handled the item to be bought in 1,2,3,,,, n companies.

"snowball social security tax (1)"=

    "social security wage tax (1, 1)"

    +"social security wage tax (1, 2)"

    +"social security wage tax (1, 3)"

       +

       +

       +

    +"social security wage tax (1, k1)"

> **k1 is the number of worker's social security wage taxes in company (1) that are included in the cost of the item. The k1 worker social security wage taxes are delivered to the market place.**

"snowball social security tax (2)"=

    "social security wage tax (2,1)"

    +"social security wage tax (2, 2)"

    +"social security wage tax (2, 3)"

       +

       +

       +

    +"social security wage tax (2, k2)"

> **k2 is the number of worker's social security wage taxes in company (2) that are included in the cost of the item. The k2 worker social security wage taxes are delivered to the market place.**

"snowball social security tax (3)"=

    "social security wage tax (3,1)"

    +"social security wage tax (3, 2)"

    +"social security wage tax (3, 3)"

       +

       +

       +

    +"social security wage tax (3, k3)"

       +

       +

       +

> **k3 is the number of worker's social security wage taxes in company (3) that are included in the cost of the item. The k3 worker social security wage taxes are delivered to the market place.**

"snowball social security tax (n)"=

    "social security wage tax (n,1)"

    +"social security wage tax (n, 2)"

    +"social security wage tax (n,3)"

       +

       +

       +

    +"social security wage tax (n, kn)"

> **kn is the number of worker's social security wage taxes in company (n) that are included in the cost of the item. The kn worker social security wage taxes are delivered to the market place.**

196

"snowball social security wage tax"=
    "snowball social security wage tax (1)"
    +"snowball social security wage tax (2)"
    +"snowball social security wage tax (3)"
        +
        +
        +
    +"snowball social security wage tax (kn)"

> The total snowball worker's social security social security wage taxes are included in the item's cost and are delivered to the market place.

The company transmits the following to the government and the market place:
    "social security wage tax"
"gross wage earner" becomes "net wage earner."
Other companies transmit the following to the government:
    "social security wage tax"
The following develops:
    "social security wage tax" becomes "snowball social security wage tax"
The "snowball" is added in the following to the transmitted tax:
    "social security wage tax"
    "snowball social security wage tax"
The company transmits the following to the market place:
    "social security wage tax"
    "snowball social security wage tax"
A "net wage earner" who buys any product in the market place ends up paying a "triple tax."
Any "non-net wage earner" or "consumer" who buys any product in the market place pays a "double tax."

"social security wage tax"

TAXATION #1
Tax is sent to government!
Tax is sent to market place too!
"gross wage earner" becomes "net wage earner"

"social security wage tax"

TAXATION #2
"net wage earner" and consumer pay
this tax in the market place.

"social security wage tax"
"snowball social security wage tax"

TAXATION #3
Companies' whom handled or produce the
item of both snowball and regular taxes had
been sent to the government. "net wage
earner" and consumer pay these taxes in the
market place!

FUNCTION END

FUNCTIONMS2

"medicare wage tax"
"snowball medicare wage tax"

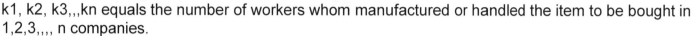

- "medicare wage tax"

k1, k2, k3,,,kn equals the number of workers whom manufactured or handled the item to be bought in 1,2,3,,,, n companies.

"snowball medicare tax (1)"=
     "medicare wage tax (1, 1)"
     +"medicare wage tax (1, 2)"
     +"medicare wage tax (1, 3)"
        +
        +
        +
     +"medicare wage tax (1, k1)"

> **k1 is the number of worker's medicare wage taxes in company (1) that are included in the cost of the item. The k1 worker medicare wage taxes are delivered to the market place.**

"snowball medicare tax (2)"=
     "medicare wage tax (2,1)"
     +"medicare wage tax (2, 2)"
     +"medicare wage tax (2, 3)"
        +
        +
        +
     +"medicare wage tax (2, k2)"

> **k2 is the number of worker's medicare wage taxes in company (2) that are included in the cost of the item. The k2 worker medicare wage taxes are delivered to the market place.**

"snowball medicare tax (3)"=
     "medicare wage tax (3,1)"
     +"medicare wage tax (3, 2)"
     +"medicare wage tax (3, 3)"
        +
        +
        +
     +"medicare wage tax (3, k3)"
        +
        +
        +

> **k3 is the number of worker's medicare wage taxes in company (3) that are included in the cost of the item. The k3 worker medicare wage taxes are delivered to the market place.**

"snowball medicare tax (n)"=
     "medicare wage tax (n,1)"
     +"medicare wage tax (n, 2)"
     +"medicare wage tax (n,3)"
        +
        +
        +
     +"medicare wage tax (n, kn)"

> **kn is the number of worker's medicare wage taxes in company (n) that are included in the cost of the item. The kn worker medicare wage taxes are delivered to the market place.**

"snowball medicare wage tax"=
     "snowball medicare wage tax (1)"
     +"snowball medicare wage tax (2)"
     +"snowball medicare wage tax (3)"
          +
          +
          +
     +"snowball medicare wage tax (kn)"

> The total snowball worker's medicare wage taxes are included in the item's cost and are delivered to the market place.

The company transmits the following to the government and the market place:
    "medicare wage tax"
"gross wage earner" becomes "net wage earner."
Other companies transmit the following to the government:
    "medicare wage tax"
The following develops:
    "medicare wage tax" becomes "snowball medicare wage tax"
The "snowball" is added in the following to the transmitted tax:
    "medicare wage tax"
    "snowball medicare wage tax"
The company transmits the following to the market place:
    "medicare wage tax"
    "snowball medicare wage tax"
A "net wage earner" who buys any product in the market place ends up paying a "triple tax."
Any "non-net wage earner" or "consumer" who buys any product in the market place pays a "double tax."

"medicare wage tax"

TAXATION #1
Tax is sent to government!
Tax is sent to market place too!
"gross wage earner" becomes "net wage earner"

"medicare wage tax"

TAXATION #2
"net wage earner" and consumer pay
this tax in the market place.

"medicare wage tax"
"snowball medicare wage tax"

TAXATION #3
Companies' whom handled or produce the item of
both snowball and regular taxes had been sent to
the government. "net wage earner" and consumer
pay these taxes in the market place!

FUNCTION END

FUNCTIONUS2

"unemployment wage tax"
"snowball unemployment wage tax"

- "unemployment wage tax"

k1, k2, k3,,,kn equals the number of workers whom manufactured or handled the item to be bought in 1,2,3,,,, n companies.

"snowball unemployment tax (1)"=
      "unemployment wage tax (1, 1)"
      +"unemployment wage tax (1, 2)"
      +"unemployment wage tax (1, 3)"
        +
        +
        +
      +"unemployment wage tax (1, k1)"

> **k1 is the number of worker's unemployment wage taxes in company (1) that are included in the cost of the item. The k1 worker unemployment wage taxes are delivered to the market place.**

"snowball unemployment tax (2)"=
      "unemployment wage tax (2,1)"
      +"unemployment wage tax (2, 2)"
      +"unemployment wage tax (2, 3)"
        +
        +
        +
      +"unemployment wage tax (2, k2)"

> **k2 is the number of worker's unemployment wage taxes in company (2) that are included in the cost of the item. The k2 worker unemployment wage taxes are delivered to the market place.**

"snowball unemployment tax (3)"=
      "unemployment wage tax (3,1)"
      +"unemployment wage tax (3, 2)"
      +"unemployment wage tax (3, 3)"
        +
        +
        +
      +"unemployment wage tax (3, k3)"
        +
        +
        +

> **k3 is the number of worker's unemployment wage taxes in company (3) that are included in the cost of the item. The k3 worker unemployment wage taxes are delivered to the market place.**

"snowball unemployment tax (n)"=
      "unemployment wage tax (n,1)"
      +"unemployment wage tax (n, 2)"
      +"unemployment wage tax (n,3)"
        +
        +
        +
      +"unemployment wage tax (n, kn)"

> **kn is the number of worker's unemployment wage taxes in company (n) that are included in the cost of the item. The kn worker unemployment wage taxes are delivered to the market place.**

"snowball unemployment wage tax"=
     "snowball unemployment wage tax (1)"
     +"snowball unemployment wage tax (2)"
     +"snowball unemployment wage tax (3)"
          +
          +
          +
     +"snowball unemployment wage tax (kn)"

The total snowball worker's unemployment wage taxes are included in the item's cost and are delivered to the market place.

The company transmits the following to the government and the market place:
     "unemployment wage tax"
"gross wage earner" becomes "net wage earner."
Other companies transmit the following to the government:
     "unemployment wage tax"
The following develops:
     "unemployment wage tax" becomes "snowball unemployment wage tax"
The "snowball" is added in the following to the transmitted tax:
     "unemployment wage tax"
     "snowball unemployment wage tax"
The company transmits the following to the market place:
     "unemployment wage tax"
     "snowball unemployment wage tax"
A "net wage earner" who buys any product in the market place ends up paying a "triple tax."
Any "non-net wage earner" or "consumer" who buys any product in the market place pays a "double tax."

"unemployment wage tax"

TAXATION #1
Tax is sent to government!
Tax is sent to market place too!
"gross wage earner" becomes "net wage earner"

"unemployment wage tax"

TAXATION #2
"net wage earner" and consumer pay this tax in the market place.

"unemployment wage tax"
"snowball unemployment wage tax"

TAXATION #3
Companies' whom handled or produce the item of both snowball and regular taxes had been sent to the government. "net wage earner" and consumer pay these taxes in the market place!

FUNCTION END

FUNCTION161

> **"16th amendment wage tax"**

- "16th amendment wage tax"

The company transmits the following to the government and the market place:
  "16th amendment wage tax"
"gross wage earner" becomes "net wage earner."
The company transmits the following to the market place:
  "16th amendment wage tax"
A "net wage earner" who buys any product in the market place ends up paying a "double tax."
Any "non-net wage earner" or "consumer" who buys any product in the market place pays a "single tax."

"16th amendment wage tax"

> TAXATION #1
> **Tax is sent to government!**
> **Tax is sent to market place too!**
> **"gross wage earner" becomes "net wage earner"**

"16th amendment wage tax"

> TAXATION #2
> **"net wage earner" and consumer pay this tax in the market place.**

FUNCTION END

FUNCTIONS1

"social security wage tax"

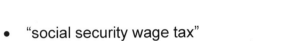

- "social security wage tax"

The company transmits the following to the government:
"social security wage tax"
"gross wage earner" becomes "net wage earner."
The company transmits the following to the market place:
"social security wage tax"
A "net wage earner" who buys any product in the market place ends up paying a "double tax."
Any "non-net wage earner" or "consumer" who buys any product in the market place pays a "single tax."

"social security wage tax"

TAXATION #1
Tax is sent to government!
Tax is sent to market place too!
"gross wage earner" becomes "net wage earner."

"social security wage tax"

TAXATION #2
"net wage earner" and consumer pay this tax in the market place.

FUNCTION END

FUNCTIONM1

"medicare wage tax"

- "medicare wage tax"

The company transmits the following to the government:
"medicare wage tax"
"gross wage earner" becomes "net wage earner."
The company transmits the following to the market place:
"medicare wage tax"
A "net wage earner" who buys any product in the market place ends up paying a "double tax."
Any "non-net wage earner" or "consumer" who buys any product in the market place pays a "single tax."

"medicare wage tax"

TAXATION #1
Tax is sent to government!
Tax is sent to market place too!
"gross wage earner" becomes "net wage earner."

"medicare wage tax"

TAXATION #2
"net wage earner" and consumer pay this tax in the market place.

FUNCTION END

FUNCTIONU1

"unemployment wage tax"

- "unemployment wage tax"

The company transmits the following to the government:
   "UNEMPLOYMENT WAGE TAX"
"GROSS WAGE EARNER" becomes "NET WAGE EARNER."
The company transmits the following to the market place:
   "UNEMPLOYMENT WAGE TAX"
A "NET WAGE EARNER" who buys any product in the market place ends up paying a "DOUBLE TAX."
Any "NON-NET WAGE EARNER" OR "CONSUMER" who buys any product in the market place pays a "SINGLE TAX."

"unemployment wage tax"

TAXATION #1
Tax is sent to government!
Tax is sent to market place too!
"gross wage earner" becomes "net wage earner"

"unemployment wage tax"

TAXATION #2
"net wage earner" and consumer pay this tax in the market place.

FUNCTION END

MATHEMATICAL
FUNCTIONS
USED
TO
PRESENT
FUNCTIONAL
TAXATION
EXAMPLES

CIVIL WAR FUNCTION2

"civil war wage tax"
"snowball civil war wage tax"

"civil war wage tax"

TAXATION #1
Consumers pay these taxes that the civil war war company sent to the market place!

"civil war wage tax"
"snowball civil war wage tax"

TAXATION #2
"Civil war companies" whom handled or produces the item of both snowball and regular taxes was sent to the market place. Consumers pay these taxes in the market place!

"civil war wage tax"

TAXATION #1
Tax is sent to government!
Tax is sent to market place too!
"gross wage earner" becomes "net wage earner."

"civil war wage tax"

TAXATION #2
"net wage earner" pays this taxes in the market place!

"civil war wage tax"
"snowball civil war wage tax"

TAXATION #3
"Civil war companies" whom handled or produces the item of both snowball and regular taxes was sent to the market place. "net wage earner" pays these taxes in the market place!

CIVIL WAR FUNCTION4

"civil war company tax"
"snowball civil war company tax"
"civil war wage tax"
"snowball civil war wage tax"

"civil war company tax"
"civil war wage tax"

TAXATION #1
Consumers pay these taxes that the "civil war company" sent to the market place!

"civil war company tax"
"snowball civil war company tax"

Note! Consumer pays "civil war company tax!"

TAXATION #2
Civil war companies whom handled or produces the item of both snowball and regular taxes was sent to the market place. Consumers pay these taxes in the market place!

"civil war company tax"
"civil war wage tax"

TAXATION #1
Taxes are sent to government!
Taxes are sent to market place too!
"gross wage earner" becomes "net wage earner"

"civil war company tax"
"civil war wage tax"

TAXATION #2
"net wage earner" pays these taxes in the market place!

"civil war company tax"
"snowball civil war company tax"
"civil war wage tax"
"snowball civil war wage tax"

TAXATION #3
"Civil war companies" whom handled or produces the item of both snowball and regular taxes was sent to the market place. "net wage earner" pays these taxes in the market place!

Note! "net wage earner" pays "civil war company tax! "

FUNCTIONCS16S10

"company tax"
"snowball company tax"
"16th amendment wage tax"
"snowball 16th amendment wage tax"
"social security wage tax"
"snowball social security wage tax"
"medicare wage tax"
"snowball medicare wage tax"
"unemployment wage tax"
"snowball unemployment wage tax"

"company tax"
"16th amendment wage tax"
"medicare wage tax"
"unemployment wage tax"

TAXATION #1
Consumers pay these taxes that the company sent to the market place!

"company tax"
"snowball company tax"
"16th amendment wage tax"
"snowball 16th amendment wage tax"
"social security wage tax"
"snowball social security wage tax"
"medicare wage tax"
"snowball medicare wage tax"
"unemployment wage tax"
"snowball unemployment wage tax

TAXATION #2
Companies' whom handled or produce the item of both snowball and regular taxes was sent to the market place.
Consumers pay these taxes in the market place!

Note! Consumer pays "company tax!"

"company tax"
"16th amendment wage tax"
"social security wage tax"
"medicare wage tax"
"unemployment wage tax"

TAXATION #1
Taxes are sent to government!
Taxes are sent to market place too!
"gross wage earner" becomes "net wage earner"

"company tax"
"16th amendment wage tax"
"social security wage tax"
"medicare wage tax"
"unemployment wage tax"

TAXATION #2
"net wage earner" pays these taxes in the market place!

"company tax"
"snowball company tax"
"16th amendment wage tax"
"snowball 16th amendment wage tax"
"social security wage tax"
"snowball social security wage tax"
"medicare wage tax"
"snowball medicare wage tax"
"unemployment wage tax"
"snowball unemployment wage tax

TAXATION #3
Companies' whom handled or produce the item of both snowball and regular taxes was sent to the market place.
"net wage earner" pays these taxes in the market place!

Note! "net wage earner" pays "company tax! "

FUNCTIONC16S9

"company tax"
"16th amendment wage tax"
"snowball 16th amendment wage tax"
"social security wage tax"
"snowball social security wage tax"
"medicare wage tax"
"snowball medicare wage tax"
"unemployment wage tax"
"snowball unemployment wage tax"

"company tax"
"16th amendment wage tax"
"medicare wage tax"
"unemployment wage tax"

TAXATION #1
Consumers pay these taxes that the company sent to the market place!

"company tax"
"16th amendment wage tax"
"snowball 16th amendment wage tax"
"social security wage tax"
"snowball social security wage tax"
"medicare wage tax"
"snowball medicare wage tax"
"unemployment wage tax"
"snowball unemployment wage tax

TAXATION #2
Companies' whom handled or produce the item of both snowball and regular taxes was sent to the market place.
Consumers pay these taxes in the market place!

Note! Consumer pays "company tax!"

"company tax"
"16th amendment wage tax"
"social security wage tax"
"medicare wage tax"
"unemployment wage tax"

TAXATION #1
Taxes are sent to government!
Taxes are sent to market place too!
"gross wage earner" becomes "net wage earner."

"company tax"
"16th amendment wage tax"
"social security wage tax"
"medicare wage tax"
"unemployment wage tax"

TAXATION #2
"net wage earner" pays these taxes in the market place!

"company tax"
"16th amendment wage tax"
"snowball 16th amendment wage tax"
"social security wage tax"
"snowball social security wage tax"
"medicare wage tax"
"snowball medicare wage tax"
"unemployment wage tax"
"snowball unemployment wage tax

TAXATION #3
Companies' whom handled or produce the item of both snowball and regular taxes was sent to the market place.
"net wage earner" pays these taxes in the market place!

Note! "net wage earner" pays "company tax!"

FUNCTION16S8

"16th amendment wage tax"
"snowball 16th amendment wage tax"
"social security wage tax"
"snowball social security wage tax"
"medicare wage tax"
"snowball medicare wage tax"
"unemployment wage tax"
"snowball unemployment wage tax"

"16th amendment wage tax"
"Social security"
"medicare wage tax"
"unemployment wage tax"

TAXATION #1
Consumers pay these taxes that the company sent to the market place!

"16th amendment wage tax"
"social security wage tax"
"medicare wage tax"
"unemployment wage tax"
"snowball 16th amendment wage tax"
"snowball social security wage tax"
"snowball medicare wage tax"
"snowball unemployment wage tax"

TAXATION #2
Companies' whom handled or produce the item of both snowball and regular taxes was sent to the market place.
Consumers pay these taxes in the market place!

"16th amendment wage tax"
"social security wage tax"
"medicare wage tax"
"unemployment wage tax"

TAXATION #1
Taxes are sent to government!
Taxes are sent to market place too! "gross wage earner" becomes "net wage earner"

"16th amendment wage tax"
"social security wage tax"
"medicare wage tax"
"unemployment wage tax"

TAXATION #2
"net wage earner" pays these taxes in the market place!

"16th amendment wage tax"
"snowball 16th amendment wage tax"
"social security wage tax"
"snowball social security wage tax"
"medicare wage tax"
"snowball medicare wage tax"
"unemployment wage tax"
"snowball unemployment wage tax

TAXATION #3
Companies' whom handled or produce the item of both snowball and regular taxes was sent to the market place. "net wage earner" pays these taxes in the market place!

FUNCTIONCS16S4

"company tax"
"snowball company tax"
"16th amendment wage tax"
"snowball 16th amendment wage tax"

"company tax"
"16th amendment wage tax"

TAXATION #1
Consumers pay these taxes that the company sent to the market place!

"company tax"
"snowball company tax"
"16th amendment wage tax"
"snowball 16th amendment wage tax"

TAXATION #2
Companies' whom handled or produce the item of both snowball and regular taxes was sent to the market place.
Consumers pay these taxes in the market place!

Note! Consumer pays "company tax!"

"company tax"
"16th amendment wage tax"

TAXATION #1
Taxes are sent to government!
Taxes are sent to market place too!
"gross wage earner" becomes "net wage earner"

"company tax"
"16th amendment wage tax"

TAXATION #2
"net wage earner" pays these taxes in the market place!

"company tax"
"snowball company tax"
"16th amendment wage tax"
"snowball 16th amendment wage tax"

TAXATION #3
Companies' whom handled or produce the item of both snowball and regular taxes was sent to the market place. "net wage earner" pays these taxes in the market place!

Note! "net wage earner" pays "company tax!"

FUNCTIONCSSS4

"company tax"
"snowball company tax"
"social security wage tax"
"snowball social security wage tax"

"company tax"
"social security wage tax"

TAXATION #1
Consumers pay these taxes that the company sent to the market place!

"company tax"
"snowball company tax"
"social security wage tax"
"snowball social security wage tax"

TAXATION #2
Companies' whom handled or produce the item of both snowball and regular taxes was sent to the market place.
Consumers pay these taxes in the market place!

Note! Consumer pays "company tax!"

"company tax"
"social security wage tax"

TAXATION #1
Taxes are sent to government!
Taxes are sent to market place too!
"gross wage earner" becomes "net wage earner"

"company tax"
"social security wage tax"

TAXATION #2
"net wage earner" pays these taxes in the market place!

"company tax"
"snowball company tax"
"social security wage tax"
"snowball social security wage tax"

TAXATION #3
Companies' whom handled or produce the item of both snowball and regular taxes was sent to the market place. "net wage earner" pays these taxes in the market place!

Note! "net wage earner" pays "company tax!"

FUNCTIONCSMS4

"company tax"
"snowball company tax"
"medicare wage tax"
"snowball medicare wage tax"

"company tax"
"medicare wage tax"

TAXATION #1
Consumers pay these taxes that the company sent to the market place!

"company tax"
"snowball company tax"
"medicare wage tax"
"snowball medicare wage tax"

TAXATION #2
Companies' whom handled or produce the item of both snowball and regular taxes was sent to the market place. Consumers pay these taxes in the

Note! Consumer pays "company tax!"

"company tax"
"medicare wage tax"

TAXATION #1
Taxes are sent to government!
Taxes are sent to market place too!
"gross wage earner" becomes "net wage earner"

"company tax"
"medicare wage tax"

TAXATION #2
"net wage earner" pays these taxes in the market place!

"company tax"
"snowball company tax"
"medicare wage tax"
"snowball medicare wage tax"

TAXATION #3
Companies' whom handled or produce the item of both snowball and regular taxes was sent to the market place. "net wage earner" pays these taxes in the market place!

Note! "net wage earner" pays "company tax!"

FUNCTIONCSUS4

"company tax"
"snowball company tax"
"unemployment wage tax"
"snowball unemployment wage tax"

"company tax"
"unemployment wage tax"

TAXATION #1
Consumers pay these taxes that the company sent to the market place!

"company tax"
"snowball company tax"
"unemployment wage tax"
"snowball unemployment wage tax"

TAXATION #2
Companies' whom handled or produce the item of both snowball and regular taxes was sent to the market place. Consumers pay these taxes in the market place!

Note! Consumer pays "company tax!"

"company tax"
"unemployment wage tax"

TAXATION #1
Taxes are sent to government!
Taxes are sent to market place too!
"gross wage earner" becomes "net wage earner"

"company tax"
"unemployment wage tax"

TAXATION #2
"net wage earner" pays these taxes in the market place!

"company tax"
"snowball company tax"
"unemployment wage tax"
"snowball unemployment wage tax"

TAXATION #3
Companies' whom handled or produce the item of both snowball and regular taxes was sent to the market place. "net wage earner" pays these taxes in the market place!

Note! "net wage earner" pays "company tax!"

FUNCTIONCSCS4

"city company tax"
"snowball city company tax"
"city wage tax"
"snowball city wage tax"

"city company tax"
"city wage tax"

TAXATION #1
Consumers pay these taxes that the city company sent to the market place!

"city company tax"
"city wage tax"
"snowball city company tax"
"snowball city wage tax"

TAXATION #2
Companies' whom handled or produce the item of both snowball and regular taxes was sent to the market place. Consumers pay these taxes in the market place!

Note! Consumer pays "company tax!"

"city company tax"
"city wage tax"

TAXATION #1
Taxes are sent to government!
Taxes are sent to market place too!
"gross city wage earner" becomes "net city wage earner."

"city company tax"
"city wage tax"

TAXATION #2
"net city wage earner" pays these taxes in the market place!

"city company tax"
"city wage tax"
"snowball city company tax"
"snowball city wage tax"

TAXATION #3
Companies' whom handled or produce the item of both snowball and regular taxes was sent to the market place.
"net city wage earner" pays these taxes in the market place!

Note! "net city wage earner" pays "company tax!"

FUNCTIONC16S3

"company tax"
"16th amendment wage tax"
"snowball 16th amendment wage tax"

"company tax"
"16th amendment wage tax"

TAXATION #1
Consumers pay these taxes that the company sent to the market place!

"company tax"
"16th amendment wage tax"
"snowball 16th amendment wage tax"

TAXATION #2
Companies' whom handled or produce the item of both snowball and regular taxes was sent to the market place.
Consumers pay these taxes in the market place!

Note! Consumer pays "company tax!"

"company tax"
"16th amendment wage tax"

TAXATION #1
Taxes are sent to government!
Taxes are sent to market place too!
"gross wage earner" becomes "net wage earner"

"company tax"
"16th amendment wage tax"

TAXATION #2
"net wage earner" pays these taxes in the market place!

"company tax"
"16th amendment wage tax"
"snowball 16th amendment wage tax"

TAXATION #3
Companies' whom handled or produce the item of both snowball and regular taxes was sent to the market place.
"net wage earner" pays these taxes in the market place!

Note! "net wage earner" pays "company tax!"

FUNCTIONCSS3

"company tax"
"social security wage tax"
"snowball social security wage tax"

"company tax"
"social security wage tax"

TAXATION #1
Consumers pay these taxes that the company sent to the market place!

"company tax"
"social security wage tax"
"snowball social security wage tax"

Note! Consumer pays
"company tax!"

TAXATION #2
Companies' whom handled or produce the item of both snowball and regular taxes was sent to the market place.
Consumers pay these taxes in the market place!

"company tax"
"social security wage tax"

TAXATION #1
Taxes are sent to government!
Taxes are sent to market place too!
"gross wage earner" becomes "net wage earner"

"company tax"
"social security wage tax"

TAXATION #2
"net wage earner" pays these taxes in the market place!

"company tax"
"social security wage tax"
"snowball social security wage tax"

Note! "net wage earner" pays
"company tax!"

TAXATION #3
Companies' whom handled or produce the item of both snowball and regular taxes was sent to the market place.
"net wage earner" pays these taxes in the market place!

FUNCTIONCMS3

"company tax"
"medicare wage tax"
"snowball medicare wage tax"

"company tax"
"medicare wage tax"

TAXATION #1
~~Consumers pay these taxes that the company sent to the market place!~~

"company tax"
"medicare wage tax"
"snowball medicare wage tax"

TAXATION #2
Companies' whom handled or produce the item of both snowball and regular taxes was sent to the market place.

note! Consumer pays "company tax!"

"company tax"
"medicare wage tax"

TAXATION #1
Taxes are sent to government!
Taxes are sent to market place too!
"gross wage earner" becomes "net wage earner"

"company tax"
"medicare wage tax"

TAXATION #2
"net wage earner" pays these taxes in the market place!

"company tax"
"medicare wage tax"
"snowball medicare wage tax"

TAXATION #3
Companies' whom handled or produce the item of both snowball and regular taxes was sent to the market place.
"net wage earner" pays these taxes in the market place!

Note! "net wage earner" pays "company tax!"

FUNCTIONCUS3

"company tax"
"unemployment wage tax"
"snowball unemployment wage tax"

"company tax"
"unemployment wage tax"

TAXATION #1
Consumers pay these taxes that the company sent to the market place!

"company tax"
"unemployment wage tax"
"snowball unemployment wage tax"

TAXATION #2
Companies' whom handled or produce the item of both snowball and regular taxes was sent to the market place.
Consumers pay these taxes in the market place!

Note! Consumer pays "company tax!"

"company tax"
"unemployment wage tax"

TAXATION #1
Taxes are sent to government!
Taxes are sent to market place too!
"gross wage earner" becomes "net wage earner"

"company tax"
"unemployment wage tax"

TAXATION #2
"net wage earner" pays these taxes in the market place!

"company tax"
"unemployment wage tax"
"snowball unemployment wage tax"

TAXATION #3
Companies' whom handled or produce the item of both snowball and regular taxes was sent to the market place.
"net wage earner" pays these taxes in the market place!

Note! "net wage earner" pays "company tax!"

FUNCTION16S2

"16th amendment wage tax"
"snowball 16th amendment wage tax"

"16th amendment wage tax"

TAXATION #1
Consumers pay these taxes that the company sent to the market place!

"16th amendment wage tax"
"snowball 16th amendment wage tax"

TAXATION #2
Companies' whom handled or produce the item of both snowball and regular taxes was sent to the market place. Consumers pay these taxes in the market place!

"16th amendment wage tax"

TAXATION #1
Taxes are sent to government!
Taxes are sent to market place too!
"gross wage earner" becomes "net wage earner."

"16th amendment wage tax"

TAXATION #2
"net wage earner" pays these taxes in the market place!

"16th amendment wage tax"
"snowball 16th amendment wage tax"

TAXATION #3
Companies' whom handled or produce the item of both snowball and regular taxes was sent to the market place.
"net wage earner" pays these taxes in the market place!

FUNCTIONSSS2

"social security wage tax"
"snowball social security wage tax"

"social security wage tax"

TAXATION #1
Consumers pay these taxes that the company sent to the market place!

"social security wage tax"
"snowball social security wage tax"

TAXATION #2
Companies' whom handled or produce the item of both snowball and regular taxes was sent to the market place. Consumers pay these taxes in the market place!

"social security wage tax"

TAXATION #1
Taxes are sent to government!
Taxes are sent to market place too!
"gross wage earner" becomes "net wage earner"

"social security wage tax"

TAXATION #2
"net wage earner" pays these taxes in the market place!

"social security wage tax"
"snowball social security wage tax"

TAXATION #3
Companies' whom handled or produce the item of both snowball and regular taxes was sent to the market place.
"net wage earner" pays these taxes in the market place!

FUNCTIONMS2

"medicare wage tax"
"snowball medicare wage tax"

"medicare wage tax"

TAXATION #1
Consumers pay these taxes that the company sent to the market place!

"medicare wage tax"
"snowball medicare wage tax"

TAXATION #2
Companies' whom handled or produce the item of both snowball and regular taxes was sent to the market place.
Consumers pay these taxes in the market place!

"medicare wage tax"

TAXATION #1
Taxes are sent to government!
Taxes are sent to market place too!
"gross wage earner" becomes "net wage earner."

"medicare wage tax"

TAXATION #2
"net wage earner" pays these taxes in the market place!

"medicare wage tax"
"snowball medicare wage tax"

TAXATION #3
Companies' whom handled or produce the item of both snowball and regular taxes was sent to the market place.
"net wage earner" pays these taxes in the market place!

FUNCTIONUS2

"unemployment wage tax"
"snowball unemployment wage tax"

"unemployment wage tax"

TAXATION #1
Consumers pay these taxes that the company sent to the market place!

"unemployment wage tax"
"snowball unemployment wage tax"

TAXATION #2
Companies' whom handled or produce the item of both snowball and regular taxes was sent to the market place.
Consumers pay these taxes in the market place!

"unemployment wage tax"

TAXATION #1
Taxes are sent to government!
Taxes are sent to market place too!
"gross wage earner" becomes "net wage earner."

"unemployment wage tax"

TAXATION #2
"net wage earner" pays these taxes in the market place!

"unemployment wage tax"
"snowball unemployment wage ta

.
Companies' whom handled or produce the item of both snowball and regular taxes was sent to the market place. "net wage earner" pays these taxes in the market place!

FUNCTION161

"16th amendment wage tax"

| "16th amendment wage tax" | TAXATION #1
Consumer pays this tax that the company sent to the market place! |

| "16th amendment wage tax" | TAXATION #1
Tax is sent to government! Tax is sent to market place too! |

| "16th amendment wage tax" | TAXATION #2
"net wage earner" pays this tax in the market place! |

FUNCTIONS1

"social security wage tax"

| "social security wage tax" | TAXATION #1
Consumer pays this tax that the company sent to the market place! |

| "social security wage tax" | TAXATION #1
Tax is sent to government! Tax is sent to market place too! |

| "social security wage tax" | TAXATION #2
"net wage earner" pays this tax in the market place! |

FUNCTIONM1

"medicare wage tax"

"medicare wage tax"
TAXATION #1
Consumer pays this tax that the company sent to the market

"medicare wage tax"
TAXATION #1
Tax is sent to government! Tax is sent to market place too!
"gross wage earner" becomes "net wage earner."

"medicare wage tax"
TAXATION #2
"net wage earner" pays this tax in the market place!

FUNCTIONU1

"unemployment wage tax"

"unemployment wage tax"
TAXATION #1
Consumer pays this tax that the company sent to the market place!

"unemployment wage tax"
TAXATION #1
Tax is sent to government! Tax is sent to market place too!
"gross wage earner" becomes "net wage earner."

"unemployment wage tax"
TAXATION #2
"net wage earner" pays this tax in the market place!

PAY COMPANY#n TAX
PAY COMPANY#1 TAX
FUNCTIONCS16S4

"company#1 tax"
"snowball company#1 tax"
"16th amendment wage tax"
"snowball 16th amendment wage tax"

"company#1 tax"
"16th amendment wage tax"

TAXATION #1
Consumer pays these taxes that the company sent to the market place!

"company#1 tax"
"snowball company#1 tax"
"16th amendment wage tax"
"snowball 16th amendment wage tax"

Note! Consumer pays "company#1 tax!"

TAXATION #2
Companies' whom handled or produces the item of both snowball and regular taxes was sent to the market place.
Consumer pays these taxes in the market place!

"company#1 tax"
"16th amendment wage tax"

TAXATION #1
Taxes are sent to government! Taxes are sent to market place too! "gross wage earner" becomes "net wage earner."

"company#1 tax"
"16th amendment wage tax"

TAXATION #2
"net wage earner" pays these taxes in the market place!

"company#1 tax"
"snowball company tax#1"
"16th amendment wage tax"
"snowball 16th amendment wage tax"

Note! "net wage earner" pays "company#1 tax!"

TAXATION #3
A company whom handled or produces the item of both snowball and regular taxes was sent to the market place. "net wage earner" pays these taxes in the market place!

PAY COMPANY#2 TAX
FUNCTIONCS16S4

"company#2 tax"
"snowball company#2 tax"
"16th amendment wage tax"
"snowball 16th amendment wage tax"

"company#2 tax"
"16th amendment wage tax"

TAXATION #1
Consumer pays these taxes that the company sent to the market place!

"company#2 tax"
"snowball company#2 tax"
"16th amendment wage tax"
"snowball 16th amendment wage tax"

NOTE! Consumer pays "company#2 tax!"

TAXATION #2
A company whom handled or produces the item of both snowball and regular taxes was sent to the market place. Consumer pays these taxes in the market place!

"company#2 tax"
"16th amendment wage tax"

TAXATION #1
Taxes are sent to government! Taxes are sent to market place too! "gross wage earner" becomes "net wage earner."

"company#2 tax"
"16th amendment wage tax"

TAXATION #2
"net wage earner" pays these taxes in the market place!

"company#2 tax"
"snowball company#2 tax"
"16th amendment wage tax"
"snowball 16th amendment wage tax"

Note! "net wage earner" pays "company#2 tax!"

TAXATION #3
Companies' whom handled or produces the item of both snowball and regular taxes was sent to the market place. "net wage earner" pays these taxes in the market place!

PAY COMPANY#3 TAX
FUNCTIONCS16S4

"company#3 tax"
"snowball company#3 tax"
"16th amendment wage tax"
"snowball 16th amendment wage tax"

"company#3 tax"
"16th amendment wage tax"

TAXATION #1
Consumer pays these taxes that the company sent to the market place!

"company#3 tax"
"snowball company#3tax"
"16th amendment wage tax"
"snowball 16th amendment wage tax"

Note! Consumer pays "company#3 tax!"

TAXATION #2
Companies' whom handled or produces the item of both snowball and regular taxes was sent to the market place. Consumer pays these taxes in the market place!

"company#3 tax"
"16th amendment wage tax"

TAXATION #1
Taxes are sent to government! Taxes are sent to market place too! "gross wage earner" becomes "net wage earner."

"company#3 tax"
"16th amendment wage tax"

TAXATION #2
"net wage earner" pays these taxes in the market place!

"company#3 tax"
"snowball company#3 tax"
"16th amendment wage tax"
"snowball 16th amendment wage tax"

Note! "net wage earner" pays "company#3 tax!"

TAXATION #3
Companies' whom handled or produces the item of both snowball and regular taxes was sent to the market place. "net wage earner" pays these taxes in the market place!

PAY COMPANY#n TAX
FUNCTIONCS16S4

"company#n tax"
"snowball company#n tax"
"16th amendment wage tax"
"snowball 16th amendment wage tax"

"company#n tax"
"16th amendment wage tax"

TAXATION #1
Consumer pays these taxes that the company sent to the market place!

"company#n tax"
"snowball company#n tax"
"16th amendment wage tax"
"snowball 16th amendment wage tax"

TAXATION #2
Companies' whom handled or produces the item of both snowball and regular taxes was sent to the market place. Consumer pays these taxes in the market place!

Note! Consumer pays "company#n tax!"

"company#n tax"
"16th amendment wage tax"

TAXATION #1
Taxes are sent to government! Taxes are sent to market place too! "gross wage earner" becomes "net wage earner."

"company#n tax"
"16th amendment wage tax"

TAXATION #2
"net wage earner" pays these taxes in the market place!

"company#n tax"
"snowball company#n tax"
"16th amendment wage tax"
"snowball 16th amendment wage tax"

TAXATION #3
Companies' whom handled or produces the item of both snowball and regular taxes was sent to the market place. "net wage earner" pays these taxes in the market place!

Note! "net wage earner" pays "company#n tax!"

"company#1 tax"
*
"company#n tax"
"16th amendment wage tax" ***1***
*
"16th amendment wage tax" ***n***

TAXATION #1
Consumer pays these taxes that the company sent to the market place!

"company#1 tax"
*
"company#n tax"
"snowball company#1 tax"
*
"snowball company#n tax"

"16th amendment wage tax" ***1***
*
"16th amendment wage tax" ***n***
"snowball 16th amendment wage tax" ***1***
*
"snowball 16th amendment wage tax" ***n***

TAXATION #2
Companies' whom handled or produces the item of both snowball and regular taxes was sent to the market place.
Consumer pays these taxes in the market place!

Consumer pays company#n taxes!

"company#1 tax"
                    *
"company#n tax"
"16th amendment wage tax" ***1***
                    *
"16th amendment wage tax" ***n***

TAXATION #1
Taxes are sent to government! Taxes are sent to market place too! "gross wage earner" becomes "net wage earner."

"company#1 tax"
                    *
"company#n tax"
"16th amendment wage tax" ***1***
                    *
"16th amendment wage tax" ***n***

TAXATION #2
"net wage earner" pays these taxes in the market place!

"company#1 tax"
                    *
"company#n tax"
"snowball company#1 tax"
                    *
"snowball company#n tax"

"16th amendment wage tax" ***1***
                    *
"16th amendment wage tax" ***n***
"snowball 16th amendment wage tax" ***1***
                    *
"snowball 16th amendment wage tax" ***n***

TAXATION #3
Companies' whom handled or produces the item of both snowball and regular taxes was sent to the market place.
"net wage earner" pays these taxes in the market place!

Note! "net wage earner" pays "company#n tax!"

PAY COMPANY#n TAX
(NO 16TH AMENDMENT TAX)
PAY COMPANY#1 TAX
FUNCTIONCS2

"company#1 tax"
"snowball company#1 tax"

"company#1 tax"

TAXATION#1
Consumer pays this tax that the company sent to the market place!

"company#1 tax"
"snowball company#1 tax"

TAXATION#2
Companies' whom handled or produces the item of both snowball and regular taxes was sent to the market place. Consumer pays this tax in the market place!

Note! Consumer pays "company#1 tax!"

"company#1 tax"

TAXATION#1
Tax is sent to government! Tax is sent to market place too! "gross wage earner" becomes "net wage earner."

"company#1 tax"

TAXATION#2
"net wage earner" pays this tax in the market place!

"company#1 tax"
"snowball company#1 tax"

TAXATION#3
Companies' whom handled produces the item of both snowball and regular taxes was sent to the market place. "net wage earner" pays these taxes in the market place!

Note! "net wage earner" pays "company#1 tax!"

PAY COMPANY#2 TAX
FUNCTIONCS2

"company#2 tax"
"snowball company#2 tax"

"company#2 tax"

TAXATION#1
Consumer pays this tax that the company sent to the market place!

"company#2 tax"
"snowball company#2 tax"

TAXATION#2
Companies' whom handled or produces the item of both snowball and regular taxes was sent to the market place. Consumer pays these taxes in the market place!

Note! Consumer pays "company#2 tax!"

"company#2 tax"

TAXATION#1
Tax is sent to government! Tax is sent to market place too! "gross wage earner" becomes "net wage earner."

"company#2 tax"

TAXATION#2
"net wage earner" pays this tax in the market place!

"company#2 tax"
"snowball company#2 tax"

TAXATION#3
Companies' whom handled or produces the item of both snowball and regular taxes was sent to the market place. "net wage earner" pays these taxes in the market place!

Note! "net wage earner" pays "company#2 tax!"

PAY COMPANY#3 TAX
FUNCTIONCS2

"company#3 tax"
"snowball company#3 tax"

"company#3 tax"

TAXATION#1
Consumer pays this tax that the company sent to the market place!

"company#3 tax"
"snowball company#3tax"

TAXATION#2
Companies' whom handled or produces the item of both snowball and regular taxes was sent to the market place. Consumer pays these taxes in the market place!

Note! Consumer pays "company#3 tax!"

"company#3 tax"

TAXATION#1
This tax is sent to government! This tax is sent to market place too! "gross wage earner" becomes "net wage earner."

"company#3 tax"

TAXATION#2
"net wage earner" pays this tax in the market place!

"company#3 tax"
"snowball company#3 tax"

TAXATION#3
Companies' whom handled or produces the item of both snowball and regular taxes was sent to the market place. "net wage earner" pays these taxes in the market place!

Note! "net wage earner" pays "company#3 tax!"

PAY COMPANY#n TAX
FUNCTIONCS2

"company#n tax"
"snowball company#n tax"

"company#n tax"

TAXATION#1
Consumer pays this tax that the company sent to the market place!

"company#n tax"
"snowball company#n tax"

TAXATION#2
Companies' whom handled or produces the item of both snowball and regular taxes was sent to the market place. Consumer pays these taxes in the market place!

Note! Consumer pays "company#n tax!"

"company#n tax"

TAXATION#1
Tax is sent to government! Tax is sent to market place too!
"gross wage earner" becomes "net wage earner."

"company#n tax"

TAXATION#2
"net wage earner" pays this tax in the market place!

"company#n tax"
"snowball company#n tax"

TAXATION#3
Companies' whom handled or produces the item of both snowball and regular taxes was sent to the market place. "net wage earner" pays these taxes in the market place!

Note! "net wage earner" pays "company#n tax!"

"company#1 tax"
*
"company#n tax"

TAXATION#1
Consumer pays these taxes that the company sent to the market place!

"company#1 tax"
*
"company#n tax"
"snowball company#1 tax"
*
"snowball company#n tax"

TAXATION#2
Companies' whom handled or produces the item of both snowball and regular taxes was sent to the market place.
Consumer pays these taxes in the market place!

Note! Consumer pays "company#n tax!"

"company#1 tax"
*
"company#n tax"

TAXATION#1
Tax is sent to government! Tax is sent to market place too!
"gross wage earner" becomes "net wage earner."

"company#1 tax"
*
"company#n tax"

TAXATION#2
"net wage earner" pays these taxes in the market place!

"company#1 tax"
*
"company#n tax"
"snowball company#1 tax"
*
"snowball company#n tax"

TAXATION#3
Companies' whom handled or produces the item of both snowball and regular taxes was sent to the market place. "net wage earner" pays these taxes in the market place!

Note! "net wage earner" pays "company#n tax!"

MATHEMATICAL

FUNCTIONAL

PROPOSED

EXAMPLES

PAY TAX FOR ONE ITEM OF GROCERY FUNCTIONCS16S10

"grocery company tax"
"snowball grocery company tax"
"16th amendment wage tax"
"snowball 16th amendment wage tax"
"social security wage tax"
"snowball social security wage tax"
"medicare wage tax"
"snowball medicare wage tax"
"unemployment wage tax"
"snowball unemployment wage tax"

"grocery company tax"
"16th amendment wage tax"
"social security wage tax"
"medicare wage tax"
"unemployment wage tax"

TAXATION #1
Consumers pay these taxes that the company sent to the market place!

"grocery company tax"
"snowball grocery company tax"
"16th amendment wage tax"
"snowball 16th amendment wage tax"
"social security wage tax"
"snowball social security wage tax"
"medicare wage tax"
"snowball medicare wage tax"
"unemployment wage tax"
"snowball unemployment wage tax

TAXATION #2
Companies' whom handled or produces the item of both snowball and regular taxes was sent to the market place. Consumers pay these taxes in the market place!

Note! Consumer pays "company tax!"

"grocery company tax"
"16th amendment wage tax"
"social security wage tax"
"medicare wage tax"
"unemployment wage tax"

TAXATION #1
Taxes are sent to government! Taxes are sent to market place too! "gross wage earner" becomes "net wage earner."

"grocery company tax"
"16th amendment wage tax"
"social security wage tax"
"medicare wage tax"
"unemployment wage tax"

TAXATION #2
"net wage earner" pays these taxes in the market place!

"grocery company tax"
"snowball grocery company tax"
"16th amendment wage tax"
"snowball 16th amendment wage tax"
"social security wage tax"
"snowball social security wage tax"
"medicare wage tax"
"snowball medicare wage tax"
"unemployment wage tax"
"snowball unemployment wage tax"

TAXATION #3
Companies' whom handled or produces the item of both snowball and regular taxes was sent to the market place.
"net wage earner" pays these taxes in the market place!

Note! "net wage earner" pays "company tax!"

PERSON ON SOCIAL SECURITY PAYS TAX ON ONE ITEM OF GROCERY!
FUNCTIONCS16S10

"grocery company tax"
"snowball grocery company tax"
"16th amendment wage tax"
"snowball 16th amendment wage tax"
"social security wage tax"
"snowball social security wage tax"
"medicare wage tax"
"snowball medicare wage tax"
"unemployment wage tax"
"snowball unemployment wage tax"

"grocery company tax"
"16th amendment wage tax"
"social security wage tax"
"medicare wage tax"
"unemployment wage tax"

TAXATION #1
Consumers pay these taxes that the company sent to the market place!

"grocery company tax"
"snowball grocery company tax"
"16th amendment wage tax"
"snowball 16th amendment wage tax"
"social security wage tax"
"snowball social security wage tax"
"medicare wage tax"
"snowball medicare wage tax"
"unemployment wage tax"
"snowball unemployment wage tax

TAXATION #2
Companies' whom handled or produces the item of both snowball and regular taxes was sent to the market place. Consumers pay these taxes in the market place!

Note! Consumer pays "company tax!"

PERSON ON MEDICARE PAYS TAX ON ONE ITEM OF GROCERY!
FUNCTIONCS16S10

"grocery company tax"
"snowball grocery company tax"
"16th amendment wage tax"
"snowball 16th amendment wage tax"
"medicare wage tax"
"snowball medicare wage tax"
"medicare wage tax"
"snowball medicare wage tax"
"unemployment wage tax"
"snowball unemployment wage tax"

"grocery company tax"
"16th amendment wage tax"
"social security wage tax"
"medicare wage tax"
"unemployment wage tax"

TAXATION #1
Consumers pay these taxes that the company sent to the market place!

"grocery company tax"
"snowball grocery company tax"
"16th amendment wage tax"
"snowball 16th amendment wage tax"
"social security wage tax"
"snowball social security wage tax"
"medicare wage tax"
"snowball medicare wage tax"
"medicare wage tax"
"snowball medicare wage tax"
"unemployment wage tax"
"snowball unemployment wage tax

TAXATION #2
Companies' whom handled or produces the item of both snowball and regular taxes was sent to the market place. Consumers pay these taxes in the market place!

Note! Consumer pays "company tax!"

PERSON ON UNEMPLOYMENT PAYS TAX ON ONE ITEM OF GROCERY!
FUNCTIONCS16S10

"grocery company tax"
"snowball grocery company tax"
"16th amendment wage tax"
"snowball 16th amendment wage tax"
"social security wage tax"
"snowball social security wage tax"
"medicare wage tax"
"snowball medicare wage tax"
"unemployment wage tax"
"snowball unemployment wage tax"

"grocery company tax"
"16th amendment wage tax"
"social security wage tax"
"medicare wage tax"
"unemployment wage tax"

TAXATION #1
Consumers pay these taxes that the company sent to the market place!

"grocery company tax"
"snowball grocery company tax"
"16th amendment wage tax"
"snowball 16th amendment wage tax"
"social security wage tax"
"snowball social security wage tax"
"medicare wage tax"
"snowball medicare wage tax"
"unemployment wage tax"
"snowball unemployment wage tax

TAXATION #2
Companies' whom handled or produces the item of both snowball and regular taxes was sent to the market place. Consumers pay these taxes in the market place!

Note! Consumer pays "company tax!"

A TOURIST VISITING THE UNITED STATES BUYS ONE ITEM OF GROCERY! FUNCTIONCS16S10

"company tax"
"snowball company tax"
"16th amendment wage tax"
"snowball 16th amendment wage tax"
"social security wage tax"
"snowball social security wage tax"
"medicare wage tax"
"snowball medicare wage tax"
"unemployment wage tax"
"snowball unemployment wage tax"

"company tax"
"16th amendment wage tax"
"social security wage tax"
"medicare wage tax"
"unemployment wage tax"

TAXATION #1
Consumers pay these taxes that the company sent to the market place!

"company tax"
"snowball company tax"
"16th amendment wage tax"
"snowball 16th amendment wage tax"
"social security wage tax"
"snowball social security wage tax"
"medicare wage tax"
"snowball medicare wage tax"
"unemployment wage tax"
"snowball unemployment wage tax

TAXATION #2
Companies' whom handled or produces the item of both snowball and regular taxes was sent to the market place. Consumers pay these taxes in the market place!

Note! Consumer pays "company tax!"

PAY TAX ON A PURCHASE OF PANTS WITH STIMULUS MONEY! FUNCTIONCS16S10

"pants company tax"
"snowball pants company tax"
"16th amendment wage tax"
"snowball 16th amendment wage tax"
"social security wage tax"
"snowball social security wage tax"
"medicare wage tax"
"snowball medicare wage tax"
"unemployment wage tax"
"snowball unemployment wage tax"

"pants company tax"
"16th amendment wage tax"
"social security wage tax"
"medicare wage tax"
"unemployment wage tax"

TAXATION #1
Consumers pay these taxes that the company sent to the market place!

"pants company tax"
"snowball pants company tax"
"16th amendment wage tax"
"snowball 16th amendment wage tax"
"social security wage tax"
"snowball social security wage tax"
"medicare wage tax"
"snowball medicare wage tax"
"unemployment wage tax"
"snowball unemployment wage tax

TAXATION #2
Companies' whom handled or produces the item of both snowball and regular taxes was sent to the market place. Consumers pay these taxes in the market place!

Note! Consumer pays "company tax!"

PAY TAX FOR ONE TIME USE OF VISA CARD

(NO SNOWBALL VISA COMPANY TAX)

FUNCTIONC16S9

"visa company tax"
"16th amendment wage tax"
"snowball 16th amendment wage tax"
"social security wage tax"
"snowball social security wage tax"
"medicare wage tax"
"snowball medicare wage tax"
"unemployment wage tax"
"snowball unemployment wage tax"

"visa company tax"
"16th amendment wage tax"
"social security wage tax"
"medicare wage tax"
"unemployment wage tax"

TAXATION #1
Consumers pay these taxes that the company sent to the market place!

"visa company tax"
 "16th amendment wage tax"
"snowball 16th amendment wage tax"
"social security wage tax"
"snowball social security wage tax"
"medicare wage tax"
"snowball medicare wage tax"
"unemployment wage tax"
"snowball unemployment wage tax

TAXATION #2
Companies' whom handled or produces the item of both snowball and regular taxes was sent to the market place. Consumers pay these taxes in the market place!

Note! Consumer pays "company

"visa company tax"
"16th amendment wage tax"
"social security wage tax"
"medicare wage tax"
"unemployment wage tax"

TAXATION #1
Taxes are sent to government! Taxes are sent to market place too! "gross wage earner" becomes "net wage earner."

"visa company tax"
"16th amendment wage tax"
"social security wage tax"
"medicare wage tax"
"unemployment wage tax"

TAXATION #2
"net wage earner" pays these taxes in the market place!

"visa company tax"
"16th amendment wage tax"
"snowball 16th amendment wage tax"
"social security wage tax"
"snowball social security wage tax"
"medicare wage tax"
"snowball medicare wage tax"
"unemployment wage tax"
"snowball unemployment wage tax"

TAXATION #3
Companies' whom handled or produces the item of both snowball and regular taxes was sent to the market place.
"net wage earner" pays these taxes in the market place!

Note! "net wage earners" pays "company tax!"

PAY AUTO TAX
FUNCTIONCS16S10

"auto company tax"
"snowball auto company tax"
"16th amendment wage tax"
"snowball 16th amendment wage tax"
"social security wage tax"
"snowball social security wage tax"
"medicare wage tax"
"snowball medicare wage tax"
"unemployment wage tax"
"snowball unemployment wage tax"

"auto company tax"
"16th amendment wage tax"
"social security wage tax"
"medicare wage tax"
"unemployment wage tax"

TAXATION #1
Consumers pay these taxes that the company sent to the market place!

"auto company tax"
"16th amendment wage tax"
"social security wage tax"
"medicare wage tax"
"unemployment wage tax"
"snowball auto company tax"
"snowball 16th amendment wage tax"
"snowball social security wage tax"
"snowball medicare wage tax"
"snowball unemployment wage tax

TAXATION #2
Companies' whom handled or produces the item of both snowball and regular taxes was sent to the market place. Consumers pay these taxes in the market place!

Note! Consumer pays "company tax!"

"auto company tax"
"16th amendment wage tax"
"social security wage tax"
"medicare wage tax"
"unemployment wage tax"

TAXATION #1
Taxes are sent to government! Taxes are sent to market place too! "gross wage earner" becomes "net wage earner."

"auto company tax"
"16th amendment wage tax"
"social security wage tax"
"medicare wage tax"
"unemployment wage tax"

TAXATION #2
"net wage earner" pays these taxes in the market place!

"auto company tax"
"snowball auto company tax"
"16th amendment wage tax"
"snowball 16th amendment wage tax"
"social security wage tax"
"snowball social security wage tax"
"medicare wage tax"
"snowball medicare wage tax"
"unemployment wage tax"
"snowball unemployment wage tax"

TAXATION #3
Companies' whom handled or produces the item of both snowball and regular taxes was sent to the market place.
"net wage earner" pays these taxes in the market place!

Note! "net wage earner" pays "company tax!"

PAY VISA CARD TAX
AND
PAY AUTO TAX

PAY VISA CARD TAX
FUNCTIONC16S9

"visa card company tax"
"16th amendment wage tax"
"snowball 16th amendment wage tax"
"social security wage tax"
"snowball social security wage tax"
"medicare wage tax"
"snowball medicare wage tax"
"unemployment wage tax"
"snowball unemployment wage tax"

"visa card company tax"
"16th amendment wage tax"
"social security wage tax"
"medicare wage tax"
"unemployment wage tax"

TAXATION #1
Consumers pay these taxes that the company sent to the market place!

"visa card company tax"
"16th amendment wage tax"
"snowball 16th amendment wage tax"
"social security wage tax"
"snowball social security wage tax"
"medicare wage tax"
"snowball medicare wage tax"
"unemployment wage tax"
"snowball unemployment wage tax

TAXATION #2
Companies' whom handled or produces the item of both snowball and regular taxes was sent to the market place. Consumers pay these taxes in the market place!

Note! Consumer pays "company tax!"

"visa card company tax"
"16th amendment wage tax"
"social security wage tax"
"medicare wage tax"
"unemployment wage tax"

TAXATION #1
Taxes are sent to government! Taxes are sent to market place too! "gross wage earner" becomes "net wage earner."

"visa card company tax"
"16th amendment wage tax"
"social security wage tax"
"medicare wage tax"
"unemployment wage tax"

TAXATION #2
"net wage earner" pays these taxes in the market place!

"visa card company tax"
"16th amendment wage tax"
"snowball 16th amendment wage tax"
"social security wage tax"
"snowball social security wage tax"
"medicare wage tax"
"snowball medicare wage tax"
"unemployment wage tax"
"snowball unemployment wage tax"

TAXATION #3
Companies' whom handled or produces the item of both snowball and regular taxes was sent to the market place.
"net wage earner" pays these taxes in the market place!

Note! "net wage earners" pays "company tax!"

PAY AUTO TAX
FUNCTIONCS16S10

"auto company tax"
"snowball auto company tax"
"16th amendment wage tax"
"snowball 16th amendment wage tax"
"social security wage tax"
"snowball social security wage tax"
"medicare wage tax"
"snowball medicare wage tax"
"unemployment wage tax"
"snowball unemployment wage tax"

"auto company tax"
"16th amendment wage tax"
"social security wage tax"
"medicare wage tax"
"unemployment wage tax"

TAXATION #1
Consumers pay these taxes that the company sent to the market place!

"auto company tax"
"16th amendment wage tax"
"social security wage tax"
"medicare wage tax"
"unemployment wage tax"
"snowball auto company tax"
"snowball 16th amendment wage tax"
"snowball social security wage tax"
"snowball medicare wage tax"
"snowball unemployment wage tax

TAXATION #2
Companies' whom handled or produces the item of both snowball and regular taxes was sent to the market place. Consumers pay these taxes in the market place!

Note! Consumer pays "company tax!"

"auto company tax"
"16th amendment wage tax"
"social security wage tax"
"medicare wage tax"
"unemployment wage tax"

TAXATION #1
Taxes are sent to government! Taxes are sent to market place too! "gross wage earner" becomes "net wage earner."

"auto company tax"
"16th amendment wage tax"
"social security wage tax"
"medicare wage tax"
"unemployment wage tax"

TAXATION #2
"net wage earner" pays these taxes in the market place!

"auto company tax"
"snowball auto company tax"
"16th amendment wage tax"
"snowball 16th amendment wage tax"
"social security wage tax"
"snowball social security wage tax"
"medicare wage tax"
"snowball medicare wage tax"
"unemployment wage tax"
"snowball unemployment wage tax"

TAXATION #3
Companies' whom handled or produces the item of both snowball and regular taxes was sent to the market place.
"net wage earner" pays these taxes in the market place!

Note! "net wage earner" pays "company tax!"

"visa card company tax"
"auto company tax"
"16th amendment wage tax"
"16th amendment wage tax"
"social security wage tax"
"social security wage tax"
"medicare wage tax"
"medicare wage tax"
"unemployment wage tax"
"unemployment wage tax"

TAXATION #1
Consumers pay these taxes that the companies sent to the market place!

"visa card company tax"
"auto company tax"
"16th amendment wage tax"
"16th amendment wage tax"
"social security wage tax"
"social security wage tax"
"medicare wage tax"
"medicare wage tax"
"unemployment wage tax"
"unemployment wage tax"
"snowball auto company tax"
"snowball 16th amendment wage tax"
"snowball 16th amendment wage tax"
"snowball social security wage tax"
"snowball social security wage tax"
"snowball medicare wage tax"
"snowball medicare wage tax"
"snowball unemployment wage tax
"snowball unemployment wage tax

TAXATION #2
Companies' whom handled or produces the item of both snowball and regular taxes was sent to the market place. Consumers pay these taxes in the market place!

Note! Consumer pays "company tax!"

"visa card company tax"
"auto company tax"
"16th amendment wage tax"
"16th amendment wage tax"
"social security wage tax"
"social security wage tax"
"medicare wage tax"
"medicare wage tax"
"unemployment wage tax"
"unemployment wage tax"

TAXATION #1
Taxes are sent to government! Taxes are sent to market place too! "gross wage earner" becomes "net wage earner."

"visa card company tax"
"auto company tax"
"16th amendment wage tax"
"16th amendment wage tax"
"social security wage tax"
"social security wage tax"
"medicare wage tax"
"medicare wage tax"
"unemployment wage tax"
"unemployment wage tax"

TAXATION #2
"net wage earner" pays these taxes in the market place!

"visa card company tax"
"auto company tax"
"16th amendment wage tax"
"16th amendment wage tax"
"social security wage tax"
"social security wage tax"
"medicare wage tax"
"medicare wage tax"
"unemployment wage tax"
"unemployment wage tax"
"snowball auto company tax"
"snowball 16th amendment wage tax"
"snowball 16th amendment wage tax"
"snowball social security wage tax"
"snowball social security wage tax"
"snowball medicare wage tax"
"snowball medicare wage tax"
"snowball unemployment wage tax"
"snowball unemployment wage tax"

TAXATION #3
Companies' whom handled or produces the item of both snowball and regular taxes was sent to the market place.
"net wage earner" pays these taxes in the market place!

Note! "net wage earner" pays "company tax!"

PAY TAX FOR ONE PERSON TALK RADIO FUNCTIONC16S9

"talk radio company tax"
"16th amendment wage tax"
"snowball 16th amendment wage tax"
"social security wage tax"
"snowball social security wage tax"
"medicare wage tax"
"snowball medicare wage tax"
"unemployment wage tax"
"snowball unemployment wage tax"

"talk radio company tax"
"16th amendment wage tax"
"social security wage tax"
"medicare wage tax"
"unemployment wage tax"

TAXATION #1
Consumers pay these taxes that the company sent to the market place!

"talk radio company tax"
"16th amendment wage tax"
"social security wage tax"
"medicare wage tax"
"unemployment wage tax"
"snowball 16th amendment wage tax"
"snowball social security wage tax"
"snowball medicare wage tax"
"snowball unemployment wage tax"

TAXATION #2
Companies' whom handled or produces the item of both snowball and regular taxes was sent to the market place.
Consumer pays these taxes in the market place!

Note! Consumer pays "company tax!"

"talk radio company tax"
"16th amendment wage tax"
"social security wage tax"
"medicare wage tax"
"unemployment wage tax"

TAXATION #1
Taxes are sent to government! Taxes are sent to market place too! "gross wage earner" becomes "net wage earner."

"talk radio company tax"
"16th amendment wage tax"
"social security wage tax"
"medicare wage tax"
"unemployment wage tax"

TAXATION #2
"net wage earner" pays these taxes in the market place!

"talk radio company tax"
"16th amendment wage tax"
"social security wage tax"
"medicare wage tax"
"unemployment wage tax"
"snowball 16th amendment wage tax"
"snowball social security wage tax"
"snowball medicare wage tax"
"snowball unemployment wage tax"

TAXATION #3
Companies' whom handled or produces the item of both snowball and regular taxes was sent to the market place.
"net wage earner" pays these taxes in the market place!

Note! "net wage earner" pays "company tax!"

PAY TAX FOR ONE RADIO CHANNEL
FUNCTIONC16S9

"radio channel company tax"
"16th amendment wage tax"
"snowball 16th amendment wage tax"
"social security wage tax"
"snowball social security wage tax"
"medicare wage tax"
"snowball medicare wage tax"
"unemployment wage tax"
"snowball unemployment wage tax"

"radio channel company tax"
"16th amendment wage tax"
"medicare wage tax"
"unemployment wage tax"

TAXATION #1
Consumers pay these taxes that the company sent to the market place!

"radio channel company tax"
"16th amendment wage tax"
"social security wage tax"
"medicare wage tax"
"unemployment wage tax"
"snowball 16th amendment wage tax"
"snowball social security wage tax"
"snowball medicare wage tax"
"snowball unemployment wage tax

TAXATION #2
Companies' whom handled or produces the item of both snowball and regular taxes was sent to the market place. Consumers pay these taxes in the market place!

Note! Consumer pays "company

"radio channel company tax"
"16th amendment wage tax"
"social security wage tax"
"medicare wage tax"
"unemployment wage tax"

TAXATION #1
Taxes are sent to government! Taxes are sent to market place too! "gross wage earner" becomes "net wage earner."

"radio channel company tax"
"16th amendment wage tax"
"social security wage tax"
"medicare wage tax"
"unemployment wage tax"

TAXATION #2
"net wage earner" pays these taxes in the market place!

"radio channel company tax"
"16th amendment wage tax"
"social security wage tax"
"medicare wage tax"
"unemployment wage tax"
 "snowball 16th amendment wage tax"
"snowball social security wage tax"
"snowball medicare wage tax"
"snowball unemployment wage tax"

TAXATION #3
Companies' whom handled or produces the item of both snowball and regular taxes was sent to the market place.
"net wage earner" pays these taxes in the market place!

Note! "net wage earner" pays "company tax!"

PAY TAX FOR A RADIO ADVERTISEMENT FUNCTIONCS16S10

"advertisement company tax"
"snowball advertisement company tax"
"16th amendment wage tax"
"snowball 16th amendment wage tax"
"social security wage tax"
"snowball social security wage tax"
"medicare wage tax"
"snowball medicare wage tax"
"unemployment wage tax"
"snowball unemployment wage tax"

"advertisement company tax"
"16th amendment wage tax"
"social security wage tax"
"medicare wage tax"
"unemployment wage tax"

TAXATION #1
Consumers pay these taxes that the company sent to the market place!

"advertisement company tax"
"16th amendment wage tax"
"social security wage tax"
"medicare wage tax"
"unemployment wage tax"
"snowball advertisement company tax"
"snowball 16th amendment wage tax"
"snowball social security wage tax"
"snowball medicare wage tax"
"snowball unemployment wage tax

TAXATION #2
Companies' whom handled or produces the item of both snowball and regular taxes was sent to the market place. Consumers pay these taxes in the market place!

Note! Consumer pays "company tax!"

"advertisement company tax"
"16th amendment wage tax"
"social security wage tax"
"medicare wage tax"
"unemployment wage tax"

TAXATION #1
Taxes are sent to government! Taxes are sent to market place too! "gross wage earner" becomes "net wage earner."

"advertisement company tax"
"16th amendment wage tax"
"social security wage tax"
"medicare wage tax"
"unemployment wage tax"

TAXATION #2
"net wage earner" pays these taxes in the market place!

"advertisement company tax"
"16th amendment wage tax"
"social security wage tax"
"medicare wage tax"
"unemployment wage tax"
"snowball advertisement company tax"
"snowball 16th amendment wage tax"
"snowball social security wage tax"
"snowball medicare wage tax"
"snowball unemployment wage tax"

TAXATION #3
Companies' whom handled or produces the item of both snowball and regular taxes was sent to the market place.
"net wage earner" pays these taxes in the market place!

Note! "net wage earner" pays "company tax!"

"16TH AMENDMENT WAGE TAX ONLY"

PAY TAX FOR ONE PERSON TALK RADIO
AND
PAY TAX FOR ONE RADIO CHANNEL
AND
PAY TAX FOR A RADIO ADVERTISEMENT
(NO SNOWBALL TALK RADIO COMPANY)
PAY TAX FOR ONE PERSON TALK RADIO
FUNCTIONC16S3

"talk radio company tax"
"16th amendment wage tax"
"snowball 16th amendment wage tax"

"talk radio company tax"
"16th amendment wage tax"

TAXATION #1
Taxes are sent to government! Taxes are sent to market place too! "gross wage earner" becomes "net wage earner."

"talk radio company tax"
"16th amendment wage tax"
"snowball 16th amendment wage tax"

TAXATION #2
Companies' whom handled or produces the item of both snowball and regular taxes was sent to the market place. Consumers pay these taxes in the market place!

Note! Consumer pays "company tax!"

TAXATION #1

"talk radio company tax"
"16th amendment wage tax"

Taxes are sent to government! Taxes are sent to market place too! "gross wage earner" becomes "net wage earner."

TAXATION #2

"talk radio company tax"
"16th amendment wage tax"

"net wage earner" pays these taxes in the market place!

TAXATION #3

"talk radio company tax"
"16th amendment wage tax"
"snowball 16th amendment wage tax"

Companies' whom handled or produces the item of both snowball and regular taxes was sent to the market place.
"net wage earner" pays these taxes in the market place!

Note! "net wage earner" pays "company tax!"

PAY TAX FOR ONE RADIO CHANNEL FUNCTIONC16S3

"radio channel company tax"
"16th amendment wage tax"
"snowball 16th amendment wage tax"

TAXATION #1

"radio channel company tax"
"16th amendment wage tax"

Taxes are sent to government! Taxes are sent to market place too! "gross wage earner" becomes "net wage earner."

TAXATION #2

"radio channel company tax"
"16th amendment wage tax"
"snowball 16th amendment wage tax"

Companies' whom handled or produces the item of both snowball and regular taxes was sent to the market place. Consumers pay these taxes in the market place!

Note! Consumer pays "company tax!"

270

"radio channel company tax"
"16th amendment wage tax"

TAXATION #1
Taxes are sent to government! Taxes are sent to market place too! "gross wage earner" becomes "net wage earner."

"radio channel company tax"
"16th amendment wage tax"

TAXATION #2
"net wage earner" pays these taxes in the market place!

"radio channel company tax"
"16th amendment wage tax"
"snowball 16th amendment wage tax"

TAXATION #3
Companies' whom handled or produces the item of both snowball and regular taxes was sent to the market place.
"net wage earner" pays these taxes in the market place!

Note! "net wage earner" pays "company tax!"

PAY TAX FOR ONE RADIO ADVERTISEMENT FUNCTIONC16S3

"advertisement company tax"
"16th amendment wage tax"
"snowball 16th amendment wage tax"

"advertisement company tax"
"16th amendment wage tax"

TAXATION #1
Taxes are sent to government! Taxes are sent to market place too! "gross wage earner" becomes "net wage

"advertisement company tax"
"16th amendment wage tax"
"snowball 16th amendment wage tax"

Note! Consumer pays "company tax!"

TAXATION #2
Companies' whom handled or produces the item of both snowball and regular taxes was sent to the market place. Consumers pay these taxes in the market place!

"advertisement company tax"
"16th amendment wage tax"

TAXATION #1
Taxes are sent to government! Taxes are sent to market place too! "gross wage earner" becomes "net wage earner."

"advertisement company tax"
"16th amendment wage tax"

TAXATION #2
"net wage earner" pays these taxes in the market place!

"advertisement company tax"
"16th amendment wage tax"
"snowball 16th amendment wage tax"

Note! "net wage earner" pays "company tax!"

TAXATION #3
Companies' whom handled or produces the item of both snowball and regular taxes was sent to the market place. "net wage earner" pays these taxes in the market place!

"talk radio company tax"
"radio channel company tax"
"advertisement company tax"
"16th amendment wage tax"
"16th amendment wage tax"
"16th amendment wage tax"

TAXATION #1
Taxes are sent to government! Taxes are sent to market place too! "gross wage earner" becomes "net wage earner."

"talk radio company tax"
"radio channel company tax"
"advertisement company tax"
"16th amendment wage tax"
"16th amendment wage tax"
"16th amendment wage tax"
"snowball 16th amendment wage tax"
"snowball 16th amendment wage tax"
"snowball 16th amendment wage tax"

TAXATION #2
Companies' whom handled or produces the item of both snowball and regular taxes was sent to the market place. Consumers pay these taxes in the market place!

Note! Consumer pays "company taxes!"

"talk radio company tax"
"radio channel company tax"
"advertisement company tax"
"16th amendment wage tax"
"16th amendment wage tax"
"16th amendment wage tax"

TAXATION #1
Taxes are sent to government! Taxes are sent to market place too! "gross wage earner" becomes "net wage earner."

"talk radio company tax"
"radio channel company tax"
"advertisement company tax"
"16th amendment wage tax"
"16th amendment wage tax"
"16th amendment wage tax"

TAXATION #2
"net wage earner" pays these taxes in the market place!

"talk radio company tax"
"radio channel company tax"
"advertisement company tax"
"16th amendment wage tax"
"16th amendment wage tax"
"16th amendment wage tax"
"snowball 16th amendment wage tax"
"snowball 16th amendment wage tax"
"snowball 16th amendment wage tax"

TAXATION #3
Companies' whom handled or produces the item of both snowball and regular taxes was sent to the market place.
"net wage earner" pays these taxes in the market place!

Note! "net wage earner" pays "company taxes!"

PAY UNITED STATES TAX
FUNCTIONCS16S10

"united states company tax"
"snowball united states company tax"
"16th amendment wage tax"
"snowball 16th amendment wage tax"
"social security wage tax"
"snowball social security wage tax"
"medicare wage tax"
"snowball medicare wage tax"
"unemployment wage tax"
"snowball unemployment wage tax"

"united states company tax"
"16th amendment wage tax"
"medicare wage tax"
"unemployment wage tax"

TAXATION #1
Consumers pay these taxes that the company sent to the market place!

"united states company tax"
"16th amendment wage tax"
"social security wage tax"
"medicare wage tax"
"unemployment wage tax"
"snowball united states company tax"
"snowball 16th amendment wage tax"
"snowball social security wage tax"
"snowball medicare wage tax"
"snowball unemployment wage tax

TAXATION #2
Companies' whom handled or produces the item of both snowball and regular taxes was sent to the market place. Consumers pay these taxes in the market place!

Note! Consumer pays "company taxes!"

"united states company tax"
"16th amendment wage tax"
"social security wage tax"
"medicare wage tax"
"unemployment wage tax"

TAXATION #1
Taxes are sent to government! Taxes are sent to market place too! "gross wage earner" becomes "net wage earner."

"united states company tax"
"16th amendment wage tax"
"social security wage tax"
"medicare wage tax"
"unemployment wage tax"

TAXATION #2
"net wage earner" pays these taxes in the market place!

"united states company tax"
"16th amendment wage tax"
"social security wage tax"
"medicare wage tax"
"unemployment wage tax"
"snowball united states company tax"
"snowball 16th amendment wage tax"
"snowball social security wage tax"
"snowball medicare wage tax"
"snowball unemployment wage tax"

TAXATION #3
Companies' whom handled or produces the item of both snowball and regular taxes was sent to the market place.
"net wage earner" pays these taxes in the market place!

Note! "net wage earners" pays company tax in the market placees!

PAY NEW YORK STATE TAX
FUNCTIONCSSS4

"state company tax"
"snowball state company tax"
"state wage tax"
"snowball state wage tax"

"state company tax"
"state wage tax"

TAXATION #1
Consumers pay these taxes that the state company sent to the market place!

"state company tax"
"snowball state company tax"
"state wage tax"
"snowball state wage tax"

TAXATION #2
Companies' whom handled or produces the item of both snowball and regular taxes was sent to the market place. Consumers pay these taxes in the market place!

Note! Consumer pays "state company tax!"

"state company tax"
"state wage tax"

TAXATION #1
Taxes are sent to government! Taxes are sent to market place too! "gross state wage earner" becomes "net state wage earner"

"state company tax"
"state wage tax"

TAXATION #2
"net state wage earner" pays these taxes in the market place!

"state company tax"
"snowball state company tax"
"state wage tax"
"snowball state wage tax"

TAXATION #3
Companies' whom handled or produces the item of both snowball and regular taxes was sent to the market place.
"net state wage earner" pays these taxes in the market place!

Note! "net state wage earner" pays "state company tax!"

PAY NEW YORK CITY TAX FUNCTIONCSCS4

"city company tax"
"snowball city company tax"
"city wage tax"
"snowball city wage tax"

"city company tax"
"city wage tax"

TAXATION #1
Consumers pay these taxes that the city company sent to the market place!

"city company tax"
"snowball city company tax"
"city wage tax"
"snowball city wage tax"

TAXATION #2
Companies' whom handled or produces the item of both snowball and regular taxes was sent to the market place. Consumers pay these taxes in the market place!

Note! Consumer pays "city company tax!"

"city company tax"
"city wage tax"

TAXATION #1
Taxes are sent to government! Taxes are sent to market place too!
"gross city wage earner" becomes "net city wage earner"

"city company tax"
"city wage tax"

TAXATION #2
"net city wage earner" pays these taxes in the market place!

"city company tax"
"snowball city company tax"
"city wage tax"
"snowball city wage tax"

TAXATION #3
Companies' whom handled or produces the item of both snowball and regular taxes was sent to the market place.
"net city wage earner" pays these taxes in the market

Note! "net city wage earner" pays "city company tax!"

PAY UNITED STATES TAX
AND
PAY NEW YORK STATE TAX
AND
PAY NEW YORK CITY TAX

PAY UNITED STATES TAX
FUNCTIONCS16S10

"united states company tax"
"snowball united states company tax"
"16th amendment wage tax"
"snowball 16th amendment wage tax"
"social security wage tax"
"snowball social security wage tax"
"medicare wage tax"
"snowball medicare wage tax"
"unemployment wage tax"
"snowball unemployment wage tax"

"united states company tax"
"16th amendment wage tax"
"medicare wage tax"
"unemployment wage tax"

TAXATION #1
Consumers pay these taxes that the company sent to the market place!

"united states company tax"
"16th amendment wage tax"
"social security wage tax"
"medicare wage tax"
"unemployment wage tax"
"snowball united states company tax"
"snowball 16th amendment wage tax"
"snowball social security wage tax"
"snowball medicare wage tax"
"snowball unemployment wage tax

TAXATION #2
Companies' whom handled or produces the item of both snowball and regular taxes was sent to the market place. Consumers pay these taxes in the market place!

Note! Consumer pays "united states company tax!"

"united states company tax"
"16th amendment wage tax"
"social security wage tax"
"medicare wage tax"
"unemployment wage tax"

TAXATION #1
Taxes are sent to government! Taxes are sent to market place too! "gross wage earner" becomes "net wage earner."

"united states company tax"
"16th amendment wage tax"
"social security wage tax"
"medicare wage tax"
"unemployment wage tax"

TAXATION #2
"net wage earner" pays these taxes in the market place!

"united states company tax"
"16th amendment wage tax"
"social security wage tax"
"medicare wage tax"
"unemployment wage tax"
"snowball united states company tax"
"snowball 16th amendment wage tax"
"snowball social security wage tax"
"snowball medicare wage tax"
"snowball unemployment wage tax"

TAXATION #3
Companies' whom handled or produces the item of both snowball and regular taxes was sent to the market place.
"net wage earner" pays these taxes in the market place!

Note! "net wage earners" pays "united states company tax!"

PAY NEW YORK STATE TAX
FUNCTIONCSSS4

"state company tax"
"snowball state company tax"
"state wage tax"
"snowball state wage tax"

"state company tax"
"state wage tax"

TAXATION #1
Consumers pay these taxes that the state company sent to the market place!

"state company tax"
"snowball state company tax"
"state wage tax"
"snowball state wage tax"

TAXATION #2
Companies' whom handled or produces the item of both snowball and regular taxes was sent to the market place. Consumers pay these taxes in the market place!

Note! Consumer pays "state company tax!"

"state company tax"
"state wage tax"

TAXATION #1
Taxes are sent to government! Taxes are sent to market place too! "gross state wage earner" becomes "net state wage earner"

"state company tax"
"state wage tax"

TAXATION #2
"net state wage earner" pays these taxes in the market place!

"state company tax"
"snowball state company tax"
"state wage tax"
"snowball state wage tax"

TAXATION #3
Companies' whom handled or produces the item of both snowball and regular taxes was sent to the market place.
"net state wage earner" pays these taxes in the market place!

Note! "net state wage earner" pays "state company tax!"

PAY NEW YORK CITY TAX
FUNCTIONCSCS4

"city company tax"
"snowball city company tax"
"city wage tax"
"snowball city wage tax"

"city company tax"
"city wage tax"

TAXATION #1
Consumers pay these taxes that the city company sent to the market place!

"city company tax"
"snowball city company tax"
"city wage tax"
"snowball city wage tax"

TAXATION #2
Companies' whom handled or produces the item of both snowball and regular taxes was sent to the market place. Consumers pay these taxes in the market place!

Note! Consumer pays "city company tax!"

"city company tax"
"city wage tax"

TAXATION #1
Taxes are sent to government! Taxes are sent to market place too!
"gross city wage earner" becomes "net city wage earner"

"city company tax"
"city wage tax"

TAXATION #2
"net city wage earner" pays these taxes in the market place!

"city company tax"
"snowball city company tax"
"city wage tax"
"snowball city wage tax"

TAXATION #3
Companies' whom handled or produces the item of both snowball and regular taxes was sent to the market place.
"net city wage earner" pays these taxes in the market

Note! "net city wage earner" pays "city company tax!"

"united states company tax"
"state company tax"
"city company tax"
 "state wage tax"
"city wage tax"
"16th amendment wage tax"
"social security wage tax"
"medicare wage tax"
"unemployment wage tax"

TAXATION #1
Consumers pay these taxes that the companies sent to the market place!

"united states company tax"
"state company tax"
"city company tax"
"16th amendment wage tax"
"social security wage tax"
"medicare wage tax"
"unemployment wage tax"
"state wage tax"
"city wage tax"
"snowball united states company tax"
"snowball state company tax"
"snowball city company tax"
"snowball 16th amendment wage tax"
 "snowball social security wage tax"
"snowball medicare wage tax"
"snowball unemployment wage tax"
"snowball state wage tax"
"snowball city wage tax"

TAXATION #2
Companies' whom handled or produces the item of both snowball and regular taxes was sent to the market place. Consumers pay these taxes in the market place!

Note! Consumer pays "company taxes!"

"united states company tax"
"state company tax"
"city company tax"
"16th amendment wage tax"
"social security wage tax"
"medicare wage tax"
"unemployment wage tax"
"state wage tax"
"city wage tax"

TAXATION #1
Taxes are sent to government! Taxes are sent to market place too! "gross wage earner" becomes "net wage earner."

"united states company tax"
"state company tax"
"city company tax"
"16th amendment wage tax"
"social security wage tax"
"medicare wage tax"
"unemployment wage tax"
"state wage tax"
"city wage tax"

TAXATION #2
"net wage earner" pays these taxes in the market place!

"united states company tax"
"state company tax"
"city company tax"
"16th amendment wage tax"
"social security wage tax"
"medicare wage tax"
"unemployment wage tax"
"state wage tax"
"city wage tax"
"snowball united states company tax"
"snowball state company tax"
"snowball city company tax"
"snowball 16th amendment wage tax"
"snowball social security wage tax"
"snowball medicare wage tax"
"snowball unemployment wage tax"
"snowball state wage tax"
"snowball city wage tax"

TAXATION #3
Companies' whom handled or produces the item of both snowball and regular taxes was sent to the market place. "net wage earner" pays these taxes in the market place!

Note! "net wage earners" pays "company taxes!"

PAY TAX FOR ONE GALLON OF GASOLINE
FUNCTIONCS16S10

"gasoline company tax"
"snowball gasoline company tax"
"16th amendment wage tax"
"snowball 16th amendment wage tax"
"social security wage tax"
"snowball social security wage tax"
"medicare wage tax"
"snowball medicare wage tax"
"unemployment wage tax"
"snowball unemployment wage tax"

"gasoline company tax"
"16th amendment wage tax"
"social security wage tax"
"medicare wage tax"
"unemployment wage tax"

TAXATION #1
Consumers pay these taxes that the company sent to the market place!

"gasoline company tax"
"snowball gasoline company tax"
"16th amendment wage tax"
"snowball 16th amendment wage tax"
"social security wage tax"
"snowball social security wage tax"
"medicare wage tax"
"snowball medicare wage tax"
"unemployment wage tax"
"snowball unemployment wage tax

TAXATION #2
Companies' whom handled or produces the item of both snowball and regular taxes was sent to the market place. Consumers pay these taxes in the market place!

Note! Consumer pays "gasoline company tax!"

"gasoline company tax"
"16th amendment wage tax"
"social security wage tax"
"medicare wage tax"
"unemployment wage tax"

TAXATION #1
Taxes are sent to government! Taxes are sent to market place too! "gross wage earner" becomes "net wage earner."

"gasoline company tax"
"16th amendment wage tax"
"social security wage tax"
"medicare wage tax"
"unemployment wage tax"

TAXATION #2
"net wage earner" pays these taxes in the market place!

"gasoline company tax"
"snowball gasoline company tax"
"16th amendment wage tax"
"snowball 16th amendment wage tax"
"social security wage tax"
"snowball social security wage tax"
"medicare wage tax"
"snowball medicare wage tax"
"unemployment wage tax"
"snowball unemployment wage tax"

TAXATION #3
Companies' whom handled or produces the item of both snowball and regular taxes was sent to the market place.
"net wage earner" pays these taxes in the market place!

Note! "net wage earner" pays "gasoline company tax!"

TAXES ON BUILDING A HOUSE
FOR
CONSUMER
AND
NET WAGE EARNER
FUNCTIONCS16S10

"house company tax"
"snowball house company tax"
"16th amendment wage tax"
"snowball 16th amendment wage tax"
"social security wage tax"
"snowball social security wage tax"
"medicare wage tax"
"snowball medicare wage tax"
"unemployment wage tax"
"snowball unemployment wage tax"

"house company tax"
"16th amendment wage tax"
"social security wage tax"
"medicare wage tax"
"unemployment wage tax"

TAXATION #1
Consumers pay these taxes that the company sent to the market place!

"house company tax"
"snowball house company tax"
"16th amendment wage tax"
"snowball 16th amendment wage tax"
"social security wage tax"
"snowball social security wage tax"
"medicare wage tax"
"snowball medicare wage tax"
"unemployment wage tax"
"snowball unemployment wage tax

TAXATION #2
Companies' whom handled or produces the item of both snowball and regular taxes was sent to the market place. Consumers pay these taxes in the market place!

Note! Consumer pays "house company tax!"

"house company tax"
"16th amendment wage tax"
"social security wage tax"
"medicare wage tax"
"unemployment wage tax"

TAXATION #1
Taxes are sent to government! Taxes are sent to market place too! "gross wage earner" becomes "net wage earner."

"house company tax"
"16th amendment wage tax"
"social security wage tax"
"medicare wage tax"
"unemployment wage tax"

TAXATION #2
"net wage earner" pays these taxes in the market place!

"house company tax"
"snowball house company tax"
"16th amendment wage tax"
"snowball 16th amendment wage tax"
"social security wage tax"
"snowball social security wage tax"
"medicare wage tax"
"snowball medicare wage tax"
"unemployment wage tax"
"snowball unemployment wage tax"

TAXATION #3
Companies' whom handled or produces the item of both snowball and regular taxes was sent to the market place.
"net wage earner" pays these taxes in the market place!

Note! "net wage earner" pays "house company tax!"

"COMPANY TAXES"
AND
"ONLY"
"16TH AMENDMENT WAGE TAXES"
PERSON PAYS TAX ON n ITEMS IN A
COMPANY STORE!
ITEM #1
FUNCTIONCS16S4

"company tax item #1"
"snowball "company tax item #1""
"16th amendment wage tax"
"snowball 16th amendment wage tax"

"company tax item #1"
"16th amendment wage tax"

TAXATION #1
Consumer pays this tax that the company sent to the market place!

"company tax item #1"
"snowball company tax item #1"
"16th amendment wage tax"
"snowball 16th amendment wage tax"

TAXATION #2
Companies' whom handled or produces the item of both snowball and regular taxes was sent to the market place. Consumer pays these taxes in the market place!

Note! Consumer pays "company tax item #1"

"company tax item #1"
"16th amendment wage tax"

TAXATION #1
Tax is sent to government! Tax is sent to market place too! "gross wage earner" becomes "net wage earner."

"company tax item #1"
"16th amendment wage tax"

TAXATION #2
"net wage earner" pays this tax in the market place!

"company tax item #1"
"snowball "company tax item #1"
"16th amendment wage tax"
"snowball 16th amendment wage tax"

Note! "net wage earner" pays "company tax item #1!"

TAXATION #3
Companies' whom handled or produces the item of both snowball and regular taxes was sent to the market place. "net wage earner" pays these taxes in the market place!

ITEM #2
FUNCTIONCS16S4

"company tax item #2"
"snowball company tax item #2"
"16th amendment wage tax"
"snowball 16th amendment wage tax"

"company tax item #2"
"16th amendment wage tax"

TAXATION #1
Consumer pays this tax that the company sent to the market place!

"company tax item #2"
"snowball company tax item #2"
"16th amendment wage tax"
"snowball 16th amendment wage tax"

TAXATION #2
Companies' whom handled or produces the item of both snowball and regular taxes was sent to the market place. Consumer pays these taxes in the market place!

Note! Consumer pays "company tax item #2!"

"company tax item #2"
"16th amendment wage tax"

TAXATION #1
Tax is sent to government! Tax is sent to market place too! "gross wage earner" becomes "net wage earner."

"company tax item #2"
 "16th amendment wage tax"

TAXATION #2
"net wage earner" pays this tax in the market place!

"company tax item #2"
"snowball "company tax item #2"
"16th amendment wage tax"
"snowball 16th amendment wage tax"

TAXATION #3
Companies' whom handled or produces the item of both snowball and regular taxes was sent to the market place. "net wage earner." pays these taxes in the market place!

Note! "net wage earner" pays "company tax item #2!"

ITEM #3
FUNCTIONCS16S4

"company tax item #3"
"snowball company tax item #3"
"16th amendment wage tax"
"snowball 16th amendment wage tax"

"company tax item #3"
"16th amendment wage tax"

TAXATION #1
Consumer pays this tax that the company sent to the market place!

"company tax item #3"
"snowball company tax item #3"
"16th amendment wage tax"
"snowball 16th amendment wage tax"

TAXATION #2
Companies' whom handled or produces the item of both snowball and regular taxes was sent to the market place. Consumer pays these taxes in the market place!

Note! Consumer pays "company tax item #3!"

"company tax item #3"
"16th amendment wage tax"

TAXATION #1
Tax is sent to government! Tax is sent to market place too! "gross wage earner" becomes "net wage earner."

"company tax item #3"
"16th amendment wage tax"

TAXATION #2
"net wage earner" pays this tax in the market place!

"company tax item #3"
"snowball "company tax item #3"
"16th amendment wage tax"
"snowball 16th amendment wage tax"

TAXATION #3
Companies' whom handled or produces the item of both snowball and regular taxes was sent to the market place. "net wage earner." pays these taxes in the market place!

Note! "net wage earner" pays "company tax item #3!"

ITEM #n
FUNCTIONCS16S4

"company tax item #n"
"snowball company tax item #n"
"16th amendment wage tax"
"snowball 16th amendment wage tax"

"company tax item #n"
"16th amendment wage tax"

TAXATION #1
Consumer pays this tax that the company sent to the market place!

"company tax item #n"
"snowball company tax item #n"
"16th amendment wage tax"
"snowball 16th amendment wage tax"

TAXATION #2
Companies' whom handled or produces the item of both snowball and regular taxes was sent to the market place. Consumer pays these taxes in the market place!

Note! Consumer pays "company tax item #n!"

"company tax item #n"
"16th amendment wage tax"

TAXATION #1
Tax is sent to government! Tax is sent to market place too! "gross wage earner" becomes "net wage earner."

"company tax item #n"
"16th amendment wage tax"

TAXATION #2
"net wage earner" pays this tax in the market place!

"company tax item #n"
"snowball "company tax item #n"
"16th amendment wage tax"
"snowball 16th amendment wage tax"

TAXATION #3
Companies' whom handled or produces the item of both snowball and regular taxes was sent to the market place. "net wage earner" pays these taxes in the market place!

Note! "net wage earner" pays "company tax item #n!"

"company tax item #1"
        *

"company tax item #n"
"16th amendment wage tax"   ***1***
        *

"16th amendment wage tax"   ***n***

TAXATION #1
Consumer pays these taxes that the company sent to the market place!

"company tax item #1"
        *

"company tax item #n"
"snowball company tax item #1"
        *

"snowball company tax item #n"
"16th amendment wage tax"   ***1***
        *

"16th amendment wage tax"   ***n***
"snowball 16th amendment wage tax"   ***1***
        *

"snowball 16th amendment wage tax"   ***n***

TAXATION #2
Companies' whom handled or produces the item of both snowball and regular taxes was sent to the market place. Consumer pays these taxes in the market place!

Note! Consumer pays all n "company taxes item!"

"company tax item #1"
      *
"company tax item #n"

"16th amendment wage tax"   ***1***
      *
"16th amendment wage tax"   ***n***

TAXATION #1
Tax is sent to government! Tax is sent to market place too! "gross wage earner" becomes "net wage earner."

"company tax item #1"
      *
"company tax item #n"

TAXATION #2
"net wage earner" pays this tax in the market place!

"16th amendment wage tax" ***1***
      *
"16th amendment wage tax"***n***

"company tax item #1"
      *
"company tax item #n"
"snowball company tax item #1"
      *
"snowball company tax item #n"
"16th amendment wage tax" ***1***
      *
"16th amendment wage tax" ***n***
"snowball 16th amendment wage tax" ***1***
      *
"snowball 16th amendment wage tax" ***n***

TAXATION #3
Companies' whom handled or produces the item of both snowball and regular taxes was sent to the market place. "net wage earner" pays these taxes in the market place!

Note! "net wage earner" pays all n "company taxes item!"

"COMPANY TAXES ONLY"

PERSON PAYS TAX ON n ITEMS IN A COMPANY STORE!

ITEM #1
FUNCTIONCS2

"company tax item #1"
"snowball company tax item #1"

"company tax item #1"

TAXATION #1
Consumer pays this tax that the company sent to the market place!

"company tax item #1"
"snowball company tax item #1"

TAXATION #2
Companies' whom handled or produces the item of both snowball and regular taxes was sent to the market place. Consumer pays these taxes in the

Note! Consumer pays "company tax item #1!"

"company tax item #1"

TAXATION #1
Tax is sent to government! Tax is sent to market place too! "gross wage earner" becomes "net wage earner."

"company tax item #1"

TAXATION #2
"net wage earner" pays this tax in the market place!

"company tax item #1"
"snowball "company tax item #1"

TAXATION #3
Companies' whom handled or produces the item of both snowball and regular taxes was sent to the market place. "net wage earner" pays these taxes in the market place!

Note! "net wage earner" pays "company tax item #1!"

ITEM #2
FUNCTIONCS2

"company tax item #2"
"snowball company tax item #2"

"company tax item #2"

TAXATION #1
Consumer pays this tax that the company sent to the market place!

"company tax item #2"
"snowball company tax item #2"

TAXATION #2
Companies' whom handled or produces the item of both snowball and regular taxes was sent to the market place. Consumer pays these taxes in the

Note! Consumer pays "company tax item #2!"

"company tax item #2"	**TAXATION #1** Tax is sent to government! Tax is sent to market place too! "gross wage earner" becomes "net wage earner."
"company tax item #2"	**TAXATION #2** "net wage earner" pays this tax in the market place!
"company tax item #2" "snowball "company tax item #2"	**TAXATION #3** Companies' whom handled or produces the item of both snowball and regular taxes was sent to the market place. "net wage earner." pays these taxes in the market place!

Note! "net wage earner" pays "company tax item #2!"

ITEM #3
FUNCTIONCS2

"company tax item #3"
"snowball company tax item #3"

"company tax item #3"	**TAXATION #1** Consumer pays this tax that the company sent to the market place!
"company tax item #3" "snowball company tax item #3"	**TAXATION #2** Companies' whom handled or produces the item of both snowball and regular taxes was sent to the market place. Consumer pays these taxes in the

Note! Consumer pays "company tax item #3!"

"company tax item #3"

TAXATION #1
Tax is sent to government! Tax is sent to market place too! "gross wage earner" becomes "net wage earner."

"company tax item #3"

TAXATION #2
"net wage earner" pays this tax in the market place!

"company tax item #3"
"snowball "company tax item #3"

TAXATION #3
Companies' whom handled or produces the item of both snowball and regular taxes was sent to the market place. "net wage earner." pays these taxes in the market place!

Note! "net wage earner" pays "company tax item #3!"

ITEM #n
FUNCTIONCS2

"company tax item #n"
"snowball company tax item #n"

"company tax item #n"

TAXATION #1
Consumer pays this tax that the company sent to the market place!

"company tax item #n"
"snowball company tax item #n"

TAXATION #2
Companies' whom handled or produces the item of both snowball and regular taxes was sent to the market place. Consumer pays these taxes in the market place!

Note! Consumer pays "company tax item #n!"

"company tax item #n"

TAXATION #1
Tax is sent to government! Tax is sent to market place too! "gross wage earner" becomes "net wage earner."

"company tax item #n"

TAXATION #2
"net wage earner" pays this tax in the market place!

"company tax item #n"
"snowball "company tax item #n"

TAXATION #3
Companies' whom handled or produces the item of both snowball and regular taxes was sent to the market place. "net wage earner" pays these taxes in the market place!

Note! "net wage earner" pays "company tax item #n!"

"company tax item #1"
*
"company tax item #n"

TAXATION #1
Consumer pays these taxes that the company sent to the market place!

"company tax item #1"
*
"company tax item #n"
"snowball company tax item #1"
*
"snowball company tax item #n"

TAXATION #2
Companies' whom handled or produces the item of both snowball and regular taxes was sent to the market place.
Consumer pays these taxes in the market place!

Note! Consumer pays all n "company tax item #n!"

"company tax item #1"
*
"company tax item #n"

TAXATION #1
Tax is sent to government! Tax is sent to market place too!
"gross wage earner" becomes "net wage earner."

"company tax item #1"
*
"company tax item #n"

TAXATION #2
"net wage earner" pays this tax in the market place!

"company tax item #1"
*
"company tax item #n"
"snowball company tax item #1"
*
"snowball company tax item #n"

TAXATION #3
Companies' whom handled or produces the item of both snowball and regular taxes was sent to the market place. "net wage earner" pays these taxes in the market place!

Note! "net wage earner" pays all n "company tax item #n!"

"16TH AMENDMENT WAGE TAXES ONLY"

PERSON PAYS TAX ON n ITEMS IN A COMPANY STORE!
ITEM #1
FUNCTION16S2

"16th amendment wage tax"
"snowball 16th amendment wage tax"

"16th amendment wage tax"

TAXATION #1
Consumer pays this tax that the company sent to the market place!

"16th amendment wage tax"
"snowball 16th amendment wage tax"

TAXATION #2
Companies' whom handled or produces the item of both snowball and regular taxes was sent to the market place. Consumer pays these taxes in the market place!

"16th amendment wage tax"

TAXATION #1
Tax is sent to government! Tax is sent to market place too! "gross wage earner" becomes "net wage earner."

"16th amendment wage tax"

TAXATION #2
"net wage earner" pays this tax in the market place!

"16th amendment wage tax"
"snowball 16th amendment wage tax"

TAXATION #3
Companies' whom handled or produces the item of both snowball and regular taxes was sent to the market place. "net wage earner" pays these taxes in the market place!

ITEM #2
FUNCTION16S2

"16th amendment wage tax"
"snowball 16th amendment wage tax"

"16th amendment wage tax"

TAXATION #1
Consumer pays this tax that the company sent to the market place!

"16th amendment wage tax"
"snowball 16th amendment wage tax"

TAXATION #2
Companies' whom handled or produces the item of both snowball and regular taxes was sent to the market place. Consumer pays these taxes in the market place!

"16th amendment wage tax"

TAXATION #1
Tax is sent to government! Tax is sent to market place too! "gross wage earner" becomes "net wage earner."

"16th amendment wage tax"

TAXATION #2
"net wage earner" pays this tax in the market place!

"16th amendment wage tax"
"snowball 16th amendment wage tax"

TAXATION #3
Companies' whom handled or produces the item of both snowball and regular taxes was sent to the market place. "net wage earner." pays these taxes in the market place!

ITEM #3
FUNCTION16S2

"16th amendment wage tax"
"snowball 16th amendment wage tax"

"16th amendment wage tax"

TAXATION #1
Consumer pays this tax that the company sent to the market place!

"16th amendment wage tax"
"snowball 16th amendment wage tax"

TAXATION #2
Companies' whom handled or produces the item of both snowball and regular taxes was sent to the market place. Consumer pays these taxes in the market place!

"16th amendment wage tax"

TAXATION #1
Tax is sent to government! Tax is sent to market place too! "gross wage earner" becomes "net wage earner."

"16th amendment wage tax"

TAXATION #2
"net wage earner" pays this tax in the market place!

"16th amendment wage tax"
"snowball 16th amendment wage tax"

TAXATION #3
Companies' whom handled or produces the item of both snowball and regular taxes was sent to the market place. "net wage earner." pays these taxes in the market place!

ITEM #n
FUNCTION16S2

"16th amendment wage tax"
"snowball 16th amendment wage tax"

"16th amendment wage tax"

TAXATION #1
Consumer pays this tax that the company sent to the market place!

"16th amendment wage tax"
"snowball 16th amendment wage tax"

TAXATION #2
Companies' whom handled or produces the item of both snowball and regular taxes was sent to the market place. Consumer pays these taxes in the market place!

"16th amendment wage tax"

TAXATION #1
Tax is sent to government! Tax is sent to market place too! "gross wage earner" becomes "net wage earner."

"16th amendment wage tax"

TAXATION #2
"net wage earner" pays this tax in the market place!

"16th amendment wage tax"
"snowball 16th amendment wage tax"

TAXATION #3
Companies' whom handled or produces the item of both snowball and regular taxes was sent to the market place. "net wage earner" pays these taxes in the market place!

"16th amendment wage tax"   ***1***
*
"16th amendment wage tax"   ***n***

TAXATION #1
Consumer pays these taxes that the company sent to the market place!

"16th amendment wage tax"   ***1***
*
"16th amendment wage tax"   ***n***
"snowball 16th amendment wage tax" ***1***
*
"snowball 16th amendment wage tax" ***n***

TAXATION #2
Companies' whom handled or produces the item of both snowball and regular taxes was sent to the market place. Consumer pays these taxes in the market place!

"16th amendment wage tax"   ***1***

*

"16th amendment wage tax"   ***n***

TAXATION #1
Tax is sent to government! Tax is sent to market place too! "gross wage earner" becomes "net wage earner."

"16th amendment wage tax" ***1***

*

"16th amendment wage tax"***n***

TAXATION #2
"net wage earner" pays this tax in the market place!

"16th amendment wage tax" ***1***

*

"16th amendment wage tax" ***n***
"snowball 16th amendment wage tax" ***1***

*

"snowball 16th amendment wage tax" ***n***

TAXATION #3
Companies' whom handled or produces the item of both snowball and regular taxes was sent to the market place. "net wage earner" pays these taxes in the market place!

CORPORATIONS AND COMPANIES TRANSMIT TAXES

CORPORATIONS AND COMPANIES DON'T PAY TAXES!!!

CORPORATION AND COMPANY TRANSMIT TAXES
SNOWBALL COMPANY TAX

Company and other companies send weekly company taxes to the Federal Government and the market place. Since the Federal Government does not pay taxes and Company only transmits taxes, the hidden sales taxes benefit Company and Federal Government.
"net wage earner and consumer pay company tax.

SNOWBALL 16TH AMENDMENT WAGE TAX

Company and other companies send weekly 16th amendment wage taxes to the Federal Government and the market place. Since the Federal Government does not pay taxes and Company only transmits taxes, the hidden sales taxes benefit Company and Federal Government.

SNOWBALL SOCIAL SECURITY WAGE TAX

Company and other companies send weekly social security tax to the Federal Government and the market place. Since the Federal Government does not pay taxes and Company only transmits taxes, the hidden sales taxes benefit Company and Federal Government.

SNOWBALL MEDICARE WAGE TAX

Company and other companies send weekly medicare wage tax to the Federal Government and the market place. Since the Federal Government does not pay taxes and Company only transmits taxes, the hidden sales taxes benefit Company and Federal Government.

SNOWBALL UNEMPLOYMENT WAGE TAX

Company and other companies send weekly unemployment wage taxes to the Federal Government and the market place. Since the Federal Government does not pay taxes and Company only transmits taxes, the hidden sales taxes benefit Company and Federal Government.

SNOWBALL COMPANY AND SNOWBALL 16TH AMENDMENT WAGE TAX

All companies send weekly company along with 16th amendment wage taxes to the Federal Government and the market place. Since the Federal Government does not pay taxes and companies transmit taxes, the hidden market sales taxes benefit company and Federal Government.
"net wage earner and consumer pay company tax.

SNOWBALL COMPANY AND SNOWBALL SOCIAL SECURITY WAGE TAX

All companies send weekly company along with social security wage taxes to the Federal Government and the market place. Since the Federal Government does not pay taxes and companies transmit taxes, the hidden market sales taxes benefit company and Federal Government.
"net wage earner and consumer pay company tax.

SNOWBALL COMPANY AND SNOWBALL MEDICARE WAGE TAX

All companies send weekly company along with medicare wage taxes to the Federal Government and the market place. Since the Federal Government does not pay taxes and companies transmit taxes, the hidden market sales taxes benefit company and Federal Government.
"net wage earner and consumer pay company tax.

SNOWBALL COMPANY AND SNOWBALL UNEMPLOYMENT WAGE TAX

All companies send weekly company along with unemployment wage taxes to the Federal Government and the market place. Since the Federal Government does not pay taxes and companies transmit taxes, the hidden market sales taxes benefit company and Federal Government.

"net wage earner and consumer pay company tax.

COMPANY AND 16TH AMENDMENT WAGE TAX

Company sends weekly company along with 16th amendment wage taxes to the Federal Government and the market place. Since the Federal Government does not pay taxes and Company only transmits taxes, the hidden sales taxes benefit Company and Federal Government.

"net wage earner and consumer pay company tax.

COMPANY AND SOCIAL SECURITY WAGE TAX

Company sends weekly company along with social security tax to the Federal Government and the market place. Since the Federal Government does not pay taxes and Company only transmits taxes, the hidden sales taxes benefit Company and Federal Government.

"net wage earner and consumer pay company tax.

COMPANY AND MEDICARE WAGE TAX

Company sends weekly company along with medicare wage tax to the Federal Government and the market place. Since the Federal Government does not pay taxes and Company only transmits taxes, the hidden sales taxes benefit Company and Federal Government.

"net wage earner and consumer pay company tax.

COMPANY AND UNEMPLOYMENT WAGE TAX

Company sends weekly company along with unemployment wage tax to the Federal Government and the market place. Since the Federal Government does not pay taxes and Company only transmits taxes, the hidden sales taxes benefit Company and Federal Government.

"net wage earner and consumer pay company tax.

COMPANY AND SNOWBALL 16TH AMENDMENT WAGE TAX

Company sends weekly company along with 16th amendment wage taxes to the Federal Government and the market place. Other companies send weekly 16th amendment wage taxes to the Federal Government and the market place. Since the Federal Government does not pay taxes and companies only transmit taxes, the hidden sales taxes benefit Company and Federal Government.

"net wage earner and consumer pay company tax.

COMPANY AND SNOWBALL SOCIAL SECURITY WAGE TAX

Company sends weekly company along with social security wage taxes to the Federal Government and the market place. Other companies send weekly social security wage taxes to the Federal Government and the market place. Since the Federal Government does not pay taxes and companies only transmit taxes, the hidden sales taxes benefit Company and Federal Government.

"net wage earner and consumer pay company tax.

COMPANY AND SNOWBALL MEDICARE WAGE TAX

Company sends weekly company along with medicare wage taxes to the Federal Government and the market place. Other companies send weekly medicare wage taxes to the Federal Government and the market place. Since the Federal Government does not pay taxes and companies only transmit taxes, the hidden sales taxes benefit Company and Federal Government.

"net wage earner and consumer pay company tax.

COMPANY AND SNOWBALL UNEMPLOYMENT WAGE TAX

Company sends weekly company along with unemployment wage taxes to the Federal Government and the market place. Other companies send weekly unemployment wage taxes to the Federal Government and the market place. Since the Federal Government does not pay taxes and companies only transmit taxes, the hidden sales taxes benefit Company and Federal Government.

"net wage earner and consumer pay company tax.

16TH AMENDMENT WAGE TAX

Companies send 16th amendment wage tax weekly to the Federal Government and the market place. Since the Federal Government does not pay taxes and companies only transmit taxes, the hidden sales taxes benefit companies and Federal Government.

"net wage earner and consumer pay company tax.

SOCIAL SECURITY WAGE TAX

Companies send social security wage tax weekly to the Federal Government and the market place. Since the Federal Government does not pay taxes and companies only transmit taxes, the hidden sales taxes benefit companies and Federal Government.

"net wage earner and consumer pay company tax.

MEDICARE WAGE TAX

Companies send medicare wage tax weekly to the Federal Government and the market place. Since the Federal Government does not pay taxes and companies only transmit taxes, the hidden sales taxes benefit companies and Federal Government.

"net wage earner and consumer pay company tax.

UNEMPLOYMENT WAGE TAX

Companies send unemployment wage tax weekly to the Federal Government and the market place. Since the Federal Government does not pay taxes and companies only transmit taxes, the hidden sales taxes benefit companies and Federal Government.

"net wage earner and consumer pay company tax.

SNOWBALL 16TH AMENDMENT WAGE TAX

Companies send 16th amendment weekly wage tax to the Federal Government and the market place. Since the Federal Government does not pay taxes and companies only transmit taxes, the hidden sales taxes benefit Company and Federal Government.

"net wage earner and consumer pay company tax.

SNOWBALL SOCIAL SECURITY WAGE TAX

Companies send social security weekly wage tax to the Federal Government and the market place. Since the Federal Government does not pay taxes and companies only transmit taxes, the hidden sales taxes benefit Company and Federal Government.

"net wage earner and consumer pay company tax.

SNOWBALL MEDICARE WAGE TAX

Companies send medicare weekly wage tax to the Federal Government and the market place. Since the Federal Government does not pay taxes and companies only transmit taxes, the hidden sales taxes benefit Company and Federal Government.

"net wage earner and consumer pay company tax.

SNOWBALL UNEMPLOYMENT WAGE TAX

Companies send unemployment weekly wage tax to the Federal Government and the market place. Since the Federal Government does not pay taxes and companies only transmit taxes, the hidden sales taxes benefit Company and Federal Government.

"net wage earner and consumer pay company tax.

TAX

TABLES

USED

TO

DESCRIBE

TAXATION#1

TAXATION#2

TAXATION#3

16th amendment wage tax
TAXATION #1

The company transmits the "16th amendment wage tax" to the government weekly.

The "gross wage earner" becomes a "net wage earner."

The "net wage earner" pays the following 16th amendment wage tax:

Tax Rate	
10%	$0 – $8,375
15%	$8,376 – $34,000
25%	34,001 – $82,400
28%	$82,401 – $171,850
33%	$82,401 – $171,850
35%	$373,651+

TAXATION #2

The company transmits the "16th amendment wage tax" to the market place weekly too.

The "net wage earner" pays the following 16th amendment wage tax:

Tax Rate	
10%	$0 – $8,375
15%	$8,376 – $34,000
25%	34,001 – $82,400
28%	$82,401 – $171,850
33%	$82,401 – $171,850
35%	$373,651+

TAXATION #3

Other companies transmit their "16th amendment wage taxes" to the government and market place weekly. Other companies "16th amendment wage tax" become "snowball16th amendment wage taxes"

Consumer and "net wage earner" pay the following 16th amendment wage taxes:

Tax Rate	
10%	$0 – $8,375
15%	$8,376 – $34,000
25%	34,001 – $82,400
28%	$82,401 – $171,850
33%	$82,401 – $171,850
35%	$373,651+

The "net wage earner" pays the following:

> TAXATION #1
> TAXATION #2
> TAXATION #3

The "consumer" pays the following:

> TAXATION #1
> TAXATION #3

Increasing the 16th amendment wage tax will increase the price of the item in the market place.

Decreasing the 16th amendment wage tax will decrease the price of the item in the market place.

social security wage tax

TAXATION #1

The company transmits the "social security wage tax" to the government weekly.
The "gross wage earner" becomes a "net wage earner."

TAXATION #2

The company transmits the "social security wage tax" to the market place weekly too.
The consumer and "net wage earner" pays the "social security wage tax:"

TAXATION #3

Other companies transmit their "social security wage taxes" to the government and market place weekly. Other companies "social security wage tax" become "snowball social security wage taxes"
The consumers and "net wage earners" pay the "social security wage taxes:"
Increasing the social security wage tax will increase the price of the item in the market place.
Decreasing the social security wage tax will decrease the price of the item in the market place.
The "net wage earner" pays the following:

TAXATION #1

TAXATION #2

TAXATION #3

The "consumer" pays the following:

TAXATION #1

TAXATION #3

Medicare wage Tax

TAXATION #1

The medicare taxes are 1.45% which has no wage base limit and medicare taxes will increase to 2.35% due to the new Health Care Reform Bill for high earners. "medicare wage tax rate"=1.45%

TAXATION #2

The company transmits the "medicare wage tax" to the government weekly.
The "gross wage earner" becomes a "net wage earner."

TAXATION #3

The company transmits the "medicare wage tax" to the market place weekly and becomes: "medicare sale tax." The "net wage earner" pays the "medicare sale tax:"
Other companies transmit their "medicare wage taxes" to the government and market place weekly. Other companies "medicare wage tax" become "snowball medicare sales taxes" The consumers and "net wage earners" pay the "medicare sales taxes:" Increasing the medicare sale tax will increase the price of the item in the market place. Decreasing the medicare sale tax will decrease the price of the item in the market place. The "medicare sale tax" in the market place becomes a "profit tax!!!"
The "net wage earner" pays the following:

TAXATION #1

TAXATION #2

TAXATION #3

The "consumer" pays the following:

TAXATION #1

TAXATION #3

Since the companies are the money makers selling their products in the market place, they bear the burden of fully paying the following entitlement taxes:
"16th amendment wage tax"
"social security wage tax"
"medicare wage tax"

unemployment wage tax
TAXATION #1
The company transmits the "unemployment wage tax" to the government weekly.

The "gross wage earner" becomes a "net wage earner."
TAXATION #2
The company transmits the "unemployment wage tax" to the market place weekly too.

The consumer and "net wage earner" pays the "unemployment wage tax:"
TAXATION #3
Other companies transmit their "unemployment wage taxes" to the government and market place weekly. Other companies "unemployment wage tax" become "snowball unemployment wage taxes"

The consumers and "net wage earners" pay the "unemployment wage taxes:"

Increasing the unemployment wage tax will increase the price of the item in the market place.

Decreasing the unemployment wage tax will decrease the price of the item in the market place.

The "net wage earner" pays the following:

> ## TAXATION #1
> ## TAXATION #2
> ## TAXATION #3

The "consumer" pays the following:

> ## TAXATION #1
> ## TAXATION #3

1913
PROGRESSISM BEGINS!!!
A PRODUCT OF THE 16TH AMENDMENT!!!
THE FOLLOWING ARE HIDDEN SALES TAXES IN THE MARKET PLACE:

- COMPANY SALES TAX
- 16TH AMENDMENT SALE TAX
- SOCIAL SECURITY SALE TAX
- MEDICARE SALE TAX
- UNEMPLOYMENT SALE TAX
- SNOWBALL COMPANY SALE TAX
- SNOWBALL 16TH AMENDMENT SALES TAX
- SNOWBALL SOCIAL SECURITY SALE TAX
- SNOWBALL MEDICARE SALE TAX
- SNOWBALL UNEMPLOYMENT SALE TAX

A NET WAGE EARNER PAYS A "TRIPLE TAXATION SALES TAX!!!"
A CONSUMER PAYS A "DOUBLE TAXATION SALES TAX!!!"

THE 16TH AMENDMENT BENEFITS CORPORATIONS
AND
FEDERAL GOVERNMENT!!!

THE 16TH AMENDMENT
PUT
THE AMERICAN PEOPLE INTO TAX BONDAGE!!!
WHERE DO THE SALES TAXES GO???

WHERE

DO

THE

HIDDEN

SALES

TAXES

GO

???

SUBSIDIZE IMPORT TAXES!!!

STIMULUS PACKAGES!!!

SENATORS EARMARKS!!!

AIRFORCE ONE!!!

STATE AND CITY GOVERNMENT IMPOSES WAGE AND COMPANY TAX PLACE

STATE AND CITY CITIZENRY INTO TAX BONDAGE WITHIN THE STATE AND CITY TERRITORY!!!

This logical mathematical algorithm is very accurate in describing the tax path of the 16th amendment.

The profit of the following hidden sale taxes:

- company sales tax
- 16th amendment sales tax
- social security sales tax
- medicare sales tax
- unemployment sales tax
- snowball company sales tax
- snowball 16th amendment sales tax
- snowball social security sales tax
- snowball medicare sales tax
- snowball unemployment sales tax

go to corporations and Federal Government. The corporations employ lobbyist to protect their interest. Not so, with small companies, that didn't sell enough of their products to offset the taxes paid to the Federal Government on a weekly basis.

These sales' taxes are sent to the Federal Reserve Bank unidentified. This hidden sale's tax collection began in 1913 and exists today over 90 plus years. The tax on wage and company bountifully and dramatically increase the Federal Government income to continue the "civil war."

At the 1910 Jekyll Island meeting, those tyrannical conspirators realized the tax bountifulness of the wage tax in the civil war. In 1913, the 16th Amendment was approved producing the hidden sale tax.

Like the "civil war," the 16th Amendment proved to be helpful in World War I, World War II and all wars since.

During World War II, "cost plus" for factories was used to produce war products increasing the hidden sale's tax.

TAXES ARE UNIDENTIFIED IN THE FEDERAL RESERVE

COMPANY SALE'S TAX
SNOWBALL COMPANY SALE'S TAX

16TH AMENDMENT WAGE SALE'S TAX
SNOWBALL 16TH AMENDMENT WAGE
SALE'S TAX

SOCIAL SECURITY WAGE SALE'S TAX
SNOWBALL SOCIAL SECURITY WAGE
SALE'S TAX

MEDICARE WAGE SALE'S TAX
SNOWBALL MEDICARE WAGE SALE'S
TAX

UNEMPLOYMENT WAGE SALE'S TAX
SNOWBALL UNEMPLOYMENT WAGE
SALE'S TAX

FEDERAL RESERVE
BANK

OR

TREASURY

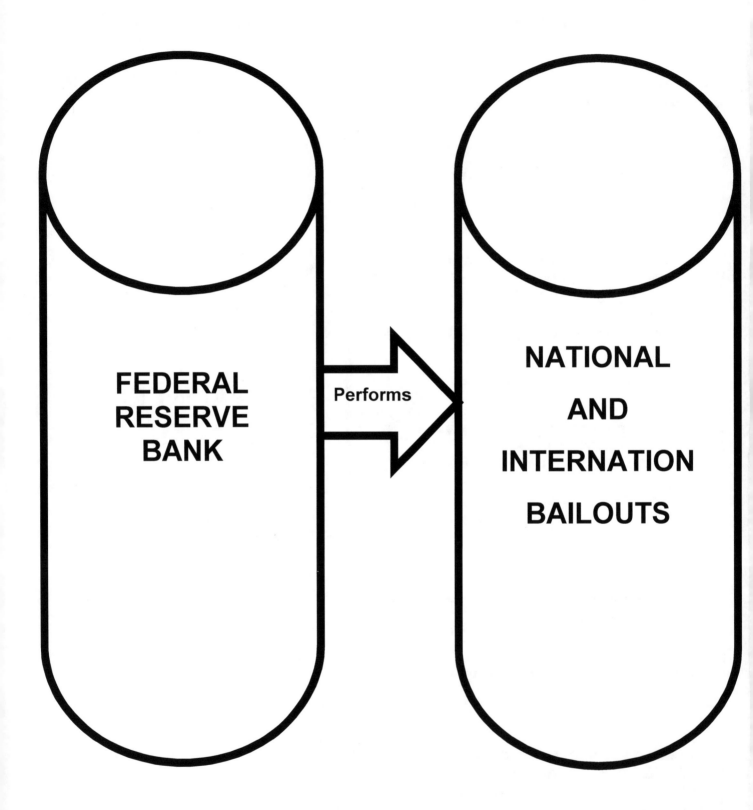

FEDERAL
RESERVE
BANK

Performs

NATIONAL

AND

INTERNATION

BAILOUTS

IN THE MARKET PLACE

COMPANY SALES TAX

SNOWBALL COMPANY SALES TAX

16TH AMENDMENT WAGE SALES TAX

SNOWBALL 16TH AMENDMENT WAGE SALES TAX

SOCIAL SECURITY WAGE SALES TAX

SNOWBALL SOCIAL SECURITY WAGE SALES TAX

MEDICARE WAGE SALES TAX

SNOWBALL MEDICARE WAGE SALES TAX

UNEMPLOYMENT WAGE SALES TAX

SNOWBALL UNEMPLOYMENT WAGE SALES TAX

PUT

MAN

ON

MOON

NOT

CORPORATION TAXES

NOR

COMPANY TAXES!!!

"…, what more is necessary to make us a happy and prosperous people? Still one more thing, fellow citizens — a wise and frugal government which shall restrain men from injuring one another, shall leave them otherwise free to regulate their own pursuits of industry and improvement, and shall not take from the mouth of labor the bread it has earned. This is the sum of good government, and this is necessary to close the circle of our felicities."

"Single acts of tyranny may be ascribed to the accidental opinion of a day; but a series of oppressions, begun at a distinguished period and pursued unalterably through every change of ministers, too plainly prove a deliberate, systematic plan of reducing [a people] to slavery."

"A wise and frugal government … shall not take from the mouth of labor the bread it has earned" – Thomas Jefferson

SNOWBALL COMPANY
SALES TAX
16TH AMENDMENT WAGE
SALES TAX
SNOWBALL 16TH AMENDMENT WAGE
SALES TAX
SOCIAL SECURITY WAGE
SALES TAX
SNOWBALL SOCIAL SECURITY WAGE
SALES TAX
MEDICARE WAGE
SALES TAX
SNOWBALL MEDICARE WAGE
SALES TAX
UNEMPLOYMENT WAGE
SALES TAX
SNOWBALL UNEMPLOYMENT WAGE
SALES TAX
TAKES BREAD FROM
THE MOUTH OF BABIES AND
ENSLAVES PARENTS
TO GO OFF TO WORK!!!

THIS BOOK IS DEDICATED TO THE FUTURE MARRIED FAMILY COUPLE WHERE ONE PARTNER GOES OFF TO WORK WHILE THE OTHER STAYS HOME TAKING CARE OF THE FAMILY!!!